Spirit and Truth

Understanding beyond Reason

Roland J. Lowther

Copyright © 2020 Roland J. Lowther

26 25 24 23 22 21 20   7 6 5 4 3 2 1

First published 2020 by Paternoster
Paternoster is an imprint of Authentic Media Ltd
PO Box 6326, Bletchley, Milton Keynes MK1 9GG.
authenticmedia.co.uk

The right of Roland J. Lowther to be identified as the
Author of this Work has been asserted in accordance with
the Copyright, Designs and Patents Act 1988.
All rights reserved.

No part of this publication may be reproduced, stored
in a retrieval system, or transmitted in any form or by any means,
electronic, mechanical, photocopying, recording or otherwise, without
the prior permission of the publisher or a licence permitting restricted
copying. In the UK such licences are issued by the Copyright Licensing
Agency, 5th Floor, Shackleton House, 4 Battle Bridge Lane, London SE1 2HX.

British Library Cataloguing in Publication Data
A catalogue record for this book is available from the British Library
ISBN 978-1-78893-113-7
978-1-78893-114-4 (e-book)

Unless otherwise noted, Scripture quotations are taken from The Holy Bible, New
International Version Anglicised Copyright © 1979, 1984 by International Bible Society.
Used by permission of Hodder & Stoughton Publishers, a division of Hodder Headline Ltd.
All rights reserved. 'NIVUK' is a registered trademark of International Bible Society. UK
trademark number 1448790.

Scripture quotations marked RSV are taken from Revised Standard Version of the Bible,
copyright © 1946, 1952, and 1971 National Council of the Churches of Christ in the United
States of America. Used by permission. All rights reserved worldwide. nrsvbibles.org

Cover design by Pete Barnsley (CreativeHoot)

Contents

	Introduction	1
1.	**Truth and Reason**	7
	Truth, Reason and the Mind: Rationalism	8
	Truth, Reason and the Senses: Empiricism	16
	Truth, Reason and Action: Pragmatism	25
	Truth, Reason and Human Existence: Existentialism	30
	Reason and the False Quest for Truth	36
2.	**Truth and Divine Revelation**	42
	Uncertainty, Faith and Revelation: The Story of Job	42
	The Spirit, Divine Power and Wisdom: Paul's Philosophy	52
	The Spirit and Truth: John's Teaching	61
	Summary: The Truth that Seeks Us	66
3.	**The Spirit, Truth and the Material World**	72
	The Spirit, Understanding and Materiality	72
	The Spirit, Creation and Divine Revelation	78
	The Spirit, History and Divine Purpose	84
	The Spirit, the Consecration of Nature, and Wisdom	89
	Summary	93
4.	**The Spirit, Truth and the Church**	97
	The Spirit and the Church	98
	The Spirit-created Church	104
	The Spirit-gifted Church	111
	The Spirit-ordered Church	117
	Summary	120

5.	**The Spirit, Truth and Personal Experience**	**122**
	Human-oriented Spiritual Experience	122
	Divine Initiative and the Conditions for Experience	131
	The Power of God's Direct Engagement through Experience	136
	Summary	142
6.	**The Spirit, Truth and Holy Scripture**	**144**
	What is Truth?	145
	What Gives Holy Scripture Its Authority?	151
	What 'Really' Gives Holy Scripture Its Truth and Authority?	158
	Why Does God Give Us Holy Scripture?	166
	Summary	171
7.	**The Spirit, Truth and Practical Obedience**	**173**
	Doing and Knowing	174
	Humility: Breaking the Power of Human Pride	178
	Self-control: Maintaining the Spirit's Power over the Flesh	183
	Obedience: The Mindset of the Spirit	188
	Summary	193
	Conclusion: Two Ways to Truth	194
	Bibliography	200
	Notes	206

Introduction

What is truth? Confronted with the decision concerning Jesus' fate, Pontius Pilate was forced to question the alleged Jewish Messiah about the legitimacy of claims he was a king. Jesus affirmed that he was a king, but not the kind of king Pilate imagined. Jesus then asserted that he was born a king, and had come into the world with the express intent of testifying to *the truth*. He declared that everyone who seeks to align with *the truth* listens to him. Pilate – greatly vexed by conflict of the Jewish claims with Jesus' response, and by his apparent innocence – found himself at a crossroads of reason and faith. Reason dictated he do the convenient thing, faith he do the right thing. But what was the right thing? Before he encountered Jesus he might have been sure; now, following the encounter he seemed less so! Hence his question: 'What is truth?' Now, let the reader not miss the irony. We cannot be certain whether Pilate's question represented a genuine request or merely a rhetorical exclamation. What we can be certain of, though, while asking Jesus about the *nature* of truth, Pilate failed to apprehend that the very *essence* of truth stood before him. Truth, it seems, is not what it seems!

Like Pilate, people have been 'seeking' truth for millennia. For many, the quest has consistently followed the pathway of reasoned inquiry. As rational creatures humans are hard-wired to think, yet on account of their natural resistance to God, the capacity to think is turned 'self-ward'. Beginning with their own existence, humans invariably reason toward an ultimate reality that enables them to make sense of their existence independent of God. Indeed, there is no shortage of theories enabling people to justify such an independent life, on 'reasonable' grounds. Rationalism, empiricism, pragmatism, existentialism, just to name a few, have all been offered up as the theoretical means of 'making sense' of life. Philosophers invent methods of describing truth, and then define the truth by the same methods, to validate their claims. These contrived philosophical systems are often so convincing that their adherents may actually believe the possibility of human sovereignty by employing them. However, it's not that straightforward.

What happens when the unpredictable occurs? What happens to the logical consistency when life deals a hand of uncertainty? The clearest example of the failure of human reason in the face of uncertainty is the life of the ancient patriarch, Job. Job was a God-fearing man and, like many around him, believed if a person was obedient to God and faithful to his values then life would go well. For the most part he was right, but one day Job's world inexplicably fell apart. Without warning Job's belief system disintegrated when he lost everything dear to him: his family, his wealth and his health. Being a devout man, Job refused to blame God, choosing to accept the anomaly as God's will. Job's well-meaning friends, however, were not slow in offering reasons for the calamity and solutions that seemed to make sense to the reasoning mind. Yet, nothing could assuage the anguish, no amount of reason could make sense of things.

As Job's lament turns to resentment, he surprisingly suffers a rebuke from a young man under the influence of God's Spirit, Elihu. Following the rebuke, Job personally encounters God in a storm, being further rebuked for the futility of his reasoning. Utterly broken, he finally concedes, 'Surely I spoke of things I did not understand, things too wonderful for me to know' (Job 42:3). In Job's case, human reason had failed to make sense of his reality, a reality that transcended the logic of metaphysical systems, a reality in which human rational certainty fell apart. All that Job could do was accept God's word in faith, knowing that God was right even if his actions in the world never made sense to the rational mind.

As with Job and his friends, human reason, in attempting to construct a reality without absolute faith in God, consciously or unconsciously resists the truth. Yet God does not leave humanity in ignorance. Like Job's storm revelation, God graciously breaks into human existence, by revealing a reality beyond rational comprehension – a reality that requires faith in a personal God to be fully grasped.

Having the faith to understand this reality and the God that created it requires the divine intervention of the Holy Spirit. Only the Spirit can reveal truth to the hardened human heart, only the Spirit can provide the means of making sense of things when the contingencies of life reach the limit of rational conception. God, through his powerful Spirit, breaks into the material world, working in and through its materiality to provide humanity with the opportunity to discover God's truth. Although many might argue that the spiritual and the material are unrelated, in God's view they are related. In fact, God readily uses the material world as the means of revealing himself. The Spirit orders the circumstances of life through nature and offers the means of interpreting these circumstances in light of God's truth. The Spirit is at work everywhere, pointing humanity to the truth, whether they choose to acknowledge it or not.

This divine guidance becomes more explicit as truth inquirers find themselves within the orbit of God's community – the church. In drawing people into a relationship with Jesus Christ through the gospel, the Spirit invariably draws them into the community of faith. In the church a person encounters a certain dynamic that exists nowhere else – the presence of Jesus Christ through the Spirit-endowed believers. The church is created by the Spirit to fulfil God's divine purposes in revealing divine truth for the edification of his people. The Spirit equips individuals with specific 'spiritual gifts', special abilities that enable them to reveal God's truth to each other: teaching, serving, prophecy, leadership, mercy, etc. are all examples of how the Spirit endows individual Christians. These gifts are put to work collectively, such that anyone who encounters God can have the truth affirmed from many difference perspectives. For example, the truth of God's love might be taught as well as demonstrated – both serving to validate it. In the church, divine truth is encountered in ways it cannot be encountered outside, that is why it is indispensable for knowing the truth.

The individual who encounters God's revelation in the world and discovers God's truth in and through the community of faith will invariably personally encounter the Spirit in a 'real' way. Those of an overly rational persuasion are all too ready to dismiss the power of religious experience as something subjective, a phenomenon merely manufactured by the emotions. This, however, is a clear misunderstanding of how God engages people. When we observe the accounts of Holy Scripture, it becomes clear that divinely initiated experience, as the means of revealing truth, is far from being the exception to the rule. In multiple instances, God powerfully engages individuals with a spiritual experience to reveal his truth to them. We only have to read the stories of Abraham, Elijah, Jesus, Paul, Peter and a multitude of others to see that experience is a valid means of truth revelation. Indeed, it could be argued that the truth does not become truly convincing until it has impacted the inquirer in a powerful experiential manner. For example, Paul knew about Jesus, but not until his powerful experiential encounter with him on the Damascus road did the truth of Jesus 'really' transform his life. The Spirit powerfully reveals truth through experience.

At this point, the question arises: How can a person be sure that their spiritual experiences, their engagements in the Christian community, and the revelation of God in and through the material world are not simply a construct of their own imagination? This is a valid concern, except in the case of the Christian faith; there is an 'objective' standard that comes from outside our own experience of reality, a standard that serves to validate or deny the truth we lay claim to: Holy Scripture. The same Spirit that is at work in the world, in the church and in individual lives powerfully inspired chosen authors to write the 'very words of God', as a means of providing a reliable testimony against the vicissitudes of human life and experience in the world. Although the word of God may be no more 'true' than a genuine religious experience or truth revelation through the church, it is more reliably consistent. In fact, the testimony of the Holy Spirit, through Holy Scripture, is the most certain of the Spirit's truth mediums, and is considered the standard by which all other means of revelation are to be measured.

Having said all that, to know about the truth the Spirit reveals through the previously discussed means is necessary and helpful. But there is a dimension to knowing truth that transcends passive observation and intellectual reflection; a dimension in which the truth is discovered for what it really is – personal knowledge of God. This is the dimension of doing, of practising what is revealed. In Christian terms, *living by the Spirit* is an existence in which the Spirit of God animates the thoughts and desires of a believer, is the means that they know the truth as a lived reality. In the practising of truth, the reality of God truly comes to life.

The apostle John states that the Spirit is the truth, and to live in the power and under the guidance of the Spirit is to live out the truth as Jesus did, intimately knowing truth through a personal dependency on God – who is truth. Truth ultimately is not a thing to intellectually grasp, but an intimate state of relationship with the One who called all existence into being, a life of conformity with God, through Christ, in the power of the Spirit.

So, in returning to our opening reflections, Pilate's engagement with Jesus provides the perfect metaphor for coming to terms with the truth and the quest to discover it. For many seekers, truth is seen as rational propositions, a set of abstract principles, rules, laws or maxims; codified ideas that allow them to make some kind of logical link between human existence and ultimate reality – connecting the world as it is to them with the world as it really is. Truth, in this case, is an intellectual system that provides the fundamental blueprint for human existence within an ultimate reality that has little or no place for God.

As in the case of Pontius Pilate, these alleged truth-seekers miss the obvious. In seeking out a set of principles, fixed laws or timeless maxims that fit into their own self-oriented intellectual constructs, the 'real' truth is missed. Truth is not simply an idea, it is a divine being.

Many fail to see that God's presence is right before them and that his handiwork constantly testifies to the truth, offering signposts that lead directly to him. Finding the truth and coming to terms with ultimate reality, then, is not about finding the 'secret laws' of the universe through theoretical inquiry; rather it's about finding the One who powerfully created them. More than this, it's about finding and living out an obedient relational intimacy with the Creator, and this through an intimate dependency on the person to whom Pontius Pilate first posited his fateful question – Jesus Christ. Truth is a person. Finding truth involves moving beyond the quest for rational certainty based on logical propositions, into the realm of relational intimacy and complete moral conformity with God – the source and essence of truth. But to find this truth, fallible humans need help; they need the powerful intervention of God to remove the 'scales' of ignorance from their eyes – they need what Jesus calls 'the Spirit of truth' (John 14:17).

1

Truth and Reason

Reason has ruled the quest for truth from antiquity. Since Adam and Eve's rejection of God's revealed truth in Eden, choosing to abandon God's command in favour of more rationally appealing solutions, humanity's quest to grasp truth has followed that familiar pathway. Of course, most people believe that through the independent use of human rationality they can define ultimate reality, order their existence within it, and consequentially provide security against every contingency they might encounter. In this regard, philosophy has played a key role, providing the logical justification for these premises. Philosophies take many forms; some argue that truth is innate, a phenomenon resident in the subconscious memory to be extracted through education. Others suggest truth is best discovered outside the inquirer through practical experiment. Still others advocate that truth is discerned from pragmatic utility – what is useful ultimately proving to be ultimately true. There is also a school of thought that argues truth is discovered by reflection on one's inner experiences.

Significantly, each of these schools of thought has been integrated also into Christian thinking, serving to shape how Christians perceive God, truth and life in the world. Reason, it seems, is also quite comfortable within the realms of 'faith'. In light of the ubiquitous influence of philosophy on humanity in general and Christians in particular, it is therefore necessary to briefly critique these key philosophical movements, to see if their influence might help or hinder the quest for truth.

Truth, Reason and the Mind: Rationalism

Rationalism is common in the Western tradition, and has been highly influential on Christian theology. In its purest form, it promotes the idea that truth is something pre-existent in the human mind. The rationalist challenge is to understand the foundational unifying principle of this embedded truth as it exists a priori (before experience), within the mind. In the Western tradition, this journey began with the ancient Greeks.

The ancient pre-Socratic philosophers were obsessed with discovering the primary element undergirding the 'flux' of observable change, as seen in the multiplicity of elements within the world they encountered. Heraclitus believed that fire was the primordial element in all things. For Thales, the unifying element of reality was water, which could take the modes of solid, liquid and gas. Anaximenes suggested that air might be the primitive element, whereas Empedocles believed the unity could incorporate earth, fire, air and water.[1]

To the post-scientific modern thinker, the notion that the unifying principle of reality might be water or fire seems absurd. However, the significance of these early contributions lies not in the outcome of the inquiry, but in the nature of the questions asked; questions emanating from the desire to relate basic human existence to a greater and more ultimate reality. While not fully aware of the implications, the pre-Socratics introduced into the tradition of Western thought the notion of metaphysics; that is, the idea that an over-arching reality, distinct from the things that exist to the naked eye, provides an explanation of why things are as they are. In philosophy, this became known as the idea of 'the one and the many'.

In developing this notion further, the seminal mathematician Pythagoras conceived that numbers were essentially of two kinds: odd and even. The unit 'one' had the power to make odd even, and even odd. The next step, as C.B. Armstrong suggests, 'was to invest the unit with constructive power, calling it the One as distinct from the numerical unit, and to regard the dyad [two] as the indefinable and infinite material on which the activity of the monad [one] was exercised'.[2] For Pythagoras then, odd numbers represented the 'many' concrete things of the material world, created by the 'one' out of an undefined material substrate. As such, Thales's natural inquiry could become more sophisticated as these ideas developed theoretically.

However, it was Parmenides who gave this notion true philosophical import. Parmenides argued that behind the flux of material reality there is a *true reality* called *being* or the One. The senses reveal a changing material world, but the mind enables us to contemplate ultimate reality, or the true unchanging being. What was most revolutionary about Parmenides' contribution was the role that reason played in his understanding. Accordingly, only pure reason provided the means of attaining knowledge of the being that lies behind material existence. Thus, for the pre-Socratics reality was not a unified whole where change is an illusion (monism) or merely a variegated reality in which the particulars are conceptually unrelated (nominalism); rather it must have abstract forms or universals, that is ideas that provide order to the reality that humans perceive.

In the end, it was Plato, the famous disciple of Socrates, who ventured to develop a fully-fledged metaphysical system predicated on pure reason. In approaching the subject raised by the Pre-Socratics, 'the one and the many', Plato introduces categories that enable a logical distinction between these two: reality and existence. Existence is what we tangibly experience (life in the material world); reality is above and beyond us and provides the metaphysical forms or the pure ideas that give reason the existence we experience. Plato advanced that these pure forms exist (somewhere) beyond our experience, and are not dependent on the human mind for their primary conception, as Armstrong explains: 'independent entities outside the space-time stream of becoming, they are manifested in it, since all things "partake of" their reality'.[3] For Plato, the human soul (the inner self / mind), which pre-exists our natural life, has access to these pure forms through the process of cognitively recalling them from latent memory; triggered by conscious reflection on sense data (things we see). These ultimate forms provide the fundamental blueprint for all the material particulars humans experience e.g. the pure form of tree enables us to relate all trees, to a common form of 'treeness', despite their markedly different shapes.

Thus, pure reason provides the bridge between mundane existence and ultimate reality. Moreover, for Plato, there is also a distinct duality between body and soul, and it is the necessary integration of these two things that hinders crossing to the side of grasping the truth of reality. The mundane body holds the soul captive to the baser desires of the human condition, hindering it from attaining a clear perception of this true reality. Plato himself indicates as much in *Phaedo*: 'as long as we have a body, and our soul is fused with such an evil we shall never adequately attain what we desire, which we affirm to be the truth.'[4] To attain an understanding of pure reality, and by extension the truth, Plato suggests the inquirer must escape attempts at understanding it by mere empirical observation, and aspire to the higher art of rational reflection: 'Then he will do this most perfectly who approaches the object with thought alone, without associating any sight with his thought, or dragging in any sense perception with his reasoning, but who, using pure thought alone, tries to track down each reality pure and by itself.'[5] For Plato, the body actually confuses the soul, hindering it from acquiring truth, and so the life of philosophers represents the noblest calling, a station where they can devote themselves to the act of pure rational reflection away from the corrupting influences of bodily desires. Therefore, to attain pure knowledge one must escape from the body and observe things as they are in themselves by means of the soul itself and in so doing a vision of the real can be more adequately attained.[6]

But how is this done? Where does the reasoning inquirer seek it? Through his conception of the soul as being pre-existent, Plato is able to posit that the knowledge of the truth is embedded within the resident soul-memory, as he indicates, 'When did our souls acquire this knowledge of them? . . . Our souls existed apart from the body before they took on human form, and they had intelligence.'[7] This knowledge of pure form (truth), which we attained prior to our earthly existence, was not lost at birth but became suppressed by our human nature. Again he says, 'we have not forgotten it, we remain knowing and have knowledge throughout life.'[8] Consequently, the truth is not something we learn anew but something that is recollected, it is a discovery of that which is buried in our minds by the burden of the sense material we have taken in, but is still available to the mind through concerted rational reflection. This notion is evident in this statement of the Socrates character in *Phaedo*:

> But when the soul investigates by itself it passes into the realm of what is pure, ever existing, immortal and unchanging, and being akin to this, it always stays with it whenever it is by itself and can do so; it ceases to stray and remains in the same state as it is in touch with things of the same kind, and its experience then is what is called wisdom?[9]

For Plato, then, it is the process of education that enables the uninformed inquirer, caught up in the vague and mundane affairs of this sense world, to climb out of ignorance into the light of understanding. This is famously illustrated by his cave analogy. In this analogy, he describes people dwelling in a cave with their backs toward the opening who have an understanding based on the images that are vaguely projected as shadows on the cave wall. Plato describes it thus, 'The visible realm should be likened to a prison dwelling.'[10] However, climbing out of the cave the inquirer observes the 'actual' reality of the projected shadows, and the light of the sun that casts these shadows. The sun represents 'the good', the ultimate reality: 'Once one has seen, however, one must conclude that it is the cause of all that is correct and beautiful in anything, and it provides both light and its source in the visible realm, and that in the intelligible realm it controls and provides truth and understanding.'[11] Education then is the process of ascending from the shadowy cave of ignorance with the vague forms of the sense world and into the light of understanding of the ideal world – reality. Armed with this metaphysical construct, Plato has provided the seminal framework for rationalism within Western thought.

However, rationalism's development was far from finished with Plato. The next 'major' revolution in rationalism occurred in the seventeenth century. Philosophers such as Descartes, Leibniz and Spinoza were key figures in the new Enlightenment movement. Of particular interest to us is the contribution of Rene Descartes. Where Plato used metaphysics to arrive at rational philosophy, Descartes used epistemology (the theory of knowledge) as the means of developing his rationalism. Basically, Descartes was a foundationalist, which meant his principal goal is to 'drill down' through the dross of superficial understanding, in order that he might arrive at the pure bedrock of solid understanding – the clear and distinct basis of truth. Descartes's principal 'drilling' method for attaining this clear and distinct basis of truth is the instrument of scepticism – doubt.

For Descartes, doubt is employed to discover that which is beyond doubt; therefore everything should be tested by doubt to ascertain its veracity. Basically, after having doubted everything, the foundation of the undoubtable must be attained. Descartes doubted the validity of the senses (even straight things can look bent under water). He even doubted the physical world (are we awake or dreaming? which is it?). For Descartes then, the way of negation (removing doubt by doubting) enabled the foundation of all truth to be discovered, for indubitably the last undoubtable thing was the sceptical mind. For Descartes the ultimate foundation became conscious human thought.

Descartes's ultimate 'undoubtable' fact is that 'I doubt'. That is to say, 'I' can doubt everything except the fact that I doubt. From this, Descartes derived his famous maxim *Cogito ergo sum*: I am thinking therefore I exist [as a thinking thing]. Fundamentally, this meant that only the reasoned consciousness is able to doubt, which for Descartes represented a clear and distinct fact beyond refutation. 'I' the thinking consciousness am thinking, which can only be true by virtue of a priori reason (reason without the benefit of sense data). That all such clear and distinct cognitions may be deemed beyond all doubt is *necessarily true*. So, as far as he was concerned, Descartes had discovered the foundation of all truth, the a priori rational consciousness. Like Plato before him, Descartes advocated a dualism of mind and body, such that the mind remained an independent entity that thought. So when Descartes suggests 'I' am thinking, he actually thinks of 'the mind' as a non-physical entity, a thinking thing that can exist independently of the body. As such, what humans really are *in essence* (the real us) is, in fact, a thinking consciousness. Our senses may deceive us, and we may be unsure as to whether we are awake or dreaming, but we cannot deny that we are thinking.

Descartes's quest toward the foundation of truth consequently involved deconstruction of the validity of sense perception (the veracity of what we see), as he says, 'Everything that I accepted as being true up to now I acquired from the senses . . . However I have occasionally found they deceive me, and it is prudent never to trust those who have deceived us, even if only once.'[12] To ensure he has removed the deception of the senses, Descartes imagined a worst-case scenario, where a hypothetical, all-powerful, cunning, evil deceiver exists as one constantly dedicated to misleading him. He then admitted he might be deceived in every possible way, but he could not deny that he has a conscious existence of being deceived: 'Therefore, it is indubitable that I also exist, if he deceives me.'[13] From this Descartes could conclude that his existence is a thinking existence: 'I am a genuine thing and I truly exist. But what kind of thing? I just said; a thinking thing.'[14] Consequently, the highest order of ideas are innate ideas, those 'I just know'. Among such ideas is the existence of God. While Descartes agrees that 'I' can pretend God does not exist, 'I' cannot avoid the idea of God existing; this is clear and distinct: 'It is also clear and distinct to the highest degree because whatever I perceive clearly and distinctly as real and true, and is containing some perfection, is completely included in it.'[15]

It is from the basis of exhausting all doubt to arrive at the truth as an existing thinking being that Descartes posits his clearest and most distinct of rational ideas – the existence of God. From this affirmation, Descartes positively constructs his theory of knowledge. Strangely, God appears within Descartes's system in a deus ex machina manner, enabling him to escape a regression into an abyss of scepticism. Interestingly, having arrived at the position that rational thought is the supreme foundational truth, he suddenly legitimizes it through an appeal to divine validation.

Descartes advances the idea that God is the perfect being, and as such it is actually impossible for God to deceive him.[16] God, obviously being on his side, has granted him a capacity for clear rational judgement: 'Next, I experience a certain faculty of judgement in myself, which, just like everything else that is in me, I received from God.'[17] This is his primary presupposition, 'Since God does not wish me to be mistaken he honestly did not give me a faculty such that, when I use it correctly, I could ever be mistaken.'[18] So, as long as the rational inquirer acknowledges God as the validating source of their reasoning and wisdom, and applies the right methods, there is no cause to disbelieve that their rational reflections could ever be erroneous.[19] For Descartes then, innate reason is the divinely appointed method of ascertaining truth.

Despite Descartes's insights there is no denying the naïvety in it. Yet, the reflections of the eighteenth-century philosopher Immanuel Kant take rationalism to a whole new level of sophistication. Kant's level of nuance in his *Critique of Pure Reason* make Plato and Descartes's rationalism look primitive by comparison, even though he is dependent on the prior contributions of both.

Kant effectively ushers in a Copernican revolution in rational philosophy by considering the conditions of understanding, not just the process. Prior to Kant, all knowledge must conform to objects based on abstract forms; with Kant all objects are 'ordered' to conform to the rational mind. Kant confessed he was awakened from his 'dogmatic slumber' (blind adherence to the rationalism of Descartes, Spinoza and Leibniz) by the challenge of the empiricist David Hume. Hume argued that all knowledge was either *synthetic a posteriori* (facts formulated from empirical observation e.g. some bachelors are old) or *analytic* a priori (self-evident truths e.g. bachelors are unmarried). For Hume the latter category was trivial and, as an empiricist, only synthetic a posteriori truths had value. Kant offered a radical challenge to Hume's thesis, arguing for the possibility of synthetic a priori knowledge; knowledge that exists as a synthesis of things a priori (prior to any sense observation).

Kant sought to show that knowledge is synthetic a priori. For example the simple mathematical equation 1 × 3 = 3 might appear to be analytically *self-evident*; however, when we try to compute 2,345 × 5,678 = 13,314,910 we must engage in some synthesis (calculation) to arrive at the answer, which suggests that even maths, though analytically true, must involve synthesis to be so (for us). Kant's philosophy is therefore predicated on this question, 'How are synthetical judgments *a priori* possible?'[20]

Kant classifies his system as transcendental, as it relates to the internal conditions of ideas. The first part he calls the transcendental aesthetic, which relates to the conditions in which we appropriate sense data; because, as he suggests, 'That all our knowledge begins with experience there can be no doubt.'[21] That we are able to gain sense data is not dependent on the innate forms of 'things', as Plato might suggest, but on the preconditional 'forms' of time and space, existent as *pure intuitions*. For Kant, space is, 'the subjective condition of the sensibility, under which alone external intuition is possible'.[22] Space is limited to external phenomena, time is not! Time is a formal condition a priori of all phenomena (external or otherwise). Time is a pure intuition, within us. Pure intuitions of space and time, then translate as empirical intuitions, where humans intuitively apprehend particular sensations e.g. if a ball is thrown to us, we intuitively know that the ball exists in space, and intuitively through time, have an awareness that it will soon arrive at us.

The second part of Kant's system is the transcendental logic. Sensation (perception) has no value without the benefit of understanding (conception). Sense requires the logical mind to order it for meaningful understanding to exist. As with the transcendental aesthetic, the transcendental logic contains pure and empirical categories, in this case pertaining to thought.[23] Regarding pure thought, Kant advances a table of four categories, each with three subcategories, as the means by which the mind orders its thought a priori: quality (e.g. unity, plurality and totality), quantity, relations and modality.[24] With these categories pure logic is able to engage pure intuition, and subsequently form conceptions, which pertain to empirical thought about real objects. Thus, with the a priori pure intuitions synthesized with the a priori pure thought, synthetic a priori understanding is possible.

This may be likened to the inner workings of a computer operating system, which provide the possibility of computing, even before any programs are loaded or data inserted. As applied with reference to empirical understanding, the pure intuition in concert with pure logic, loaded with the data of empirical objects can now conceptualize them, such that we are able to think and reason about a ball being thrown toward us.

However, there is a further qualification to Kant's rational system. The understanding we have spoken about *only* applies to the world as we know it, the Phenomenal – the reality of 'the thing for me'. That is to say, this system of knowledge posits the possibility of a form of subjectively derived objectivity, only as it is to us, not as it really is! Roger Scruton describes it in this manner, 'The essence of Kant's "transcendental" method lies in its egocentricity. All the questions that I can ask I must ask from the standpoint that is mine . . . which the perspective of "possible experience" is.'[25] True reality is defined by Kant as the Noumenal – 'the thing itself'. The Noumenal cannot be known in any absolutely objective sense. Although the observer might conclude they are watching a particular event, what they are really watching is an event synthetically ordered by the hard-wired a priori faculties of their inner self; what is actually happening is ultimately unknowable to them. Thus, according to Kant's system: 'There is no description of the world that can free itself from the reference of experience . . . it cannot be known except from the point of view which is ours.'[26] Pure reason, then, is ultimately subjective.

Truth, Reason and the Senses: Empiricism

Empiricism is most commonly related to what we know as science. The empiricist seeks truth through the assimilation of sense data after experience. Empiricists typically believe that there are no universal a priori forms determining phenomena – a thing is simply a thing. Truth is only knowable through observation, experiment and experience. Empiricism, like rationalism, originated in ancient Greece. The Sophists rejected abstract rational speculation and took on the concrete reality of human life and the experience of society as more valid objects of inquiry, while the Stoics believed that a child at birth was devoid of conceptions. Only through an interaction with sense data via direct experience were conceptions developed. Sense perception represented an interaction between the human soul and the object being sensed, with the object being stamped as an impression on the blank mind. Epicurus acquired from Democritus the idea of atomism, which implies the world we know is atomic in structure. Sense perception, then, is enabled by atomic films, which are constantly floating off all objects, and impinging themselves on our sense organs.[27]

The most famous and influential empiricist was Aristotle. Over and against Plato's theory of forms (the blueprint for the things of the world through innate reason), Aristotle considered that material things possess potentiality, which, when fully developed, becomes pure actuality – the true form.[28] As such, Aristotle pioneered the bottom-up inductive method of discovery. Operating with the senses, Aristotle was convinced that perception was the principal means of arriving at truth. Jonathan Barnes defines Aristotle as a true empiricist for two reasons, 'First, he held that the notions or concepts with which we seek to grasp reality are all ultimately derived from perception . . . Secondly, he thought that the science of knowledge on which our grasp of reality consists is ultimately grounded on perceptual observations.'[29] While perception may be the source of knowledge for Aristotle, it does not represent knowledge in and of itself. Perceptions become impressions on the mind, then memories, which are then correlated with others to become experience. In its reified (consolidated) form, experience becomes knowledge – the generalized principle extracted from the perception of particulars. This, of course, is what we ordinarily know as inductive reason.

For Aristotle, the primary means of knowing is the faculty of sense (touch, taste, smell, etc.): 'All men by nature desire to know. An indication of this is the delight we take in our senses.'[30] Against rationalism, Aristotle argued for the primary value of sense experience, and in his work *Metaphysics* cites examples of how success through experience is greater than success through abstract theory. In one such case, he cites the futility of a physician seeking to bring about healing based on theoretical generalizations: 'If, then, a man has a theory without experience, and knows the universal but does not know the individual included . . . he will often fail to cure.'[31] For Aristotle, the senses – sight, hearing, touch, smell, taste – all give the body different sensations, enabling the mind to gain 'impressions' from these different senses: 'we can say that a sense is what has the power of receiving into itself the sensible forms of things without the matter, in the way in which a piece of wax takes on the impress of a signet-ring without the iron or gold.'[32] While different human senses may grant different kinds of impressions, Aristotle argues for a unity of 'the soul' that assimilates them: 'We must conclude, therefore, that there is, as has been stated before, some one faculty in the soul with which the latter perceives all its precepts . . . we must assume also, in the case of the soul, that the faculty of perception in general is in itself numerically one and the same.'[33]

Thus, perceiving is the first step toward knowledge. Impressions gained from the senses, when intentionally gained, come from a form of organized method. In this regard, Aristotle was somewhat akin to a research scientist, devoting large amounts of energy to meticulous, hands-on gathering of data and recording of observations, literally and figuratively dissecting the evidence.[34] At the time that Aristotle conducted his research, there were few writings to be drawn upon, and most of his data was gathered from first-hand experiment or second-hand observations. Consequently, making sense of how an animal or human functioned meant detailed dissection and cataloguing of the objects of inquiry, as some of his anatomical notes suggest, 'The heart has three cavities, and is situated above the lung at the division of the windpipe, and is provided with a fatty and thick membrane where it fastens on to the great vein and the aorta.'[35] Thus beginning with detailed perceptions of the component parts of creatures, plants and humans, Aristotle was able to formulate the nature of the interaction between all the component parts, and for this task he developed a complete system for categorization.

For Aristotle to properly analyse a subject of inquiry, he must be able to classify the things that are predicated of it, that is the things that make the subject what it is. This enables everything to be ordered in a consistent manner. Predicates that answer the question 'What is . . .?' of a subject under investigation are called substance, and the things that belong to the category are called substances.[36] For example, Aristotle might begin with the subject, man. The predicate of 'man' is animal (i.e. 'man' is a category of animal). A man also has qualities: we might say the man is dark. Quantity is also predicated of him, such that the man in question has dimensions: weight, height, width, etc. Another category of the subject is relations: 'All things then are relative which are called just what they are, of or than something else – or in some other way in relation to something else.'[37] Thus we might say the man is taller, shorter, heavier, etc. than another man. Armed with all this 'ordered' information, Aristotle is now able to move toward the final goal, of defining what a thing really is.

Causality was also indispensable. Aristotle was aware that things change, and reasoned there must be something that causes change. In order to understand the changing nature of the subject, Aristotle devised a scheme that represented causality in four ways. The first cause of a thing is its '*material* cause'; that is to say, for example, the bronze that the statue is shaped from. The second cause is designated the '*formal* cause': 'The form or pattern, i.e. the formula of the essence';[38] we may liken this to the design of the statue. The third, the catalogue of causality, is the '*efficient* cause'; this relates to the agent of change. In the example of the bronze statue, the efficient cause is the craftsman. Finally, there is the '*final* cause'. This relates to the purpose of the cause, what we would liken to purpose or goal; in the case of the statue it is to honour someone. The introduction of this final stage represented Aristotle's most original and influential idea, enabling his system to be designated teleological.³⁹ Thus, when the final cause realizes its full potential, it becomes actualized into what it really is – in this state, the thing is the thing, not merely a vague representation of a higher form (as in Plato's schema).

Empiricism, however, took a significant leap forward with the contribution of David Hume. What Kant did for rationalism, Hume did for empiricism. In fact, it was Hume's critique of philosophy that actually prompted Kant's influential work. In 1734, at the age of twenty-three, Hume began writing *A Treatise of Human Nature*, aimed at introducing an experimental (scientific) method to the study of human nature. Hume believed the ancient philosophers set forth theories that were ostensibly hypothetical and speculative, depending more on invention and superstition than verifiable facts. In response to these fanciful ideologies, Hume advocated a philosophical method that sought to verify the nature of human understanding on the grounds of science. As Morris and Brown suggest: 'Hume is proposing an empiricist alternative to a priori metaphysics. His empiricism is naturalistic in that it refuses countenance to any appeal to the supernatural in the explanation of the human nature.'⁴⁰ Hume's project for conceiving the basis of truth was relatively straightforward: no reliance on mystery, superstition, speculation or the supernatural, but simply a carefully set out formulation of what we experience.

If Descartes conceived of the self as a thinking thing, the 'I' (which is pure rationality), how did an empiricist like Hume account for it? Well, fundamental to Hume's understanding of the self is the nature of understanding itself. We understand everything through perceptions: 'Every idea of a quality in an object passes through an impression.'⁴¹ Things are what we perceive them to be, which is then true of the soul. The mental impression of the soul (inner self) on our mind enables us to perceive it as real, even though we cannot attribute to it any substance. Given the dynamic nature of perceptions, Hume concludes that 'motion' is the cause of thought and perception.⁴² This lays the foundation of his understanding of the self, as he writes, 'I never can catch myself at any time without a perception, and never can observe anything but the perception.'⁴³ In fact, the mind is a perception of dynamic perceptions: 'The mind is a kind of theatre, where several perceptions successively make their appearance; pass, repass, glide away, and mingle in an infinite variety of postures and situations.'[44] Hume asserts that the mind is not a thing, but a constitution of successive perceptions. In this regard Hume is actually a phenomenologist. The self, then, is really what we perceive it to be – what we experience of ourselves.

Fundamentally, Hume believes that the way we think and the thoughts we have are attributable to our engagement with the world of experience. This world impresses on us phenomena, which we then correlate and order into a system of thought. Hume differentiates between impressions and ideas; the difference between the two relates to the force with which they strike the mind.[45] The impressions from sensation engage us directly (things we see, taste, touch, hear, etc.), and under this category Hume puts the emotions and passions, which impress themselves directly on the soul. An idea, then, is a representative echo of the original impression on the mind.[46] Hume states it thus: 'all our simple ideas in their first appearance, are derived from simple impressions; which are correspondent to them, and which they exactly represent'.[47] Hume uses the example of taste. Can you ever imagine the taste of a pineapple from innate reason? Hume responds, 'We cannot form to ourselves a just idea of the taste of a pineapple, without having actually tasted it.'[48] Hume reasons that, in the first instance, ideas are dependent on prior experience.

Of course, this theory rings true for simple ideas; but what of complex ideas? How do we account for the fact that simple impressions can eventually lead to complex ideas? Hume reasons as follows: Human nature has two faculties at its disposal, through which the association of ideas is possible: memory and imagination. The memory recalls the impressed ideas, and the imagination associates them. The imagination draws upon three qualities in the association of these ideas: resemblance, contiguity, and cause and effect.[49] Hume suggests that the imagination easily runs from one idea to another that resembles it (what we would call analogy). As it does so the imagination operates in time and space, so contiguity comes into it along the way;

impressed ideas associate with those that are spatially next to or in a temporal sequence to them. Cause and effect are, by far, the greatest factor in association. One thing may be related to another as a thing that is caused by, or is the cause of another. However, for Hume, 'causation' is not an innate principle: 'For as that action or motion is nothing but the object itself, considered in a certain light, and as the object continues the same in all its different situations, it is easy to imagine how such an influence of objects upon one another may connect them in the imagination.'[50]

In essence, Hume's basic question is one of meaning, not absolute truth. He is striving to ask the question 'What does it mean?' rather than 'What is the truth?' As such, truth is more accurately conceived as belief, a belief that is arrived at empirically. A complex association of ideas derived from impressions can soon be formed into a custom or habit. Belief then is a further reification of custom or habit. If a custom or habit remains consistent long enough, we 'believe' it to be consistently true. Belief is a sentiment, which is impossible to empirically observe, but is a firmer, more consistent, and more vivid conception of a phenomenon. For example, if my experience of the sun rising of a morning is valid, and it proves to be consistently so, then I can form a firm belief that the sun will rise every morning. As such what is 'believed' to be true, through consistently empirical investigation, is consequently true. As such, it is easy to see why only observable facts can be conceived of as being true!

There are other notable empiricists. In the twentieth century, Ludwig Wittgenstein took up Hume's concept of meaning, but with specific reference to language. Following a time at Cambridge in 1911–13 under the influence of Bertrand Russell, Wittgenstein composed his most famous work, *Tractatus Logico-Philosophicus* (in note form), during the war years. This work became influential on a group called the Vienna Circle, which was originally formed on the basis of the logical positivism of Ernst Mach, aiming to free scientific inquiry from metaphysical dependencies.[51] The group came to embrace the idea that the starting point for philosophy was not epistemology but a kind of mathematical logic, developed by Gottlob Frege and Bertrand

Russell. The group was then heavily influenced by Wittgenstein's *Tractatus*, developing a school of thought that saw that logic was more dependent on the form of reasoning rather than its subject matter, leading to the notion that the validity of conclusions does not depend on terms but on symbols that represent a shorthand version of the formal structure of the argument. Thus, rather than individual words being receptacles for meaning, they only had meaning in relation to a material context, such that meaning was tied to the empirical facts of the context.

Wittgenstein proceeds on the basis that the logic of our language is misunderstood. When we make individual words the primary conveyors of meaning this leads to equivocation, as one word can mean many things to different interpreters. Take for example the word 'law'; it can mean rule, principle, moral command, etc. and is highly subject to prevarication. For Wittgenstein the only words that truly carry meaning must be clear, as his introduction to *Tractatus* suggests: 'The whole sense of the book might be summed up in the following words: what can be said at all can be said clearly, and what we cannot talk about we must pass over in silence.'[52] The world is the totality of facts, not things. For Wittgenstein a fact is the existence of a state of affairs, and states of affairs are a combination of things; as for individual words, they simply name things, the things which make up the state of affairs, which in turn lead to facts. A fact is something we can picture, as we picture the state of affairs; therefore reality is something we can picture, and words only have meaning with reference to the state of affairs with constitute fact (the picture): 'In logic nothing is accidental: if a thing can occur in a state of affairs, the possibility of the state of affairs must be written into the thing itself.'[53]

For empiricists such as Wittgenstein, meaning over abstract truth is paramount. He would ask not what truth is revealed, but rather what does it mean: 'What is the meaning of a word?'[54] We should not confuse the sign (word) with the meaning; meaning is derived from a process, not simply a sign. For Wittgenstein, we don't simply interpret words, as the interpretation is necessarily bound up in the processes of language.[55] Indeed, the signs of these words are dead without the association of the process. With reference to propositions he notes: 'what must be added to the dead signs in order to make a live proposition is something immaterial [intangible], with properties different from all mere signs.'[56] He adds, 'But if we had to name anything which is the life of the sign, we should have to say that it was its use.'[57] Wittgenstein argues that the primary problem with our attempt to understand the meaning of words is we are looking for the use (meaning) of a sign as though it were an object coexisting with the sign. However, he suggests that signs (words, sentences, etc.) get their significance from the 'system' of signs, from the language to which they belong: 'Roughly; understanding a sentence means understanding a language.'[58] Thus the meaning of the word is not associated with an abstract metaphysical theory of signs that imposes itself on existence, but rather the word's use in relationship to the language game.

Wittgenstein is able to effectively conceptualize the meaning of words, by describing language as a game. For example, the game of football has a language all of its own; certain phrases and expressions only find their true meaning with reference to that game. There is an implicit understanding of meaning that the players adopt, such that those listening from the side lines (who are not familiar with the game) would have no comprehension of the meaning. For example, the players have predetermined plays they wish to execute during the game, to which they might give code names, and there might be moves within the play that also can be abbreviated. If the team is pressing forward and one of the key players shouts 'ball-right', implying the ball should be passed out to the right, the rest of the team would instinctively 'know the meaning', even though the term 'ball-right' is completely nonsensical when abstracted from the context of the game. Then, 'ball-right', which may be abbreviated further to 'B-R', would be meaningless to those who were ignorant of the game.

As you can now see, meaning is found in the context of the dynamic language process. As such Wittgenstein is able to convey the idea that meaning determines truth. What is true is that which has meaning with reference to a particular tangible context, which, invariably, leads to the notion of truth being entirely relative.

Truth, Reason and Action: Pragmatism

Truth is sometimes perceived and valued in terms of its 'useful' outcome. Pragmatism promotes the idea that the value of what we think must be conceived in terms of what we do and the practical value of it. It is a philosophy increasingly influencing Christian thought and practice, necessarily linking truth to practical religious outcomes. This school of thought formally came into being in the United States in the 1870s, promoted by thinkers such as Charles Sanders Peirce, William James and John Dewey. With Immanuel Kant, the possibility of conceiving 'reality' entirely in terms of a human point of view was established, and although some pragmatists (such as Peirce) might reject Kant's metaphysics, he makes use of Kant's notion of the 'world for me', as Cornelius van Til suggests, 'Thus pragmatism has consistently worked out the Kantian idea that man must furnish his own a priori.'[59] In reaction to speculative metaphysics, which in the mind of the pragmatist seems to promote 'useless' ideas about ideas (such as Descartes's clear and distinct ideas), pragmatism seeks to demonstrate that clarity of thought comes when reflection on an 'object' takes into account the practical effects of the 'object'. As such, pragmatism is a form of phenomenology, enabling the interpreter to understand the object in relation to the practical outworking of their understanding; as such, the practical goal of philosophical reflection is utility.

Charles Sanders Peirce was the first to formally set out the philosophy of pragmatism. Over and against the alleged 'nonsense' of Cartesian rationalism, Peirce technically avoids the quest to establish 'the truth' as some abstract absolute, in favour of formulating a method by which we can establish the relative certitude of what we believe: 'Your problems would be greatly simplified, if, instead of saying that you want to know the "truth", you simply say that you want to attain a state of belief unassailable to doubt.'[60] As for the logical basis of his endeavour, he posits that to 'infer' anything is determined by some habit of mind. The passage from premise to conclusion must be governed by some 'general principle', which is encapsulated in the notion of habit of mind: 'the particular habit of mind which governs this or that inference may be formulated in a proposition whose truth depends on the validity of the inference which the habit determines; and such a formula is called a guiding principle of inference.'[61] The practical nature of the philosophy is evident in that 'habits' are constitutive of the interpretation of certitude, in his terms 'settling opinion' (what is popularly accepted).

But how is such 'settling of opinion' determined? He advocates four potential candidates: the method of tenacity (bigotry), the method of authority (social convention), the method a priori (rationalism), and the method of science (empirical observation). Peirce advocates a conceptual system that makes provision for the legitimate reality of external objects that exist independent of our thinking or perceiving them. That these objects exist is most aptly validated by a general consensus; what is real is what most people through a consensus of scientific investigation come to see and believe as real. The notion of practical consensus seems to be his undergirding guiding principle: 'he thinks we should decide in favour of science . . . best adapted to our social needs . . . the practice of method by all inquirers must in the long run lead to all disputed questions being settled.'[62] Thus by means of a practical investigation through scientific method, which has been tested and approved by the consensus of the many, the truth (as it can be best approximated) can be arrived at, as Peirce states, 'The opinion which is fated to be ultimately agreed to by all who investigate, is what we mean by the truth, and the object represented in this opinion is the real.'[63]

If the method of Peirce's pragmatism is scientific investigation, then its goal is practical utility. For Peirce the goal of philosophy is never mere rational speculation; such an endeavour he considers as useless. Rather he suggests that his conception of truth was developed out of an original impulse to 'act' consistently and with definite intention; that is to say that his philosophy is purposeful.[64] In fact Peirce's maxim of pragmatism is clear: 'Consider what effects that might conceivably have practical bearings we conceive the object of our conception to have; then, our conception of those effects is the whole of our conception of the object.'[65] Thus, for Peirce the significance and value of any conception lies in its practical bearings as they relate conceivable circumstances and how we should act in a practical way, and not merely how we would act with regard to affirming or denying the conception under investigation.[66] Therefore, in Peirce's estimation, the goal of the pragmatist's quest for truth (or believable certitude) is to provide a theoretical justification for some practice or action that most people consent to seeing its veracity and value.

William James, a fellow-American contemporary of Peirce, found in pragmatism the solution to what he considered the fundamental problem in philosophy – the clash between two ideologies of rationalism and empiricism. On the one side was empiricism, which James categorized as 'tough-minded'. Empiricism related to hard sciences, matters of fact, and concrete observations of phenomena, and had little interest in metaphysics or time for ethics. On the other side, rationalism fell into the category of 'tender-minded'. The tender-mindedness of rationalism tended to be idealistic, ethical and religious; it was interested in the over-arching structures, how things held together, and whether things were right or wrong – to those with a bias toward the former it had little value. The tough-minded empiricists were naturally sceptical, whereas the tender-minded rationalists tended toward dogmatism, notions of truth in abstraction, and virtue.[67] Rather than dispensing with rationalism, as his pragmatic bias might have suggested, James saw it as necessary to incorporate, with Kant before him, the idea that the rational a priori gave meaning to the empirical. In his version of pragmatism (radical empiricism), James advocated a mediating system; a philosophy that removed the ambiguities by clarifying their practical value, and allowed both to exist in harmony, as they complemented each other.

In understanding James's philosophy, it is helpful to understand his view of 'the self'. As opposed to Descartes's view of 'self', which represented the rational consciousness in abstraction from material reality, James's appraisal is grounded: 'In its widest possible sense, however, a man's Self is the sum total of all that he CAN call his, not only his body and his psychic powers, but his clothes and his house, his wife and children, his ancestors and friends, his reputation and works, his lands and horses, and yacht and bank-account.'[68] James actually divides 'the self' into distinct categories: the material self, social self, spiritual self and pure ego. The material self includes the body, clothes, family, home, etc.; all that can be called mine! The social self is the self as recognized by others in relationship with 'me'. The spiritual self is a person's inner subjective being, psychic faculties or dispositions; this is the felt self that knows and can be known through emotions, etc. The pure ego is the 'I' identity, which might be compared to the soul or mind; it is not a substance, and as such is not subject to empirical observation. Unlike Descartes's abstracted self, James's self is holistic, integrated, relational and dynamic.

Rather than the self standing in stark differentiation from phenomena, with Descartes, James's self stands interpretively engaged. James advocates a radical empiricism, in which he argues that ideas, which are part of our experience, become true in as much as they assist us to get into 'satisfactory' relations with other parts of our experience: 'To be radical, an empiricism must neither admit into its constructions any element that is not directly experienced, nor exclude from them any element that is directly experienced.'[69] This effectively means that if a new idea enters into a relationship with the 'stock' of our current ideas and dynamically proves by experience to have value for the concrete life it will be true (in a limited experiential sense). How far they may be determined as being truer will depend on further empirical verification and relations to other truths. Therefore, true ideas are those that a person can assimilate and validate; the more they are socially validated the more true they become – no idea is intrinsically true until it is validated. Therefore in James's conceptualization, truth is something that happens to an idea, and its veracity is a process, an event; its validity is the process of its verification.[70] Absolute or objective truth is something being worked toward; it represents the ideal vanishing point at which someday all of our provisional truths will converge.[71]

We can already anticipate what this kind of thinking will produce. Truth is determined with respect to utility. Something is provisionally true until a new idea sheds light on it, and alters the veracity of the previous truth by proving 'more' useful. Truth, then, progressively shifts according to increasingly valuable utility. Rational concepts do not necessarily serve as correctives against this continual drift toward the 'vanishing point' of truth, but actually augment the process. James sees them as having three functions: 'provide an immense map of relations among the elements of things . . . which may steer us practically . . . They bring new values into our perceptual life, they reanimate our wills . . . The map which the mind frames out of them is an object which possesses, when once it has been framed, an independent existence.'[72]

With regard to truth, reason doesn't correct the flux of experience, but supports and validates it. Whatever the 'value' of the rational idea validating this pragmatic system of logic, this then determines the truth-value of the practical outcome. Therefore, if economic rationalism (the value of things determined by their economic benefits) is adopted, it then becomes the dominant logic feeding the system of belief, which in turn argues that what is 'true' is what becomes most economically efficient, which in turn becomes more true, the more economically efficient (profitable) it appears to be – and so on.

But, as with Plato's rationalism, pragmatism needs education to give it legs. The degree to which pragmatism became assimilated into the public consciousness was in no small part due to the efforts of John Dewey, a philosopher dedicated to the field of education. Dewey believed that pragmatism, being an active philosophy, needed a context in which to develop, because an idea was not an idea in the fullest sense until it was applied and enacted in an actual situation toward some constructive purpose, as William Kilpatrick suggests, 'this philosophy properly required its own incarnation in order to be itself and to get itself adequately studied and criticized.'[73] Education became that incarnation.

Standing over and against a top-down authoritarian system of traditional education that focused on dogmatically presenting content that should be memorized, Dewey, in accord with his philosophy, introduced an interactive model of learning. In Dewey's thinking, knowledge results from human efforts to deal with the actual world: 'As man seeks to meet his wants, his past experiences in the shape of accumulated habits and ideas will come forward to help him analyse the situation at hand and suggest promising ways of dealing with it.'[74] Learning is not simply acquiring principles, but represents an interactive engagement, assimilating past experience and new ideas to gain greater knowledge, the teacher being the guide.

Truth, Reason and Human Existence: Existentialism

Existentialism is a philosophical movement that approaches the quest for truth with reference to 'personal' human existence and the inner experience of considering it. Although Jean-Paul Sartre may have formally coined the term in his post-war literature, its heritage long predates him. Opposing the dualism of Descartes, where the self is a thinking thing abstracted from material reality, existentialism addresses a more holistic self (heart, soul, emotions, etc.). Of course, this does not imply the dismissal of the empirical sciences and an engagement in the concrete affairs of life, but it does suggest they are not enough.[75] Existentialism seeks out an understanding of the inner human self in its engagement with reality, because it advocates there is something authentic to life over and above abstract rational reflection and material life – an existence that transcends the world of the mind and senses. This being so, it comes as no surprise that seminal existentialists were actually Christian. The Christian faith, as a spiritual phenomenon, provides the perfect framework for conceptualizing the true existence of the 'inner self', as it transcends merely 'human' categories.

What we know as existentialism, for all intents and purposes, has its heritage in the Augustinian tradition. Augustine was not an existentialist in the modern sense of the word; in fact his reliance on Platonic dualism would probably set him at odds with contemporary manifestations of it. Yet, this seminal thinker was one of the first to authentically address the holistic (including non-rational) self in relationship to truth, as his reflection on the futility of his former beliefs suggests: 'Truth! Truth! How the very marrow of my soul within me yearned for it as they dinned it in my ears over and over again!'[76] Existentialism, for Augustine, related to an 'inward turn', that he might get in touch with his soul and through contemplation attain a higher state of existence in communion with God. And while this in a contemplation finds justification in the New Testament, it is his Platonic heritage that truly gives it methodological legs, as Phillip Cary suggests: 'The inward turning of Augustine has a Christological theme, but is no less philosophical for that. On the contrary, it is in the inward turn that we can see most clearly how Augustine's Platonist philosophical conviction shaped his understanding of Christ.'[77]

Ultimate existence for Augustine did not pertain to life in this material world, but in the escape from it; an idea heavily indebted to Plato, as Ronald Nash intimates: 'Man's ultimate goal should be union with the One, but in order to attain this union, the soul must rise upward – it must free itself from its bondage to the body, pleasure, and sensation. As a soul leaves behind the realm of sensation, it becomes closer to its ultimate goal, the One. This view was derived from Plato.'[78] Of course, for Augustine, Plato's idea of 'the One' was replaced by God. For this seminal thinker, there were two kinds of knowledge to be embraced, *scientia* (relating to the realm of material things), and *sapientia* (wisdom related to higher matters). While he saw value in *scientia* with respect to ordinary life, it is the focus on *sapientia*; the contemplative life always being superior to the active life: 'The upper path of knowledge for Augustine involves the passage from sensation to the rational cognizance of temporal things (scientia) to the intellectual cognizance of eternal reality (sapientia).'[79] And yet, in this process of contemplation, we find some of Augustine's most grounded, honest and authentically human reflections.

But, it is the honesty and openness of these reflections that enable him to be most readily identified with existentialism. His words have all the existential thrust of Jean-Paul Sartre, but the poetic eloquence of a deeply religious thinker: 'But while my hunger was few, for truth itself, these were the dishes in which they served me up the sun and the moon, beautiful works of yours . . . For your spiritual works are greater than these material things, however brightly they may shine in the sky.'[80] In the following quote we see his Platonic ontology dressed up in highly existential language: 'My soul was a burden, bruised and bleeding. It was tired of the man who carried it, but I found no place to set it down to rest. Neither the charm of the countryside or the sweet sense of the garden could soothe it.'[81] But it is Augustine's incredible openness that sets him apart as an existentialist; his willingness to bear his soul, perhaps, remained uneclipsed: 'My heart lies before you, O my God. Look deep within. See these memories of mine, for you are my hope. You cleanse me when uncleaned humours such as these possess me, by drawing my eyes to yourself and saving my feet from the snare.'[82] Augustine was not intentionally an existentialist, but one who would take up his mantle could be described thus – Soren Kierkegaard.

Kierkegaard was a nineteenth-century Christian philosopher, credited as being the father of modern existentialism. Kierkegaard's upbringing, early life and cultural context set his philosophical tenor. First, his family situation shaped his strongly introspective disposition: 'What was unusual in the Kierkegaard home was the strict religious upbringing combined with the father's melancholia, a melancholia that Kierkegaard felt had been projected onto himself.'[83] Then there was Kierkegaard's controversial separation from his fiancée, Regine. Despite his passion to marry, the young Soren felt torn between choosing two destinies: marriage and life in a country parish, or the solitary life of the philosopher that he felt the times demanded. His choice to set aside the 'normal' life for the extraordinary set the tone for his writing.

Finally, the philosophical and religious climate was strongly determinative of his calling. The monist Hegel strongly shaped the thinking of the times, justifying the homogenization of the individual self within the social 'whole'. Moreover, Hegel's dialectic logic promised the capacity to access the mind of God without compromising human reason, one could have both/and; doubtless the impetus behind the title of one of Kierkegaard's more famous works: 'Either/Or'!

Furthermore the religious climate reflected Hegelian influences. This was the era of Schleiermacher, and resultant theologies that saw Christ as merely an example, and good works as the means of progression toward God. A strongly introspective early life, and being thrust into a culture climate of homogenization set Kierkegaard at odds with his time.

Within a form of Christendom that had capitulated to culture that was merging the individual into an homogenous social identity, Kierkegaard felt the need to invent a style of rhetoric that challenged people to not only see the problems, but also identify these problems and take responsibility for their own existential choices.[84] In this matter Kierkegaard was inspired by the methods of Socrates, whose use of irony was able to undermine the dogmatism naïvely embraced by his audience, as William McDonald notes, 'Kierkegaard sought to provide a similar service for his own contemporaries. He used irony, parody, satire, humor, and deconstructive techniques in order to make conventionally accepted forms of knowledge and value untenable.'[85] Like the apostle Paul, Kierkegaard presented Christianity as diametrically opposed to the Christian ethos that sought to make it rationally acceptable, by emphasizing the transcendence of God and the necessity of the individual to personally engage him. The human is not simply a representation of the whole working toward God, but one who stood in stark contrast to a transcendent holy being.

Kierkegaard's greater project emphasized and engaged three stages of human existence. The first stage or category he qualified as the aesthetic stage. In this stage the human is a mere spectator, one who is enamoured by the mundane sensate world, who simply goes along with the crowd, content to meld into a lacklustre society: 'Let others complain that the age is wicked; my complaint is that it is wretched, for it lacks passion . . . This is why my soul always turns back to the Old Testament . . . I feel that those who speak there are at least human beings.'[86] The second stage is the ethical. In this stage the human moves beyond the baser desires of life, and sees value in having a social conscience; such a person sees the value in family responsibility, civic duty, social stewardship and religious devotion (in so far as it encourages a sober life that can benefit society at large). Although nobler than the former stage, this 'existence' falls short of the third and highest state of life: the religious state animated by a passionate faith in God.

This final stage Kierkegaard sees as exemplified by Abraham's 'leap of faith'. God commands Abraham to break the rules (ignore the former promise and innate moral imperative), in what Kierkegaard might deem as a teleological suspension of the ethical, in order to ascend to a greater calling of absolute abandonment to God in faith. Such a moment of passion is decisive for human existence, for in the paradox of the abandonment of self in absolute trust (against all reason), the human discovers an unparalleled form of existence. It is Abraham's example that then becomes the Christian paradigm for true existence. Such a philosophical 'move' enables value to be bestowed on the 'non-cognitive' aspects of the human 'inner life' as the means of arriving at the highest form of truth. This kind of truth cannot be learned, studied or acquired in any second-hand manner; it has to be appropriated by being involved, by giving over. This is not a truth acquired by the 'rational self', but requires an experience of self-abandonment. An existential engagement is therefore indispensable for truth to be appreciated and understood. Such a move then opens the door for further development in the field, which leads us to the work of another prominent twentieth-century existentialist, Martin Heidegger.

Heidegger initiated the 'ontological turn' in philosophy, instigating a significant break from a tradition extending from Descartes to Husserl. Thus, with Heidegger the dominance of epistemology came under the challenge of hermeneutics. Heidegger was a prior disciple of Edmund Husserl, who pioneered modern phenomenology. Husserl's phenomenology represented the zenith of a form of philosophizing that began with Descartes. Rather than simply thinking in terms of a subject / object relationship, where the object projects qualities toward the perceiving subject, Husserl argued that the subject, in the act of interpretation, intentionally 'constitutes' the object being interpreted. Integrating the 'act of understanding' into the object being understood gives another level of nuance to the transcendental idealism of Kant. To prevent the object or the act of understanding merging, Husserl advocates a theory called 'bracketing' where the subject can 'stand aloof' from the process and, in a Cartesian fashion, bring objectivity to the event. Yet, in identifying the weakness of such a system – that 'existence' was simply assumed – Heidegger took his cue to introduce a new way of thinking about understanding.

In his most famous work, *Being and Time*, Heidegger lays out a new ontology (understanding of being) and by extension a new way of approaching the 'truth quest'. For Heidegger, we do not begin the truth endeavour as an abstracted reasoning mind relating to objects as a superior subject, but rather we start with our 'being-in-the-world', as McGrath suggests: 'This task is nothing less than the grounding of ontology in a faithful analysis of everyday living.'[87] The notion of 'being' as substance (corporeal or incorporeal) in traditional philosophy, that may be abstracted, is challenged by Heidegger, as he affirms that being must 'be' somewhere. For this task he employs the term *Dasein* (being there): 'Being lies in the fact that something is, and in its Being as it is; in Reality; in presence-at-hand; in subsistence; in validity; in Dasein.'[88] The implication is that thinking, in the Cartesian sense, cannot predate existence or being-in-the-world; existence is a pre-critical given and cannot simply be inferred through rational thought: 'Dasein always understands itself in terms of its existence – in terms of a possibility of itself: to be itself or not itself.'[89] This notion of possibility hints at the other key element of his ontology, the relationship of being to time.

Heidegger's view of being (*Dasein*) implies that being is conditioned by time. For something to 'be there' (somewhere), and not simply be being in ethereal abstraction, it must be subject to the temporal: 'Time must be brought to light – and genuinely conceived – as a horizon for all understanding of Being and for any way of interpreting it.'[90] As such, the idea of being in time conditions the idea of being itself. Thinking in this way Heidegger seeks to ground all philosophical inquiry in human existence that is subject to the limitations of time (proven by the fact that we all die). As such, people cannot simply launch into metaphysical speculation without first coming to terms with their own existence in the world, as beings in 'time'. With this approach Heidegger is able to take philosophical inquiry one step back to our unconscious or pre-critical existence, before we engage in the rational process.

Heidegger's thinking was developed in the context of everyday life. He would argue that, in our naïve thinking, we often take for granted that which predates interpretation; we are thrown into the world and find ourselves in a concrete existence, simply 'knowing' things we are not conscious of. As such, in the experience of using things, we understand the nature of being. This concept Heidegger calls 'readiness-to-hand'. In using a hammer, a carpenter understands the purpose of the hammer in a real, 'non-theoretical' way. Even without a theory of 'hammering', knowledge of the hammer and its purpose is clearly known.[91] In another example, consider a child who is born into a family that speaks the French language. The child will grow up learning habits of speech, understanding and speaking the language, even developing a particular accent, without any conscious awareness of that language. Only when the child goes to school does she get to critically examine language by learning to write, understanding grammar, etc. In this case, as in the case of many things, understanding precedes interpretation; our existence in the world offers a kind of understanding that precedes critical knowing.

Reason and the False Quest for Truth

When I speak of reason in this context, I am referring to reason as that human intellectual and/or sensual capacity that seeks to make sense of things independent of God's revealed truth; either by ignoring that revelation, minimizing it or relativizing it as insignificant. This does not imply that the use of reason has no value; indeed it does, for no human can think or feel without reasoning. But, as we have seen, the quest for truth has largely been a human attempt to independently make sense of what is real with reference to known existence without primary reference to and complete dependence on God. Our primary focus has been on independent human reason as it has manifested itself in the Western philosophical consciousness, and because of its ubiquitous influence on the culture in which contemporary Christianity operates.

However, extinguishing all reference to the divine in an attempt to understand reality is ultimately naïve, as at some point the notion of God must be taken into account (as in the case of Descartes). In view of this, the nature of Western thought could not be considered strictly atheistic, but more accurately a-theistic, in as much as it seeks to make the human interpreter the primary point of reference, leaving the divine on the fringe or bracketing it out of the philosophical equation. Consequently, the quest assumes that human thinkers must work with the phenomena encountered, and on the assumption that they 'themselves' must come to terms with it, resolutely thinking their way toward truth or meaning. This is a quest that effectively attempts to define reality in terms of what is agreeable to, but not limited by, the existence they know – truth as they want it to be!

Rationalism pays credence to the fact that humans are rational beings, advocating an innate capacity for the authority of reason. However, in the Western tradition, it is predicated on the pre-Socratic notion of the one and the many, the idea that there must be one unifying constant behind the many particular things that are constantly in flux. Viewed sceptically, this is nothing more than a metaphysical projection of the individual self, trying to make sense of the multitude of particulars encountered. Plato's notion of pure forms as the basis of material existence, with the soul having access to the meaning of pure forms via memory, actually presents more like a religious ideology evacuated of a divine modus operandi. While Descartes attempts to add credibility with a system to support the notion of pure reason as the basis of truth, with 'I' (the thinking thing) capable of knowing that rationality is the basis of truth, he also resorts to the 'outside' idea of the divine to validate the capacity of reason to arrive at a credible position of truth.

Kant's sophisticated critique, in contrast to the prior contributions, exposes that the true starting point for rationalism is not 'pure reason' at all, but actually human experience. He openly states, at the outset of *The Critique*, that all knowledge invariably begins with experience. Moreover, Kant's contribution reveals that rationalism is really a highly egocentric endeavour; where the 'thing' observed is in fact the 'thing for me' – a reality 'I' form. Ironically, despite its attempt to provide a basis for discerning truth objectively, rationalism is perhaps the most subjective of all the philosophical disciplines. Reality (from without or within) imposes itself on existence, giving it 'form', while it remains itself beyond complete comprehension. In the end, it is a sophisticated way for humans to justify what they want to see as real.

Empiricism, as we have seen, represents a way of arriving at truth / meaning on the premise that the human mind is a blank canvas on which sense data, through sensed perception, makes its impression on the human mind. These sense-based impressions form the basis of ideas, aided by the use of memory and imagination. This philosophy is inherently naturalistic, viewing the human being as little more than an intelligent animal, which comprehends things, albeit complex, from a direct engagement with the natural world. Reason is 'naturally' conditioned by experience, as Hume's example of the pineapple suggests – we have no concept of what it tastes like until we have tasted it!

For the empiricist the concept of truth is not really important, what is of greater value is the notion of meaning: what a thing means in my understanding is what I finally believe to be true. For example, if physical violence has a valid meaning in any context, then it is legitimate to enact (as per evolutionary theory). A true fact is not something we derive from innate reason, but is validated by context in which we find it. As a consequence, morality is something that develops in a given setting and has no absolute reference point to determine it. For empiricism, reality is what the experiencing subject finds to be consistently meaningful in their experience of the material existence they consistently encounter. Truth is seen almost entirely in materialistic terms, and is created by a reasoned formulation of sensed 'facts'. Ironically, like the rationalism it seeks to counter, it relies on independent human rationality to arrive at its formulation of reality.

Pragmatism, as a radical form of empiricism perceives truthfulness as a state of belief oriented toward practical utility. A philosophy well suited to the twenty-first century, pragmatism enables the validation of views of truth, based on ever-changing consensus and usefulness. Truth (as accepted belief) becomes socially validated when enough people agree that something seems useful to the whole group. As such, truth is never a static thing, never absolute; it is always progressing toward that illusory vanishing point of a greater truth.

Pragmatism provides an ideology that validates ever-changing views on matters such as technology, economics, sexuality and medicine, to the degree that new advances leading to new understanding should be embraced, if they prove useful to the perceived good of the majority. This is the quintessential doctrine for the practical and progressive thinker. It is ever moving toward an allegedly better and more satisfactory view of truth – often ignoring the long-term costs. However, whenever progress and utility drive truth, the potential exists for new 'revelations of truth' to become a runaway train, no longer subject to any absolute standard that provides moral regulation. For pragmatism then, reality is an existence of progressive utility, despite consequences. Its subtle embracing by many Christians will have disastrous consequences.

Existentialism is the most introspective and emotive of all the philosophical schools that seek to find truth independently. In its most introspective form, truth can simply become 'my' existence with reality disengaged, having a penchant toward nihilism. Whilst having the potential to be the most delusional, it also has the potential to be the most honest and revelatory of the philosophical movements. Pushing aside the delusion of rational control, existentialism is able to recognize aspects of truth that are non-rational that we accept as valid (faith, intuition, emotiveness, etc.) even if they cannot be rationally defined. We see this in Kierkegaard's portrayal of Abraham's faith, where in a complete abandonment to God, Abraham suspends the power of human reason in favour of the Lord's wisdom. Through a non-rational apprehension of faith, Abraham is able to accept the truth of God's call, knowing it to be completely valid, even if it is rationally non-verifiable. Furthermore, Heidegger's version of existentialism being strictly a-theistic, carries with it a similar epistemic humility to Kierkegaard's. Heidegger recognizes that human subjects find themselves 'thrown' into the world, into an existence that is bigger than the rational perception can grasp – an existence in which understanding is known before it can be defined. For the existentialist, reality is an existence in a dimension unconstrained by rational constructs, a reality that I provisionally understand, but through faith and action seek greater revelation to make sense of it. In this sense, existentialism is the least sceptical of all the philosophies.

Of course, all humans 'reason'; we are rational beings and that is the nature of our being. Indeed, the quest for truth along the pathway of reason is helpful in wrestling with vital questions of human understanding, and offers up some interesting and valid answers. However it is the failure to deliver substantive answers to life's conundrums that reveals the emptiness of independent reason.

Indeed, the processes of human reasoning, sophisticated as they might seem, actually serve to obscure truth and its meaning, by creating an artificial view of reality where God does not exist, is impotent in existence, or only serves human purposes and its ends through his existence. When the 'I' becomes the sovereign truth seeker, the quest is invariably limited to human capacities and can never reach beyond what 'I' can reasonably want to comprehend. At best it defines truth within the limitations of human capacity, a truth agreeable to the human ego. Ultimately it is an attempt to define reality from a limited and fallible perspective and, as such, fails to acknowledge and submit to the divine revelation that surrounds it, and always seeks to define a controllable reality independent of God.

In human philosophy, there seems to be an inherent bias not to be open to truth / meaning that cannot be fully quantified and controlled by the human subject. As such, in deliberately excluding divine revelation in its full potency, from the quest, we might say that the quest for the truth is actually a quest to mask the divine within human existence, by pulling over it an artificial reality concomitantly agreeable to the limited agendas of human reason. As such, the goal, albeit unintended, is actually the concealment of the truth in favour of independent human control. We could say that human reason constructs a reality through which the interpreter shapes existence in the world or reality as 'I' want it to be.

If this is the state of affairs, then the discovery of truth can never come from the independent human self and its reliance on reason. Truth must be revealed from outside; it must break into our false reality through the initiative of one who transcends the human condition – truth must be shown to us by God.

2

Truth and Divine Revelation

What if truth was not something 'we' discovered? Through the use of independent reason, humans ultimately desire quantifiable control of an existence within a contrived reality. Every philosophical system is fundamentally oriented toward ordering human existence according to the reality it has constructed for itself. Indeed, all philosophical systems provide the logical blueprints for an imagined *world* that is both quantifiable and predictable; a world in which *the self* can be sovereign. These contrived 'worlds' are so convincing that those who embrace them actually believe in the possibility of controlling *everything* within them. Consequently, human existence becomes entirely explicable in terms of its own 'infinite' power. But there is a problem. While human control seems 'hypothetically' possible within these frames of reference, it actually is not! Invariably human finitude is shown up by its faltering response to the inexplicable. The extent of human impotence is truly exposed when the harsh experiences of life reveal certainty through control is simply an illusion. What then is the truth-seeker to make of this misalignment between 'real' human existence and those idealized philosophical realities? Is there another way of making sense of things? Could it be that God just might have something to say about the misalignment we encounter? What if we were open to a truth that wasn't our own?

Uncertainty, Faith and Revelation: The Story of Job

God reveals truth, and does so through powerful stories. When we consider the nature of God's revelation as it engages ultimate reality and human existence, the Old Testament story of Job is unsurpassed. The narrative of Job sets out to discuss the supremacy of divine wisdom by referencing one man's calamitous life and his struggle to come to terms with the divine reality in the midst of an existence of human suffering. John Goldingay suggests that the story of Job takes the form of a play in which various characters act out their ideologies by offering up varying human insights in an attempt to make sense of Job's tragic experience, and the relationship between reality and existence with reference to divine truth and justice.[1] In this 'play', the principal actor is God, the one in the divine drama with the most at stake, having laid his reputation on the line as he 'bets' against Satan on Job's integrity. Satan also takes a leading role, at least in the initial stages, acting out the role of the quintessential sceptic, arguing that even the noblest human will invariably fail in the face of calamity, readily abandoning a faith-dependency on God when their testing removes all divine privileges.

Then there is Job, a model of human integrity around whom the entire drama unfolds. Despite Job's exemplary character, there appears to be, at least initially, a negative element of 'the fear of the Lord' motivating his obedience; a certain dread that haunts him: 'What I feared has come upon me; what I dreaded has happened to me' (Job 3:25). Only at the end of the calamitous chain of events does Job come to terms with this dread by fully embracing God's word in 'absolute' faith. Playing key roles are also Job's three friends and would-be comforters / counsellors. These three men represent the voice of the conventional human wisdom of the day. Not insignificantly, arriving on the stage late in the drama is the enigmatic figure of Elihu, who serves to provide a powerful prophetic precursor to God's revelatory speech.

As the story unfolds, various dialogues set out different forms of wisdom (truth); each appearing to make sense in its own way, each offering up knowledge with a degree of cogency. However, as we shall see, even the most 'reasonable' human wisdom reaches a limit when attempting to make sense of this anomalous existence ordered by the unseen divine powers.

In the beginning Job's perception of reality aligned perfectly with the experiences of his own life to date. That God favoured the good and punished the wicked, represented a status quo belief to Job and his contemporaries – a solid belief on which one could build their entire existence. From Job's perspective, his life of blessing was attributable to God favouring Job's own righteousness. Moreover, it should be noted that Job was not indifferent to this favour, nor did he take it for granted, as he genuinely responded to God with gratitude, faithfulness and regular fervent devotion. This seemed to be an arrangement that worked, divine justice ordering human existence – the righteous prosper, the wicked suffer.

Yet, this understanding of human existence was seriously ruptured when the forces 'above' imparted on Job's state of affairs a significant anomaly. Unbeknown to Job, divine forces of good and evil (God and Satan) had conferred over the nature of his life and the motives for his actions. Satan argued that Job merely worshipped God as a response to his material blessings, and that removing them would soon reveal his selfish side. In response to this challenge, God gave Satan the power to remove Job's blessings, such that all that he held dear (family and material wealth) was taken from him. However, consistent with God's prior affirmation of Job, the man did not falter. He affirms his faith in God: 'Naked I came from my mother's womb, and naked I shall depart. The LORD gave and the LORD has taken away; may the name of the LORD be praised' (Job 1:21). Even after his health was sorely afflicted, Job remained true to God, consistent with his prior record of integrity.

However, such an anomalous event could not be easily dismissed. Job's calamity ruptured more than his material life; it seriously challenged conventional human wisdom about human existence. Of course, the conventional wisdom of Job's day varies from what moderns determine as wisdom, as the modern view of truth is often represented as rationally defined propositions – 'statements, ideas or things' by which all other things are measured. Indeed, such views leave little room for the divine, as Bartholomew and O'Dowd suggest:

> Our mechanistic, sterile view of the world with this critical lens orientates us to our life experienced through psychological, social or scientific

concepts. When reason and observation rule in this way, anyone who speaks seriously of mystery, the transcendent or the spiritual seems increasingly out of touch with reality. On the contrary, the ancients viewed human life in the world as a personal, holistic and non-scientific relationship with nature.[2]

But for the patriarch Job and his contemporaries, wisdom and truth took on a much more 'grounded' dimension. Truth was far more often oriented around the order of practical existence and the pattern of life under God's governance, rather than a rational abstract ordering of reality. In fact, there was never a sense that truth could be considered without reference to the divine, or one's practical and moral life. This is why wisdom in the Bible is principally presented as 'the fear' of the Lord, with morality being bound to the quality of one's existence. In such a reckoning, the biblical cornerstone of divine wisdom must be the *fear of the Lord*.

Of course, it is precisely this notion of the 'fear of the Lord' that animates the advice of Job's counsellors, as they enter the story offering their form of wisdom. Eliphaz's leading counsel represents a clear example of the conventional wisdom of the day: 'As I have observed, those who plough evil and those who sow trouble reap it' (Job 4:8). From Eliphaz's empirical perspective, Job's calamity clearly reveals the necessary consequence of some evil or sinful action and an ensuing form of divine discipline (Job 5:17). Bildad also weighs in on the side of conventional logic: 'When your children sinned against him, he gave them over to the penalty of their sin' (Job 8:4). For Bildad it's simply a matter of cause and effect. Following on, and in concert with his friends, Zophar brings this logic to bear on Job's situation, admonishing Job to acknowledge the sin, and allow God to restore him: 'if you put away the sin that is in your hand . . . then you will lift up your face without shame' (Job 11:14–15).

Quite simply, from the counsellors' reasoned perspective the cause of Job's undoing must be sin, albeit hidden. The counsel they offer cannot but suggest Job address the unmistakable facts and make amends to God: 'Submit to God and be at peace with him . . . If you return to the Almighty you will be restored' (Job 22:21,23). Of course, what undergirds such logic is the notion that God could never bring suffering to a righteous man, and he only punishes the wicked.[3]

In presenting their version of wisdom, Job's friends offered a view of reality defined in terms of the existence they have empirically found to be true, that is, according to their own experience. Based on the fundamental notion that good things happen to good people and bad things to bad people, they accrued a bank of knowledge grounded on empirical verifiable facts. Such wisdom may seem to be generally true but, as we shall see, the anomaly of Job's circumstances has completely turned this logic on its head. In the case of the wisdom of Job's friends, as in the cases of many human philosophical systems, it cannot account for all anomalies: 'There is a way that seems right to a person, but in the end it leads to death' (Prov. 14:12).

Despite their best intentions, Job remains indifferent to his friends' advice. Yes, Job could comprehend a version of suffering that came as a consequence of evil behaviour, representing a form of divine retribution; in fact this is the reason he prayed on behalf of his children (Job 1:4–5), but in his own mind this was not the cause of his present calamity. Job is resolute about his current station; as far as he can see he remains a righteous man: 'I put on righteousness as my clothing; justice was my robe and my turban. I was eyes to the blind and feet to the lame. I was a father to the needy; I took up the case of the stranger' (Job 29:14–16).

Nevertheless, Job is at a loss to reconcile himself to his new station; conventional wisdom has simply reached an end, and in a moment of sombre reflection acknowledges the futility of the human quest for truth (wisdom): 'Where then does wisdom come from? Where does understanding dwell? It is hidden from the eyes of every living thing, concealed even from the birds of the air' (Job 28:20–21). In the midst of despair, Job acknowledges that God alone knows the way to wisdom: 'And he said to all people, "The fear of the Lord – that is wisdom, and to shun evil is understanding"' (Job 28:28). Yet there is something perplexing in this affirmation, because as far as Job can ascertain, this is the very principle by which he has lived his life thus far. Why then has God abandoned him?

In point of fact, the limitation of Job's wisdom is not that it is inherently flawed on a practical level, but that it simply represents an appraisal of divine wisdom in relation to his own righteousness from a purely human perspective – an understanding of existence based on Job's own perceived anthropocentric reality. Job, in expecting God to vindicate his righteousness, actually proved that he was operating in human terms, as Samuel Terrien intimates, 'He condemned God to human finiteness in attempt to justify himself. He conceived divine justice, not in relation to our God-revolving macrocosm but as a function of his self-centred microcosm.'[4] Indeed, Job was simply living out of and thinking from the wrong centre: 'He denied the theocentricity of the universe by living anthropocentrically.'[5]

Job then represents the quintessential example of autonomous humanity, albeit in a self-righteousness form; not, of course, the hypocritical self-righteousness of the Pharisees, but a form of righteousness that represented the very best of human nature, that had oriented its existence around a human-centred reality. In this regard Job serves as example for all who purport to have 'arrived' on the grounds of naturally contrived truth, whether philosophical or religious. Yet, for all his fallibility Job had touched upon one solid truth; he knew that only God held the key to wisdom: 'God understands the way to it and he alone knows where it dwells' (Job 28:23).

Enter Elihu, a young man who presumes to lecture all concerned regarding the truth. On a superficial reading, the speeches of Elihu seem somewhat out of place within the story of Job. In fact, there has been a general consensus among many scholars that this incongruity implies that the Elihu speeches are later redaction.[6] However, in contrast to such views, Norman Whybray believes that Elihu's speeches are integral to the original text and have a significant role to play: 'Elihu is perhaps best seen as a transitional figure who quite properly disappears once his role has been played out – a counterpart to that other figure, the Satan, for whom also there was no further role in the author's scheme.'[7]

To simply dismiss the Elihu dialogues is to do a great injustice to the overall argument of the book, as it is just as valid to interpret Elihu's 'prophetic' speeches as a precursor, preparing the way for the divine speeches to follow: 'It acts as a spoiler for God's address, in a positive fashion. Elihu starts to get us thinking in God's way, or at least introduces the idea of thinking from God's angle.'[8] In fact, that Elihu seems out of place could actually be interpreted as the very point of his inclusion. As Elihu brings a form of wisdom entirely incongruous with Job's three counsellors he sets the stage for God's speeches and a deliberate challenge to conventional human wisdom.

However, what is most striking about Elihu is that the source of his claimed wisdom is not of human origin. In contrast to his learned company, Elihu is not presented as someone who has accrued wisdom through years of study, observation, practice or reflection, but represents a relatively inexperienced young person: 'I am young in years, and you are old; that is why I was fearful, not daring to tell you what I know' (Job 32:6). Elihu doesn't draw on any credentials of human wisdom to present his case, but appeals to a divine source: 'But it is the spirit in mortals, the breath of the Almighty, that gives them understanding' (Job 32:8). Indeed, Elihu does not credit his insights to his own experience or wisdom, but acknowledges the Spirit's sovereignty, even from the outset of his existence: 'The Spirit of God has made me; the breath of the Almighty gives me life' (Job 33:4).

Perhaps what is most evident as we reflect on Elihu and his non-humanistic credentials is the reminder that human wisdom, philosophy and tradition simply cannot account for all things: 'God's Spirit trumps natural human impulses, abilities, and rationales.'[9] As for his message, based on his Spirit-originated insight, Elihu reminds Job (against his indictment for God to speak) that God can speak in numerous ways, even through human suffering (Job 33:14–26), and despite his appeals to God's apparent injustice and the illogical nature of events, God's ways are simply beyond human comprehension: 'How great is God – beyond our understanding!' (Job 36:26).

With Elihu having 'set the stage', by emphasizing the insufficiency of human-devised truth and naturally attained wisdom, God arrives to offer his defence. The Lord makes a dramatic theophanic appearance in a thunderstorm, issuing forth a direct verbal challenge to Job (who stands out as the representative of those offering a defence in terms of human wisdom). God's address begins with a rebuke: 'Who is this that darkens my counsel with words without knowledge?' (Job 38:2). Then with a series of questions, God highlights the absolute insufficiency of human knowledge in making sense of reality: 'Do you know the laws of the heavens? Can you set up God's dominion over the earth?' (Job 38:33).

Following this sequence of questioning Job is asked to respond. He says: 'I am unworthy – how can I reply to you? (Job 40:4). Again God spoke from the storm inciting him to adorn the attributes of God if he wished to justify himself against God and save himself (Job 40:1–13). After further questioning that still further set the impotence of humanity in its place, Job relents to God's superiority: 'Surely I spoke of things I did not understand, things too wonderful for me to know . . . Therefore I despise myself and repent in dust and ashes' (Job 42:3,6). The story then abruptly concludes with Job's prosperity being reinstated.

Strangely, there is no resolution with reference to human wisdom, no attempt to verify it against the divine testimony; the narrative simply ends with Job admitting God's absolute superiority and humbling himself before the presence of an omniscient divine being.

Yet we must not hastily pass over this, for the ending of Job's story serves to establish the beginning of wisdom, as the proverb states, 'The fear of the LORD is the beginning of wisdom, and knowledge of the Holy One is understanding' (Prov. 9:10). From God's point of view, human wisdom devoid of obedient submission to God has no power to reconcile the nature of ultimate reality against the existence it experiences; on the contrary the beginning of wisdom is to admit that one has no capacity for wisdom and hence must humbly submit to God as one with a child-like faith.

Thus, an understanding of truth only 'truly' begins when the human inquirer has come to an end of himself or herself and acknowledges the insufficiency of human reason in the face of life's anomalies, and then by faith proceeds to walk in obedience before God, leaving the outcome entirely to him: 'Trust in the LORD with all your heart and lean not on your own understanding; in all your ways acknowledge him, and he will make your paths straight' (Prov. 3:5–6). Indeed, there is a way to understand reality beyond reason; this is the way that responds to divine revelation with complete brokenness, faith and humility.

The story of Job reminds us that the real is not rational, quite simply because rationality fails to make sense of human experience when that experience becomes quantifiable. Job's story challenges all who would depend on the capacity of human rationality to provide certitude by quantifying life according to human logic – whatever it might be. In the final analysis, reason (independent of faith in God) is at a loss to explain anomalous events that humans encounter.

Reason may provide a measure of understanding, and to a degree (as Job and his friends suggested) it is true that good things happen to good people, but the mysterious purposes of God ensure that this is not always the case: 'God is indeed good, and his purposes will be accomplished in the end; but this journey must be lived by embracing the mystery and wonder of human life in this world. This is the great contribution of a book like Job; it places us in a dilemma to teach us about our own limitations.'[10] Job's story reminds us that that reason can only ever be a subsection of God's revelation and humans should never presume to rise above it and encapsulate it. Reason is an integral part of human functioning, but it has a limit. Yes, God plans may coincidently align with it in many circumstances but, as Job's circumstances remind us – not all.

Moreover, the story of Job reminds us that a right understanding of existence cannot be anthropocentric – human-centred. Prior to his theophanic revelation of God, Job had a view of human existence that placed God above it, but not at the controlling centre of it. Through this calamitous encounter with God, Job was able to let go of his self-righteous quest for justification and be content to trust God, despite not knowing why: 'Job does not know how, but spiritually he is in a position to accept that God can make even this situation work for his good purposes.'[11]

Samuel Terrien beautifully sums up the lesson here, 'Existence is fulfilled when man is aware, not of his ultimate concern but of becoming the concern of the ultimate. The derelict knows himself to be accepted by the creator of the universe; the orphan discovers the heart of a father; God's lonely man is received into the Society of God.'[12] In not trying to encapsulate existence within the limited confines of human reason, a person humbled by God's revelation is opened up to a new existence; a bigger and broader horizon – the majestic eternal horizon of God. Even though this new horizon is beyond human comprehension, embraced in faith it enables a certain comfort; the comfort of being released from the burden of having to know – the comfort of embracing the peace of God that passes all understanding, knowing the One who does know.

In summary, *relying* on reason necessitates that 'I' take control, and that 'I' must take the place of God. But Job had to come to terms with the fact that 'I' am not the interpreting *ego*, but actually the *ego* interpreted! In letting go of control and embracing a mysterious sense of wonder, which leads the truth-seeker to become 'open' to the author of truth, Job ultimately found himself. 'The sense of wonder, in the end, is insufficient. It is contemplation of God at work which is called for, and this is exactly what the discourses of the Lord [in Job] achieve.'[13]

To truly contemplate God and the truth he reveals, an act of absolute faith is required. Job had initially contemplated God out of his anthropocentric world-view, but following the theophanic encounter with God, and his own ensuing repentance, he comes to a position of contemplating God's reality theocentrically. Such a quantum shift can only come about through a genuinely personal encounter with God, with its resultant subversion of human rationality within the matrix of faith. Once one encounters God and his revelation, the predilection toward a *reliance* on reason gives way to a faith that embraces the mysterious revelation of God.

What the narrative of Job poignantly brings to bear on the truth quest is that following the human apprehension of divine revelation all questioning ceases, and in the realm of absolute trust, the person of faith is content to trust and obey God, even if God fails to provide reasons why. Although many theological endeavours have been described as faith seeking understanding, a personal encounter with God in true faith should engender such a deep contentment that the believing subject is willing to accept that there are some things beyond the scope of human understanding. Even when an understanding of lofty things may never be forthcoming, the believer still continues to trust.

The true person of faith, who seeks the truth, is content to embrace the mystery of God despite not fully grasping it because, as Margaret Barker rightly asserts, 'God is unfathomable and will remain so'.[14] True comprehension of reality in its relationship to one's human existence only begins when the inquirer is simply content to trust God, despite understanding, indeed, with the proviso that understanding may never follow.

The Spirit, Divine Power and Wisdom: Paul's Philosophy

At the climax of Job's epic ordeal, we were confronted with God's divine revelation exposing the limited capacities of human reason as a valid means for comprehending the link between ultimate reality and human existence. Just prior to this final theophanic revelation, we also encountered the enigmatic figure of Elihu, a person who introduces to us the epistemic role of God's Spirit: 'But it is the spirit in a man, the breath of the Almighty, that gives him understanding' (Job 32:8). Although 'spirit' could be interpreted as the human spirit (inner life force), Elihu's qualifying statement 'the breath of the Almighty' suggests that God's Spirit is in view: 'The Spirit of God has made me; the breath of the Almighty gives me life' (Job 33:4).

Elihu's further comparison of the divine wisdom, born of the Spirit, with a disposition toward wisdom that relies on human flattery

(Job 32:21–2) prepares us for the apostle Paul's discussion in the New Testament. In this case, Paul sets before the Corinthian Christians, in 1 Corinthians 1:1 – 2:16, a similar comparison; he challenges a form of human wisdom that sets itself against the wisdom of the divine Spirit. For Paul, the Spirit of God represents the supreme source of understanding, the means of unmasking human delusion and revealing the truth, raw and unvarnished.

For this apostle to the Gentiles, the search for wisdom (truth) was never a speculative endeavour, rather it was inherently bound up with eternal consequences of God's deliverance through Christ. Against the backdrop of factional divisions in the Corinthian church, Paul points out that his primary focus, contrary to cultural norms of Greek culture, was and is never personal notoriety or social status;[15] but purely and simply the gospel of Jesus Christ. In emphasizing his point, Paul stresses that the *means of* promoting the gospel, let alone its counter-cultural content, necessarily clash with worldly wisdom (*sophia logou*). For Paul to preach the gospel according to worldly wisdom would be to contradict the inherent truth of the gospel; which, on the one hand, is enshrouded in the humility of Christ's self-deprecating action, and on the other is based on the inability of human power vis-à-vis salvation. For Paul, then, the wisdom of the gospel stood at odds with the wisdom of the day, as Stephen Pogoloff affirms: 'In Paul's narrative world, the normal cultural narratives of eloquence and status are radically reversed . . . Paul's rhetoric of the cross thus opposes the cultural values surrounding eloquence.'[16] Paul's counter-cultural gospel of Christ provides the epistemic context for divine wisdom, such that to grasp the truth the inquirer cannot escape identifying with the crucified and risen Christ – God's supreme revelation of truth.

For those seeking to order their human existence according to humanly contrived philosophies, the message of the cross was folly. Indeed, the fact that a divine being would take on the humility of humanity, and through the *means* of humility redeem humanity, appeared as totally absurd to those who oriented their thinking around 'this world's' wisdom: 'Jews demand miraculous signs and Greeks look for wisdom, but we preach Christ crucified: a stumbling block to the Jews and foolishness to the Gentiles, but to those whom God has called, both Jews and Greeks, Christ the power of God and the wisdom of God' (1 Cor. 1:22–4). But, as Ian Scott suggests, once the wisdom of Christ is grasped by the believer, it is then human wisdom that is seen as folly: 'This failure of ordinary wisdom means that the tables turn, and that such wisdom can be seen for the folly which it really has become, while the gospel . . . is revealed as God's wisdom.'[17] To embrace the Christ event – expressed powerfully in his incarnation, life of obedience, crucifixion and resurrection – is to grasp a new form of wisdom and a new way of viewing existence with reference to God's eternal salvific purposes in Christ. Christ brings God's eternal reality into the present existence of humanity – foreshadowing a new and eternal existence.

Indeed for Paul, it is not enough to simply promote God's wisdom for the sake of the Corinthians' ignorance; he must also defend it by challenging the alternative. In a statement, quoting from Isaiah 29:14: 'I will destroy the wisdom of the wise; the intelligence of the intelligent I will frustrate' (1 Cor. 1:19), Paul underscores the futility of human wisdom, even in its 'wisest' manifestation. Indeed, he is quite deliberate in using Holy Scripture to bolster his argument, not merely for the superior and time-honoured content it imparts to the argument, but that he might *methodologically establish* the superior wisdom of God, as revealed in the written word of Scripture. Then in a rhetorical flourish Paul further derides the wisdom of this current age by highlighting that the wise, the scholarly and the philosophically inclined are found wanting with reference to God's wisdom: 'Has not God made foolish the wisdom of the world?' (1 Cor. 1:20). Clearly, for the apostle, the revelation of God through the *cross event* has nullified every human attempt at making sense of human existence.

Paul is not simply challenging a form of 'wisdom' operative in the culture outside the church; he is addressing those within who have become inclined to adopt it to promote the gospel, as David Garland suggests, '[the] boastful Corinthians Christians were no different from their Pagan fellow citizens, obsessed with exalting themselves.'[18] In challenging their false assumptions that worldly wisdom might, in some way, augment the works of God, the apostle makes it clear that once a person embraces God's wisdom (in the gospel of Christ) it is then futile to try and grasp or augment divine knowledge by means of worldly wisdom – the two forms of wisdom are simply incompatible. For Paul, the matter is clear-cut; only through humbly embracing the 'foolishness 'of the cross is it possible to embrace the wisdom of God; as wisdom and truth (of the kind that seeks to make sense of ultimate reality with reference to human existence) cannot be attained outside submission to God through his gospel.

Therefore, Christ is the wisdom of God – the ultimate revelation of God's truth. Yes, Jews look for a revelation of truth in miraculous signs as manifestations of God's power; Greeks look for a revelation of truth in human wisdom, manifested by way of reason. But in Paul's estimation, the revelation of Christ is the 'only true' fulfilment of both of these false attempts at wisdom: 'Christ is the power of God and the wisdom of God' (1 Cor. 1:24). Paul is not speaking of Christ as an abstract principle either, but speaks of him as the personal revelation of God – revelation that extends beyond mere theoretical knowledge, but revelation that encompasses a living relationship with real ethical and practical implications.

But are there any preconditions for appropriating the truth in Christ? In stating his case, Paul first notes that the foolishness of God through the gospel of Christ, though it makes no sense to the worldly wise, is still 'stronger' (wiser) than the cleverness of humanity (1 Cor. 1:25). He then goes on to point out to the Corinthians that, by the standards of this world, not many of them were influential or noble or wise, and yet God still chose them, moreover chose them to shame those who are wise in their own eyes: 'God chose the weak things of the world to shame the strong' (1 Cor. 1:27). The implications of such reasoning is that the precondition for embracing 'true' wisdom, the wisdom of God, stands in contrast to virtues that the world highly esteems. Thus, the precondition for attaining the wisdom of God is not a reliance on human ability, eloquence, wisdom or social status, but humility; a complete recognition of human inability to attain the knowledge of God, and a commensurate recognition of the sovereignty of God in providing it.

But to realistically engage with the risen Christ in this *personal* way, the work of the Holy Spirit is necessarily involved. William Barclay describes the Spirit in these personal terms: 'The Holy Spirit is God's introducer, the one who opens the door and brings us into the presence of God. That is to say, it is the Holy Spirit in our hearts who gives us a desire for the confidence to enter into the presence of God.'[19] Far from being an abstract 'force', Anthony Thiselton suggests that the Spirit must not be viewed as 'sub personal' either, but supra-personal.[20] Paul in stressing this personal dimension speaks of the Spirit as actually having personal attributes (Eph. 4:30). The Holy Spirit is able to personally introduce people to the person of Christ, because he shares the same 'personal' Trinitarian relationship to the Father as the Son: 'He proceeds from God as a kind of person that God is.'[21] Thus entering into an understanding of divine wisdom can only be attained by the means of the Spirit's personal engagement, where he invites the believer to embrace Christ.

Of course, as relatively simple as God's method for attaining wisdom is (an act of faith in Christ), the greatest hindrance to its appropriation is the stubbornness of human autonomy. Ian Scott suggests:

> Human beings want complete control over their own existence, and so resist the inevitable need to trust God for their security . . . The gospel may not be inherently incomprehensible; instead it is obviously designed to frustrate any attempt at confirmation from within the realm of human experience . . . So that in order to accept it one is forced to adopt a whole new frame of reference.[22]

The autonomous resistance comes because these new frames of reference necessitate the subjugation of human reasoning to the authority of God's revelation in Christ. Yet, there is a purpose behind God's method. The reason Paul stresses humility in contrast to the standards of *this world*, is expressly to exclude all human boasting vis-à-vis the attainment of God's wisdom in Christ: 'so that no-one may boast before him' (1 Cor. 1:29). Therefore, not dissimilar to Job's outcome, Paul advocates that only an absolute faith reliance on God provides the way into divine truth; only when all human pride is abandoned is the truth made accessible.

With pride being a primary hindrance to embracing the wisdom of God, then it must follow that the failure to attain truth is not intellectually but morally conditioned: 'Paul does not say here that human beings fail to know God because they are intellectually unfit or because they failed to reason properly. Rather, they fail to respond appropriately to the God they know . . .'[23] The true knowledge of God, attainable by humbly embracing the gospel of Jesus Christ, invariably requires an admission of one's own moral shortcoming, resulting in the inquirer's moral transformation, as Andre Munzinger argues, 'The truth of the gospel can only be realised in an existential realisation, which in turn means true knowledge is inherently linked to ethics.'[24] Therefore, by virtue of God's election and the believer's subsequent faith, enabling the endowment of a status of being *in Christ* (who is God's wisdom: 1 Cor. 1:30), this wisdom reveals itself in ethical and relational terms, as the believer's will is subsumed in the Christ reality; Christ who is 'our righteousness, holiness and redemption' (1 Cor. 1:30).

Having outlined the two forms of wisdom – the wisdom of God and the wisdom of the world – and pointing out the insufficiency of the latter, Paul now in 1 Corinthians 2 pays particular attention to the 'strange' *method* in which the truth is revealed – the epistemic superiority of the Holy Spirit. Having established that the *manner* of his testimony about Christ was not according to eloquence or sophisticated human wisdom, he equally makes it clear that his message came by the *means* of a human: weakness, fear and trembling (1 Cor. 2:3).

Of course, in downgrading human ability in this regard, Paul correspondingly promotes a necessary reliance on God's power – a power manifest through the Holy Spirit. His primary focus in 1 Corinthians 2 is not to establish 'what' the truth is, but rather to establish how a person may recognize and appropriate this divine truth for him or herself. The means of gaining the truth, is not by way of 'wise and persuasive words', but through a supernatural demonstration of the Holy Spirit's power (1 Cor. 2:4). For Paul then, the *content* of divine truth not only originates with God, but so does the *means* of appropriating it, that the one true foundation of faith would be God and his power (1 Cor. 2:5).

It would be correct to say that 1 Corinthians 1 – 4 may be characterized as a defence for Paul's apostolic ministry among the immature Corinthians.[25] Paul has to overcome both false appraisals and false objections and re-establish himself as a spiritual father of the church.[26] In the course of this defence, the apostle must address those who think they are mature, but in reality fall dreadfully short: 'I gave you milk, not solid food, for you were not yet ready for it' (1 Cor. 3:2). From 2:6–16 the apostle is addressing a message of wisdom for the mature, but not the 'falsely' mature (sophisticated) of this current age.

The key to grasping this true wisdom is not a superficial spirituality augmented by human philosophy and rhetoric, but a comprehension by way of divine initiative – in the Holy Spirit. Paul speaks of 'secret' wisdom that has existed from the beginning, incomprehensible to even the most prominent thinkers of this current age. The qualification for grasping such wisdom transcends human ability or education, and is located in divinely initiated revelation. The apostle wants the Corinthians to realize that the truly 'mature' are only those who have received the Spirit and embrace the truth of this wisdom in humble faith. The deep things of God are *only* comprehensible to those whom God favours (1 Cor. 2:9–10).

In Paul's estimation, the Spirit is the key factor in the apprehension of truth, the active agent in the epistemic endeavour. The Spirit is not passive, a mere instrument to be used in comprehending truth, but rather the Spirit actively 'possesses' the believer in the process of revelation.[27] The Spirit works to plumb the depths of not only God's will, but also the mind and heart of the human subject, bringing the submissive human will into alignment with God's will by illuminating, revealing and transforming, through various endowments, whether individual or corporate. As Margaret Mitchell notes, 'The spirit, as

God's own, has the ability to delve into the very "depths of God", and through the gifts of the spirit to endow those who have received the spirit with its gifts.'[28]

The Spirit exercises this function among all believers in the new covenant, whereas in the Old Testament, only those specially anointed with the Spirit could access such revelation, such as King David: 'Search me, O God, and know my heart; test me and know my anxious thoughts' (Ps. 139:23). The Spirit's active role in the process of divine revealing necessarily accords with Paul's previous assessment that human 'boasting' about their own capacities in arriving at the truth is excluded. God's Spirit only reveals the truth to those in humble submission to God – in Christ.

In making the point that no one is able to know the thoughts of God except the Spirit of God reveal it to them (1 Cor. 2:11), Paul employs the Greek philosophical principle of 'like is known by like' – only God knows the thoughts of God![29] In subverting human logic to his own cause, the apostle stresses that natural humanity simply does not have access to the thoughts of God, they are revealed by God himself to those who believe in the gospel – through the Spirit. Because all genuine Christian believers have received the Spirit of God, they have the capacity to understand what God has revealed; whereas those without (in Paul's terminology those who have the 'spirit of the world') do not have access to divine revelation (1 Cor. 2:12). This being the case, Paul can confidently assert that the content of his message is not of human derivation, but owes its provenance directly and purely to the Spirit of God. Consequently, his message of wisdom represents spiritual truths in spiritual words (1 Cor. 2:13), a form of logic incompatible with and contrary to the aforementioned human wisdom (*sophia logou*). Thus, in shifting the focus of the discussion about wisdom into the realm of the Spirit, Paul has undercut the Corinthians' appeal to sophisticated human wisdom.

Before we conclude this section on Paul, it is worth recapping that the gospel establishes the epistemic context for the Spirit revealing truth. Wisdom or truth is never revealed by God, that humans might attain a higher knowledge of things for their own intellectual stimulation or academic exultation. Revelation is always oriented towards God's ultimate purpose through the gospel; a purpose that relates to believers' life and conduct in this present age, an age conditioned by eternity, as Gordon Fee's helpful summation suggests:

> The Spirit should identify God's people in such a way that their values and worldview are radically different from the wisdom of this age. They do know what God is about in Christ; they do live out the life of the future in the present age that is passing away; they are marked by the cross forever. As such they are the people of the Spirit, who stand in bold contrast to those who are merely human and do not understand the scandal of the cross. Being spiritual does not lead to elitism; it leads to a deeper understanding of God's profound mystery – redemption through a crucified Messiah.[30]

In the final three verses of chapter 2, the apostle draws together the conceptual threads of his argument to establish the supremacy of the Spirit, in the dimension of human understanding. Without the Spirit, divine mysteries are unattainable: 'The person without the spirit does not accept the things that come from the Spirit of God, but considers them foolishness, and cannot understand them because they are spiritually discerned' (1 Cor. 2:14).

This is a truth that Paul would have personally experienced, with his Damascus road conversion establishing the stark difference between a knowledgeable man without the Spirit and an enlightened man with it.[31] Consequently, the person controlled by the Spirit of God has the capacity to discern all things, with rationality not subjugated to the judgement of any human (1 Cor. 2:15). However, this does not suggest that Paul abandons all human reason, as Ian Scott is right to suggest, 'What we must recognise in all of this is that, for Paul, the spirit's activity does not provide a license for irrationality. The spirit's revelatory activity does not remove the need for rational consideration of the gospel and its implications.'[32] In such a case, the Spirit not only reveals the truth, but also subjugates human rationality to augment its comprehension.

In Paul's logic, if Christians have access to the Spirit of God, they also have access to the mind of God; and if one has access to the mind of God, then human wisdom (as the primary epistemic arbitrator) is made redundant! Of course, Spirit-enlightened wisdom is not the kind of wisdom that grants knowledge on every subject – this is not the goal. Divine wisdom is connected to the reality of the gospel and its outworking, and can never be perceived as pure wisdom with a direct line to the mysteries of the universe unconnected to the grounded reality of life in conformity with God (a point made at the end of the book of Job). This is why Paul concludes this chapter, by stating, 'But we have the mind of Christ' (1 Cor. 2:16b). The divine wisdom granted by the Spirit always brings the believer back to the grounded reality of Christ's mindset and a life of humble, obedient submission to his will, a life of holy devotion to the cause of the gospel, and a life lived before all humanity to the glory of God. Wisdom, then, finds its terminus not in placating human kudos or satisfying human curiosity, but in the exaltation of God and the worship of the one who does exercise the power to control all things – God.

The Spirit and Truth: John's Teaching

When it comes to the matter of determining truth, and the epistemic significance of the Spirit in that endeavour, John's contribution certainly equals that of Paul. To appreciate the epistemic role of the Spirit in John's thought we need to appreciate his dualism. John contrasts conceptual polar opposites: life / death, light / darkness, truth / falsehood, belief / unbelief, etc. This dualism suggests that John views the Christian life as a struggle between good and evil, played out in a reality within two vertically defined realms: 'above' relating to all that is good, and 'below' relating to that of evil origin. As Murray Hogg suggests, 'This knowledge of God is associated with concepts on one side of the dualism (light, life, love, truth, good, etc.) whilst the world is associated with their antitheses . . . The language of descent points to the fact that the distinction between "heaven" and "earth / world" is itself part of the Johannine dualism.'[33] In John's reasoning then, the Logos, who has been with God since the beginning, comes down manifesting in human form (John 1:14), bringing heavenly truths previously hidden from humanity (John 3:31–2). It is with this revelation that has 'come down' that John connects the role of the Spirit: 'For the one whom God has sent speaks the words of God, for God gives the Spirit without limit' (John 3:34).

Furthermore, in John's Gospel the Spirit is specifically associated with truth. This might seem unremarkable given the prevalence of the *truth theme* within the gospel account, yet this prevalence has a distinct purpose. John wants to establish that Jesus is the source and revealer of divine truth: 'For the law was given through Moses; grace and truth came through Jesus Christ' (John 1:17). In doing so, John records many of Jesus' sayings introduced with the formula: 'I tell you the truth'. He also records Jesus designating right worship as being in 'spirit and truth' (John 4:23–4); that truth is the key to freedom (John 8:32); and truth is advanced as the means of sanctification and primary quality of God's word (John 17:17). John also specifically relates the ministry of the Spirit to the truth. In this regard, the action of the Spirit of truth is not seen as independent of the actions of the Father and the Son: 'When the Counsellor comes, whom I will send to you from the Father, the Spirit of truth who goes out from the Father, he will testify about me' (John 15:26). John wants to affirm that the Spirit does not bring an independent form of truth from the Godhead, but works in concert with God the Father and God the Son, to reveal truth and bring glory (John 16:12–15).

Not dissimilar to Paul, John also associates the revelation of truth with moral conduct. To embrace the revealed truth of Jesus in faith (by means of being born 'from above': John 3:3 margin) is to embrace the positive side of John's dualism: light, truth, life, and all it entails.[34] As such, knowledge of the revealed truth is intimately bound to a life of faithful obedience to Christ. In the farewell discourse in John 14, Jesus had just finished telling his disciples that he would do anything they ask in his name (v. 14), he then goes on to speak about another counsellor who he will send to be with them for ever – the Spirit of truth (v. 16). However, between these two statements he offers this exhortation: 'If you love me, you will obey what I command' (John 14:15). Jesus sends 'another counsellor' (*paraclete*), the indwelling Holy Spirit, to enable the followers of Christ not only to recall his teaching (John 14:26), but also to grant them discernment in their personal life of devotion. Therefore, the Spirit's revelation of truth is conditioned by a higher goal than mere knowledge, the goal of obedience to Christ's commands – the fruit of love and devotion. That the Spirit's revelatory role is inherently bound to a moral purpose is seen in a later statement by Jesus about the Spirit's ministry: 'When he comes, he will convict the world of guilt in regard to sin and righteousness and judgment' (John 16:8). The Spirit's revelation, the truth, obedience and love for God and others are intimately bound in John's thought, which is especially evident in 1 John.

Although there is some conjecture as to John's opponents in his first epistle, the content suggests that their error was oriented around a dualism that divided the ethereal and the material. Georg Strecker argues that Docetism was probably central to the errors being addressed: 'Docetism opposes the doctrine of the incarnation, for it is a fundamental truth that the divine cannot unite with the human, the heavenly with the earthly. This Christological conception, nourished by the Greek spirit, could be articulated in a variety of systems.'[35] This ideology invariably resulted in a divorce of theory and practice; such that truth remains an abstract concept, with no substantive connection to material reality, spatially or ethically. Of course, this is why John pays so much attention to the physicality of Jesus Christ (1 John 1:1; 2:22; 5:6–8) and to the practical ethics that pertain to following him (1 John 1:6–10; 3:6; 4:7). Furthermore, because John views the Holy Spirit as the agent of revelation, it is not surprising that he makes reference to the Spirit as a truth agent, as he counters false doctrine. For John then, the Spirit is a primary reference point for truth, and he references the Spirit's role in this regard in varying capacities in his first epistle.

The first capacity in which the Spirit authenticates truth is through a concept John calls the 'anointing': 'As for you, the anointing you received from him remains in you, and you do not need anyone to teach you' (1 John 2:27). While arguments have been set forth that the anointing is Jesus, his word or sound teaching, the most sensible interpretation is that the Spirit represents 'the anointing', as this section largely parallels what is written in John's Gospel regarding the Paraclete.[36] This anointing is granted on a personal divine initiative, as Robert Yarbrough points out: 'The anointing John has in mind derives from a person, not a place . . . grounded not least in this exalted figure bestowing on them their privileged status.'[37] As such, the Spirit's anointing is to be perceived as divine validation that one is in the truth and guaranteed of God's favour, akin to Paul's idea of the seal of ownership (2 Cor. 1:22). Moreover, the anointing brings with it more than existential affections, but a cognitive dimension: an epistemic confirmation that the knowledge the genuine believer embraces is true.[38] Furthermore, this validated knowledge becomes an effective safeguard against error, as Judith Lieu suggests, 'It is implicit to the argument that the knowledge will protect them from the danger posed . . . This becomes explicit as the author specifies what it is they will know: the truth.'[39] The Spirit's 'anointing' is validation that one is in the truth.

The second capacity in which the Spirit authenticates truth pertains to an existential 'heart' confirmation in connection with ethical conduct. In 1 John 3:19–24, John argues that obeying Jesus' commands and doing what pleases him secures peace: 'And this is his command: to believe in the name of his Son, Jesus Christ, and to love one another as he commanded us' (1 John 3:23). Not assent to theory, but heart-motivated ethical conformity to Christ ensures one's faith is genuine. However, it is not that keeping commands is *causal* with reference abiding in the truth, but necessarily *consequential* for all who do abide in the truth. There is a further existential validation beyond a cognitive affirmation of command-keeping, that of the Spirit: 'And this is how we know that he lives in us; we know it by the Spirit he gave us' (1 John 3:24). The Spirit's validation, in this case, represents a kind of 'intuitive sense'; believers just 'know' through the Spirit's indwelling presence that God lives in them and that they belong to the authentic community of faith.[40] Thus, the Spirit provides the 'capstone' in evidence, as John Painter suggests, 'If keeping the Commandments is the basis for knowing that we abide in him, the fact that he gave us his Spirit is the evidence that he abides in us.'[41]

The third authenticating dimension in which the Spirit offers truth discernment is the truth-confirming nature of the community. In 1 John 4:1–6 John exhorts the believers to 'test the spirits', exercising discernment regarding truth and error. Those who truly are in the truth have the Spirit and will correctly confess Christ: 'This is how you can recognise the Spirit of God: Every spirit that acknowledges that Jesus Christ has come in the flesh is from God' (1 John 4:2). Yet, the discernment John calls for has a corporate orientation: 'We are from God, and whoever knows God listens to us; but whoever is not from God does not listen to us. This is how we recognise the Spirit of truth and the spirit of falsehood' (1 John 4:6). Of course, genuine believers have the Spirit within, and as such should have an innate capacity to 'sense' truth, but John wants to establish the 'extra' value of the corporate confession of truth, and the Spirit's validation of it. The Spirit of God creates a culture in which the truth can be clearly discerned, as Strecker argues, 'The congregation, as a community of those who have been born of God, have the Spirit of God, and the Spirit in turn has the function of shaping the community and bringing it to insight.'[42] Thus the community shaped by the Spirit will confess the truth, and those who wish to know the truth must listen to the voice of the Spirit through the community.

The final categorization of the Spirit validating truth in 1 John is that of the witness. The apostle has already stated that he himself is a witness to Christ's reality (1 John 1:1,5), but in 1 John 5 as he brings the wider argument of the epistle to a conclusion, he draws the reader's attention to the other witnesses that validate the truth: the water, the blood and the Spirit. Although there is some conjecture over the interpretation of the water and blood, one of the most plausible explanations has the water being Jesus' baptism (where the Spirit was present: John 1:32–4), and the blood referring to his death. Marshall notes that John refers to the Spirit's testifying activity in the present tense: 'the most obvious interpretation is that the Spirit presently testifies to us, in our inward hearts . . . that the baptism and death of Jesus point to his being the Christ and the Son of God.'[43] Regarding the testifier, John describes the Spirit 'as the truth', implying whatever the Spirit testifies to is true, because the Spirit is truth, which also fits with John's prior affirmation of the Spirit's role in John 15:26. However, to state that the Spirit is the truth is not to suggest that the Spirit represents a kind of abstract principle of truth but, as Judith Lieu suggests, 'The Spirit is not truth in some absolute or independent sense, but only because it expresses and embodies God's truth in those to whom it is given.'[44]

For the apostle John, the Spirit is inseparably linked to the truth. Framed within the context of a *vertical dualism*, John notes that the truth has come down to us through the revelation of Jesus Christ. Not only is the Spirit's ministry prevalent in the incarnation and ministry of Christ, but continues as the Paraclete guiding the followers of Jesus not only to recall the truth, but also to walk in it. As such, the truth can never be represented as an abstract theory but is necessarily connected to a dynamic moral conformity with Jesus Christ (who is the truth). It is the Spirit that enables this conformity. Moreover, in the capacity of countering error and maintaining the 'walk' of truth, we observed that in 1 John, the Spirit works in a number of validating capacities: the Spirit is represented as in the anointing of God's approval, the Spirit intuitively confirms truth-validating ethical conduct, the Spirit guides the community into the truth providing the context in which the truth may be discerned, and finally the Spirit is the ultimate *witness* to the truth of Christ, so much so that John equates the Spirit with the truth (1 John 5:6).

Summary: The Truth that Seeks Us

Humanity, in their quest for reason-oriented truth, seeks quantifiable control of their daily existence. To gain this alleged control, they must define their own view of ultimate reality, and then order their practical existence in a way that is rationally definable within that contrived paradigm. At best, this grants the illusion of control. As we saw, Job's tragic story starkly challenges any such notion, reminding the reader that no matter how much we might attempt to control our existence, some things are beyond our power. In reality this approach to 'the truth' represents nothing more than a fool's errand. However, a more appropriate way of seeking out and adopting a secure existence is to come to terms with the truth that is seeking us. Rather than contriving a truth formula, the inquirer might just find having a humble openness to 'divine' revelation a more fruitful endeavour. In fact, if humanity had the humility to set aside their predilection for autonomy, then perhaps they would discover the very thing we are actually seeking – certainty and security!

Job's story offered up the challenge that even beliefs based on so-called divine principles need to be open to God's revelation. If ever there was a person in the ancient world who would have been able to gain security and certainty in his life it would have been Job – there was no one more consistent in his existence before his perception of the divine order. Yet, Job's ordeal represents the realization of the worst of human fears, reminding us that no matter how well our lives are ordered, even by religious maxims, there are greater factors beyond human understanding ordering existence. In the wake of Job's calamitous circumstances, the commonly held view that *the good prosper and the evil suffer* came apart at the seams. Despite some considered reflection by well-intentioned thinkers, there was no clear way of making sense of this unprecedented set of circumstances. These anomalous events totally ruptured conventional wisdom at every level, leaving every sensible person reeling in their wake.

However, in all this, just prior to his final encounter with God, Job correctly acknowledged that understanding and wisdom belonged to God (Job 28), even if a clear understanding of the same, vis-à-vis his own circumstances, was not available. Ultimately, Job's flaw resided in the adoption of an anthropocentric view of reality, where God was taken into account but not allowed to exist beyond the scope of human comprehension. As a precursor to God's personal divine revelation, the speeches of Elihu introduced the reader to the Spirit of God, challenging the reader with the notion that divine wisdom circumvents human experience and knowledge. Furthermore, in rebuking the futility of human reasoning, God personally challenges Job that it is beyond any human capacity to fully comprehend the divine purposes behind life in the world. On the contrary, Job is presented with the simple notion that making sense of reality and the existence that flows from it must begin with faith. In the end God offers no real explanation for Job's 'anomaly', simply implying that once a person personally encounters God in faith, the need for explanations are lost in the wonder of trusting faith. For such a person, knowing God knows is enough! Taken from this perspective, the key to truth is not reason, but faith.

While the story of Job implicitly contrasts human wisdom with divine wisdom, Paul's engagement with his readers in 1 Corinthians makes this contrast much more explicit. If the book of Job offers an introduction to the epistemic role of God's Spirit, Paul's work places it at the centre of human knowing. He emphasizes the supremacy of divine wisdom over and against the futility of human wisdom by stressing the superior role of the Holy Spirit. Consequently, the search for truth does not have as its goal a rationally cogent system of thinking, but a faith-based devotion that is inexorably linked to the eternal redemptive purposes of God, in the revelation of Jesus Christ. For Paul, to know 'the truth' one must actually know Christ, whose mode of revelation stands as the antithesis of human wisdom, in as much as the gospel comes to humanity in humility and weakness; diametrically contrasted to the kind of 'worldly' wisdom the Corinthians were tempted to embrace. Christ's self-deprecating revelation in the power of God was incomprehensible (foolishness) to those who embraced the best of 'this world's' wisdom, because it could only be attained by faith.

Paul was not simply content to advocate a 'foolish' form of wisdom, but openly challenged the futility of human wisdom. No matter how good 'it' was, it simply didn't have available to it the means of appropriating divine truth – the Spirit. To have access to the Spirit, the seeker must have the kind of faith that is willing to abandon trust in human autonomy and embrace God's 'foolishness', as revealed in Christ. Even more radically, Christ doesn't just bring words of wisdom that might be rationally apprehended, but is himself the embodiment of wisdom. To know this wisdom of God, one needs to enter into a faith-based relationship with Jesus Christ, being personally united to him by means of the Holy Spirit's secret working. The precondition for such a 'spiritual' union is not via the channel of sophisticated autonomous wisdom, simply because this is *methodologically contrary to the message of Christ*. The precondition for having access to this wisdom is the humility to recognize one's own moral and epistemic failures and, like Job, to embrace revelation in faith.

Having access to divine truth means adopting the same epistemic posture as the divine revealer adopted in making the truth known through the gospel. Gaining the truth then is inexorably linked to gaining Christ in a personal, Spirit-initiated union of faith. Only then does the thinking subject, by means of an associated spiritual indwelling, have the mindset to process ultimate reality with reference to one's existence in God's world – an existence linked with the eternal purposes of God. For Paul, the Spirit is the key factor in the apprehension of this truth, for without the regenerating power of the Spirit, and its associated abiding epistemic influence, the thinking subject would not be able to comprehend the truth made available to them in and through Christ. Moreover, this truth is not simply given for the satisfaction of one's intellectual predilections, but for the purpose of manifesting a life of moral and practical conformity to Christ and his kingdom purposes. Indeed, truth is never static, dry or technical, in the Christian conception, but is always dynamically oriented toward greater divine purposes.

Like Paul, John also challenges an alternate form of wisdom that was imposing itself on the church and corrupting the true wisdom revealed in Christ. For John, the truth was revealed explicitly with the coming of Christ; not only his teaching and his miracles, but also his incarnational presence manifested the truth of God among humanity. The revelation of 'the truth' in this manner makes an otherwise inaccessible divine reality accessible to humanity. God could now be touched, seen, heard and related to in a very real and tangible way. Far from being an abstract proposition the truth (the Logos) now represented a living being with whom even the most humble of humans could engage. Moreover, in John's conceptualization, the truth Jesus reveals to a humanity that is entrapped by a dark world of evil brings some very tangible benefits: freedom, hope, love, life. The Holy Spirit's role then, was to principally make the truth of Christ perpetually available to those who had put their faith in him.

The Holy Spirit makes the truth of Christ an ever-present reality. The commensurate outworking of embracing this truth is a life of moral conformity to Christ; a life where the truth is always manifested in faithful obedience – walking in the light as he is in the light. Contrary to the ideology of the 'false' opponents, who advocated one could hold to the truth separate from a moral life, John's view of the truth, made 'self-evident' through the Spirit, necessarily demands that theoretical beliefs must manifest themselves in practical and moral conformity to God. For John, as for Paul, truth is not an abstract principle that is attained by inventing a philosophical view of reality that can order human existence, but is someone who, under divine initiative, breaks into human existence. In breaking in, Jesus brings with him the divine reality: a reality that requires human faith and obedience, a reality that entirely changes the perspective of the believing subject, who no longer seeks to be in control, but is prepared to submit to the One who is.

When we compare the philosophically based human quest for truth and the divine revelation of truth, it becomes apparent that these two forms of connecting ultimate reality with human existence are fundamentally incompatible. The former employs the best of human reason to construct a view of reality that attempts to make sense of the existence we experience; the latter, abandons a 'reliance' on human reason (though does not abandon the use of the same absolutely) in favour of accepting divine revelation on the basis of simple faith. One trusts in the capacities of the thinking subject to arrive at the truth, the other trusts in the omniscient capacities of the divine revealer, accepting the revelation given by faith. One seeks to discover 'truth', the other is open to be discovered by it!

I posit that those who adopt the first approach to truth are actually constructing their own version of truth, designed to provide a rationally cogent view of the life they want but, as such, it can never truly account for anomalies in human existence. Those who adopt the second approach to truth open themselves up to the unlimited possibilities of God's divine reality in all its unknowability; necessarily implying that aspects of human existence will always be out of their control, which, of course, is why faith is so critical to this kind of knowing. For those who 'truly' embrace the divinely revealed truth by faith, control is no longer important. Rather, what is of supreme importance is knowing the 'one' who is in control – God. Ironically, the faith-based, Spirit-guided life gives the peace and security that the 'wise' of this world so desperately seek, but can never truly find.

3

The Spirit, Truth and the Material World

Divine truth is revealed, but this revelation is never grasped in pure abstraction. Even for the pure rationalist, truth is encountered in concrete life, coming through the means of practical engagements with the 'real' world. Comprehending truth at any meaningful level, then, must include a legitimate appreciation of the material world. Comprehending God must also include an appreciation of his involvement in the material world. In fact, Holy Scripture reveals that God is intimately engaged and purposefully involved in the world we know in grounded and meaningful ways. God's Spirit, his active presence, is powerfully engaged in creating and recreating, shaping and directing, guiding and ordering the world which humans relate to and relate in. Moreover, reflecting 'on' and reflecting 'in' the material world is unavoidable, and coming to terms with its value and significance is indispensable to the processes of human interpretation. The Holy Spirit, as the divine active agent in the world, is actually the key to the Christian's interpretive process; absolutely indispensable to understanding both the content and context of revelation. In this chapter we shall consider the Holy Spirit's engagement in, with, and through the material world we encounter; in doing so, aiming to gain a richer appreciation of how God the Spirit conditions the truth we come to understand as divine revelation – revelation that is grounded in daily life.

The Spirit, Understanding and Materiality

If Christians believe that God created and sustains the world, then more than a passing thought must be given to his ongoing interaction with it. Moreover, a deeper grasp of the Holy Spirit's ongoing engagement with the material world serves to enrich our appreciation of how this ongoing divine interaction augments our understanding of truth. However, the greatest challenge to the successful negotiation of this subject is coming to terms with the specific *nature* of the Holy Spirit's relationship to the material world. Often a dichotomy is set up between the material and the spiritual. Does the Holy Spirit reveal truth through the material reality or does the Holy Spirit reveal truth from above? The challenge is overcoming this false dichotomy. Indeed, the greatest challenge to a correct interpretation of the Spirit's engagement with material reality pertains to the unconscious adoption of philosophical assumptions that unwittingly condition the mind of the truth-seeker to frame the relationship of the Spirit to the material world in ways that limit and distort our understanding of it.

Two broad philosophical ideologies have clouded a clear perception of the Spirit / material relationship: monism and dualism. Monism is an ideology based on the belief that everything is essentially one. While there are different types of monism, fundamentally the theory advocates that 'everything', including God, is a unity; at its most basic level 'one in essence'. Whether we reflect on animistic beliefs that consider the integration of the 'spirit world' with the 'material world', the ancient philosophy of Heraclitus that considered fire the unifying element of all reality, or the modern and much more sophisticated system of Hegel that advocates the unity of all things through spirit or mind, monism fundamentally advocates that all 'things' are an essentially unity. This unity is manifest in different forms. Applied to religion in general, and Christianity in particular, this may be known as pantheism; God is in all things and all things are just an extension of God. It could even be argued that a very literal interpretation of Paul's apologetic approach to the Athenians might be pantheistic in nature: 'For in him we live and move and have our being' (Acts 17:28). Incorporated into this monistic view, the Spirit, in constituting the basic essence of all things, is integrated into *everything*. This is then embraced by the monist as useful for developing a practical belief that the truth can be encountered through examining everything in the world; God the Spirit is not only in everything, but is everything.

On the other hand, dualism represents a contrary view. In contrast to monism, it draws out a clear and distinct separation between entities such as body and soul, mind and matter, spiritual and material. Proponents of this theory have had considerable influence in Western thinking, and include substantial philosophers such as Plato and Descartes. Plato openly promoted a profound separation of body and soul, arguing that the body was little more than a prison-house for the soul, and hindered the inner person from gaining a full appreciation of the truth. For Plato then, in order to attain a clear and distinct appreciation of truth, the soul must escape from the contaminating influences of the body and material reality by climbing out of the shadowy cave of human existence into the light of pure theoretical forms: 'It really has been shown to us that, if we are ever to have pure knowledge, we must escape from the body and observe things in themselves with the soul by itself.'[1] The majority of Western Christian thinkers have been so influenced by this kind of dualism that this divide between the *physical* and *spiritual* realms is simply taken for granted in the popular Christian consciousness.

Conveniently, dualism provides a legitimate theory for confronting the difficult issues of life by bifurcating realities. Translated on a practical level, the physical dimension represents the mundane matters encountered in everyday life, whereas spiritual reality is that which is encountered through a higher experience, gained though some kind of personal religious encounter or intellectual endeavour. Consequently, apart from an acknowledgement that God has created the world and in some mysterious way sustains it, there is little impetus to seek out how God's Spirit might engage us in and through the material realm, because such an understanding might seriously compromise or complicate the carefully constructed bifurcation of reality that dualism has set up.

Because of the ease of appeal to the rational mind, both monism and dualism have found legitimate support in 'mainstream' Christian thinking. Monism, for example, is manifested in modern Christian theology most distinctly through the thinking of the eighteenth- to nineteenth-century theologian Friedrich Schleiermacher (acknowledged as the founder of 'liberal' theology). Schleiermacher relates human self-consciousness, world-consciousness and God-consciousness as one, and advocates that the human interpreter, through an innate God-consciousness, can encounter God's divine revelation everywhere:

> And just as in belief in the eternal omnipotence is implied that the world is the complete revelation of it, so in belief in the original perfection of the world it is implied that through the feeling of absolute dependence the divine omnipotence in all its livingness reveals itself everywhere in the world, as eternal omnipresent and omniscient, without any distinction of more or less, without even a contrast in respect of dependence between one part and another.[2]

In such a view, the knowledge of the truth can potentially be attained as interpreters 'get in touch' with self-conscious feelings of God-dependence, through an engagement with nature, such that human intuition becomes the basis for truth. The ultimate implication of such a belief is that divinity becomes simply a different form and higher extension of humanity, which can be engaged through religious intuition.

In stark opposition to Schleiermacher's theological monism stands Karl Barth's theological dualism, a form of thought indirectly influenced by neo-Kantianism.[3] Barth saw Schleiermacher's style of theology leading to confusion between God and humanity, that any knowledge of truth about God was too dependent on human experience, such that God can become a human construct. Barth would argue that, in such a view, divine truth ultimately becomes a projection of human thoughts and emotions, and is invariably corrupted by the human proclivity to recreate God in their own image.[4]

In challenging this monistic point of view, Barth emphasized the otherness of God; that God and his divine revelation could in no way be dependent on human experience or human interpretation. In trying to establish a strict ontological distance between divinity and humanity, Barth tended to 'objectify' humanity, advocating that humanity can only know divine truth through unidirectional revelation. In Barth's estimation then, God is 'Wholly Other', and even God's revelation through the apostolic witness cannot be corrupted by human sensibilities: 'The Spirit gives grace through him [Paul]. Possessing nothing, he has nothing of his own to offer . . . It is sufficient that what is, is – above us and behind us and beyond us.'[5] As such, Barth's dualism stressed the 'hiddenness' and 'otherness' of God, making God's revelation through the Spirit in any medium 'experientially' unattainable.

Fully aware of the implications of both the theological monism of Schleiermacher and the dualism of Barth, specifically as they relate to the Spirit's engagement with the material world, Jürgen Moltmann considers that both views misrepresent how the Spirit engages us. Moltmann argues that the former results in the Spirit being a modality of human experience and the latter is the modality of God's revelation to us:

> If the spirit is a modality of our own experience, then human experience of God is the foundation of human theology. But this can be at the cost of a qualitative difference between God and human beings. If the spirit is viewed as a modality of the divine revelation, then the foundation of theology is God's revelation of himself. But in this case the qualitative difference between God and human beings makes every immediate relation of human beings to God impossible. And so there can be no natural human theology either.[6]

Moltmann considers the dualist position potentially more damaging to a true understanding of our engagement with God through the Spirit: 'Barth undoubtedly thinks that by saying this he has formulated the spirit's true continuity to the human spirit. But his eschatology is not linked with the future of the new creation of all things; it is related to God's eternity, over against the temporality of human beings.'[7] In Barth's view the Holy Spirit does little more than place Christians in a position of expectation of the divine they can never truly experience in this life, as Moltmann suggests, 'As a subjective reality of God's self revelation, the Holy Spirit remains entirely on God's side, so it can never be experienced by human beings at all.'[8] Indeed, Moltmann suggests of Barth's position: 'Anyone who stylizes revelation and experience into alternatives, ends up with revelations that cannot be experienced, and experiences without revelation.'[9]

Although briefly, we have sufficiently identified the potential problems of relating the Spirit to the material order. On the one hand, filtered through the lens of monism, the divine Spirit may be merged into the material realm (including the human subject), such that the human is simply an extension of the divine, with knowledge of divine truth being obtained through an intimate self-conscious engagement with the divine, revealed through nature (in various forms). Of course, this is potentially an open door to the most nefarious forms of superstition, where the truth can be contrived from whatever we might 'feel or experience' it to be through an engagement with natural phenomena.

On the other hand, the objectification of the Spirit's engagement with the material realm through dualism offers no practical point of contract between the Spirit and our experience of life in the world. In much the same way as Kant's Noumenal dimension allows the divine to be unknowable, a dualistic approach ensures that revelation of truth through the Spirit within the material realm can be known about and never truly known.

Both monism and dualism represent theoretical views that correlate readily with human logic because they make sense to the reasoning mind by presenting simple solutions to an issue that, in all probability, is beyond intellectual encapsulation. When we seek to engage God and the divine truth he offers us, the limitations of human logic, despite all its best intentions (as we have already seen in the Job accounts) 'ultimately' fail to grasp that which is sought. The Spirit of God's epistemic engagement cannot be reduced to a dimension of human experience, nor can it be deemed to be aside from God's revelation and experientially unknowable. The Spirit is neither a component of the natural human essence, nor is it unrelated or separate from the human self altogether. Moreover, what is true of the human, as part of the material order, is also true of every other element within that created order. So how do we come to terms with the relationship of the Spirit to the material world?

The Spirit of God is quantitatively engaged in the material realm in an unquantifiable and mysterious sense, and is qualitatively distinct from it. Despite various attempts by scholars to grasp the nature of this relationship,[10] how this actually 'is' (as Job's encounter with the divine suggested), it is exclusive to the secret counsels of God. The Spirit of God is actively engaged in the material world – creating, redeeming, resurrecting, recreating, sustaining, guiding, gifting and empowering – but the exact manner of this operating, I believe, will remain beyond full human comprehension, and can only be satisfactorily embraced in a proximate sense from a position of absolute truth – faith.

To understand the Spirit rightly, to move toward a greater appreciation of Spirit-generated divine truth as revealed within the material order we encounter, we need to stop relying on philosophical reason and its propensity to gravitate toward monism or dualism, and seek out a standard that can determine the relationship of the spiritual to the material in a way that is more consistent with God's 'real' engagement with the material world.

The Spirit, Creation and Divine Revelation

The manner in which the Spirit engages us through the exigencies of this material world is most explicitly revealed in God's most direct form of disclosure – the Holy Scriptures. The Scriptures themselves are the product of the Spirit's revealing action, and although the manner of the Spirit's engagement with aspects of the material world and the human interpreter are the subject of a subsequent chapter, for now we shall proceed on the assumption of the Scriptures Spirit-derived authority. In appealing to Holy Scripture we are appealing to a work that is explicitly *practically oriented*. Indeed, we are not delving into writings with a principal focus on philosophical ontology and the 'how' of the Spirit's engagement with the material world, but a practical appreciation of 'what and why' the Spirit relates to the material world, so from this we must then draw our conclusions.

The concrete world has the fingerprints of the Spirit of God all over it. Even the apostle Paul alludes to this when he stresses the accountability of all humanity in light of God's revealed truth: 'For since the creation of the world God's invisible qualities – his eternal power and divine nature – have been clearly seen, being understood from what has been made, so that they [people] are without excuse' (Rom. 1:20). However, in many theological endeavours the Spirit's engagement with the created order has only received a passing mention. In fact, the focus of theology in the Western tradition, vis-à-vis the Spirit, has been mostly directed towards the Spirit's redemptive role: anointing, delivering and saving God's people from the consequences of their sin. Of course, redemption is a valid discussion, a central theme of Scripture, and a necessary part of the human story; regrettably however, other equally important aspects of the Spirit's work, particularly with reference to the created order and the importance of it for our understanding, have been quietly ignored.[11]

What then does the testimony of Scripture reveal about the Spirit's engagement with the material realm? According to the creation account, and prior to the intervention of the Spirit in the creation process, the earth was little more than a formless mass of seething matter: 'In the beginning God created the heavens and the earth. Now the earth was formless and empty, darkness was over the surface of the deep, and the Spirit of God was hovering over the waters' (Gen. 1:1–2). The Spirit here is portrayed as an active agent, giving the primal creation form and order. Although much ink has been spilt in defending and affirming God as creator and his creation *ex nihilo*, Alister McGrath believes the Old Testament prophetic tradition takes a different view on creation: 'The world is regarded as ordered on account of the divine act of creation; indeed, the emphasis within many biblical passages dealing with the theme of creation can be argued to be more concerned with "the imposition of order" than "bringing into being".'[12] Much more than creating from nothing, the Spirit's primary function, with reference to material creation, is presented as *primarily* imposing an order on creation, such that we can now speak of a 'created order'.

In the process of imposing this order, what is immediately obvious to the reader of the Genesis account is the Spirit's distinction 'from' the material world. The primal creation is formless, empty and dark; the divine Spirit 'hovers' over it, as a separate being – ready to act creatively upon it. That is to say, the Spirit of God cannot be seen as 'essentially' one with this primordial material reality, or as giving form to it from 'essentially' within. The Spirit clearly works at creating form, design and purpose from the outside, and in so doing can only be a force from the outside, a divine force, as John Calvin iterates, '[the Spirit] is accepted from the category of creatures; but in transfusing into all things his energy, and breathing into them essence, life, and movement, he is indeed plainly divine.'[13] Thus, the divine creative power of the Spirit flows in a unidirectional manner, such that the Spirit, although being distinct from the material order, mysteriously supplies the energy that animates the form and shape out of chaos; creating beauty and order – a realm in which the wonder of life can exist and flourish.

The world that we experience and recognize with its various forms – eco-systems, seasons and complex life in all its abundance – is, in essence, a product of the Spirit's working. As John Owen suggests, without the Spirit's influence life is a void: 'Without him, all was a dead sea; a rude unformed chaos; a confused heap covered with darkness: but by the moving of the Spirit of God upon it, he communicated a quickening prolific virtue.'[14] This life-enabling virtue is also powerfully revealed through the prophet Ezekiel who, when commanded by the Lord to prophesy over dry (dead) bones, sees the once-living carcasses restored (Ezek. 37:1–14). It is the breath of the Lord (the Spirit) that restores their form. Although this message is metaphorical (Ezek. 37:5), the fact that the Spirit can be spoken of as the means of bringing life and order from death and chaos suggests there is a consistency between creation and ongoing or new creation narratives. Without the quickening presence of the divine Spirit, the material order is little more than dust, primordial slime or chalky dry bones – lifeless, formless matter. Thus, we can conclude that the Spirit gives form and life to material things. Without the spiritual dimension, the material has no substantive existence!

As the transcendent Spirit of God acts on the material world, while remaining distinct from it, the 'practical' relationship between the two is nevertheless effectively indissoluble, as Eduard Schweizer suggests, 'the Holy Spirit has nothing to do with the higher life of idealism which strives to elevate itself above the level of the material world. The Holy Spirit is as close to the body as to the soul, to the bodily functions of man as to the spiritual or psychic functions.'[15] By way of the analogy, if we consider a human life, at the point of death the soul, which is 'essentially' spiritual, departs and physical decay sets in. In this case, the Spirit of God, which animated the life-connection between body and soul, has temporarily withdrawn its creative influence, enabling the decay of death to set in. Thus, the definable and recognizable form of the human being dissipates, and returns 'to the dust', practically defined as formless matter. Just as a human body ceases to live without the soul, so material reality ceases to have form, meaning, power and purpose without the Spirit. The point being, we cannot simply collapse the Spirit into a monistic view of reality, nor clinically separate it out in some dualistic sense. The Spirit's mysterious involvement in ordering and animating the material creation is as close as body and soul.

The Holy Spirit also instils in the created order beauty and design that reflect the artistic mind of the Creator. If we just view aesthetics (an appreciation of beauty) from a rationalist point of view, by looking on this beauty / design within the created order from a subject / object point of view – with the material object having representative or symbolic value – creation can be reduced to a rational concept through the mode of human language. Moreover, in its more extreme naturalist application, nature can be reduced to principles: 'consistent simplification and gradual reduction to lower and lower terms . . . to attempt to refer to all phenomena in a single, uniform mode of occurrence, which admits nothing outside at all beyond itself'.[16] Because the object is a mere carrier of meaning, when the capacity for language to define that object ceases, so does the capacity for the object to have meaning. Objects then, have no meaning outside what they can be defined as technically; they become nothing more than the effects of a greater cause, which can be determined by applying the simple 'laws of nature'. Taken naturalistically, the beauty instilled into creation by the Spirit is evacuated of meaning, and reduced to an object of human redefinition.

Even while we can look at the design and coherence of nature and derive from mere 'principle', for example, that there must be a designer; there is something more than reasoned principles being communicated through this medium. The phenomenological approach to nature enables us to transcend the subject–object relationship to nature. As a primary advocate, Hans-Geog Gadamer worked on the principle that Being exceeds knowing and linguistic Being transcends linguistic consciousness.[17] That is, beauty – or art which describes it – is not representational but presentational; that is, its meaning comes from self-presentation, and this self-presentation draws us into a 'world' of its own, where we become much more than an interpreter, we become the one interpreted. In such a view, meaning cannot be encapsulated by the mind alone. In Gadamer's estimation, no meaning is immediately revealed, because the meaning initially extracted from the engagement can be expanded upon or modified with subsequent or continual engagements.[18] That is to say, we don't simply define objects; they reveal themselves to us, and in greater detail through continual engagement.

From this point of view, we approach the material or natural world, not as an observer looking at objects which can be reduced to principles, but as one that is open to be interpreted by the 'gallery' of God's divine artwork. In so doing, there is opened up the possibility of looking at the Spirit's engagement in nature in a new light – that of a dynamic engagement of revealed truth. If indeed, as the scriptural testimony has stated, the Spirit of God exercises creative power in forming, shaping and designing the primordial mass into something ordered and beautiful, and the Spirit is still at work animating life (as the Ezekiel account suggests), then surely it must follow that there is 'potential' for the Spirit to reveal divine truth through the created order, and not just in a representational way, but presentational way, viewed and experienced as we walk through life. In our dynamic engagement in God's world, we encounter a dynamic art gallery, a vista constantly captivating us and drawing us into its interpretation; we are able to 'sense' specific truths, divine truths, being revealed (albeit imperfectly and in a limited way).

Of course, such a view would only be possible if the human, in engagement with this Spirit-animated natural world, has a spiritual capacity. Humanity, as part of God's creation, occupies a special role in as much as the human being is not only created by God, but also is created in God's very image. Moreover, the Spirit is the active agent in the special human creation, as Job, in reflecting on his state, recognizes, 'The Spirit of God has made me; the breath of the Almighty gives me life' (Job 33:4). This Spirit not only sustains life, but empowers the ability to engage in the workings of life: 'I have filled him with the Spirit of God, with skill, ability and knowledge in all kinds of crafts' (Exod. 31:3). Human life is not only animated materially by the Spirit's power, but is also quickened with a divinely created self-consciousness to actually be aware of it. As such the human has the capacity to respond to the Spirit's creative and revelatory influence through practical engagement with the material world. The human being and the created order both owe their provenance to the Spirit's creative power, and as such this Spirit-enabled human existence, both intellectual and practical, cannot be easy abstracted from the material world. Spirituality and materiality are not mutually exclusive.

Furthermore, in connecting the Spirit's engagement with the material with revelation, Proverbs personifies wisdom (practical truth) as actively involved in creation: 'By wisdom the LORD laid the earth's foundations, by understanding he set the heavens in place; by his knowledge the deeps were divided, and the clouds let drop the dew' (Prov. 3:19–20) and again: 'Then I was the master worker at his side. I was filled with delight day after day, rejoicing always in his presence, rejoicing in his whole world and delighting in the human race'

(Prov. 8:30–31). Both the Spirit and wisdom are integrated vis-à-vis the creative act.

Therefore, when considering the Spirit of God, humanity and material creation in dynamic relationship, we cannot avoid the conclusion that divine wisdom is bound to be manifest, to greater or lesser degrees, within that created order; or, as Gwyn Walters insightfully suggests, 'The Spirit of life, wisdom and power is thus at work in all men – oftentimes working despite their perverseness, and so arranging things that there is "nothing haphazard in the universe".'[19]

Consequently, if the Spirit of God animates human life and the material world by divine wisdom, then the human interpreter through the Spirit's illuminating presence should expect God to use the material dimension as a medium for revealing truth, a revelation of truth that is not static or cyclic, but is dynamically integrated into an unfolding plan.

The Spirit, History and Divine Purpose

God's engagement within history has a purpose and a goal, in technical terms it is both teleological and eschatological. Isaiah writes, 'The LORD Almighty has sworn, "Surely, as I have planned, so it will be, and as I have purposed, so it will stand"' (Isa. 14:24). Taking into account what was considered in the previous section, on the Spirit's intentional involvement in creative processes of the material world, it necessarily follows that the Spirit should play a role in the structuring of history. We capture a glimpse of this in Revelation 22, where the symbolic representation of the heavenly conditions awaiting those who remain faithful to Christ, is offered up by a call of the Spirit: 'The Spirit and the bride say, "Come!" And let those who hear say, "Come!" Let those who are thirsty come; and let all who wish take of the free gift of the water of life' (Rev. 22:17). The Spirit, operating within the bounds of temporal history, is presented as issuing a call to God's people to faithfully embrace the blessed future purposed by God. The Spirit that transcends the temporal is actively involved in human history, directing the particular focus of God's people toward the goal of that history – God's eternal kingdom.

The Spirit is purposefully involved in the unfolding of God's plan and in the lives of God's people – the direct beneficiaries of that plan's goal. However, we should be also aware of the Spirit's engagement in the affairs of the wider human population. Indeed, the Spirit's presence is not entirely inconsequential to the functioning of those that only 'appear' to be on the edge of the redemptive / restorative purposes of God. Yes, even the most reprobate has a role to play in the Spirit's unfolding of the divine drama. John Calvin identified this fact: 'we ought not to forget those most excellent benefits of the divine Spirit, which he distributes to whomever he wills, for the common good of mankind.'[20]

Of course, we must not forget that God's salvation history also unfolds along the same timeline as ordinary human history. The rise and fall of great nations and empires, even with their inherently this-worldly orientation, have played and do continue to play a role in this unfolding scheme. The scriptural accounts readily outline how Babylon, Persia, Greece, Rome and their leaders served God's ultimate purposes, as he sought to set apart a people of his own. Furthermore, this occurs, not only on a macro-scale, but also on a localized level as well. The ordinary affairs of human life (in which the actors are often entirely oblivious to the purposes of God) form the small threads in which the tapestry of God's ultimate purposes is woven.

Perhaps the most explicit teleological reference to the Spirit's engagement with the material order is seen in advent, life and ministry of Jesus Christ. The Spirit is liberally endowed in those heralding Jesus' birth (Luke 1:15 – 2:27) and explicitly portrayed as the material cause of the physical conception of Jesus (Matt. 1:18–20). Of course, such an explicit engagement of the Spirit with the material world has been readily misunderstood in history; filtered through the macro-ideologies of monism / dualism. Significantly, these errors were identified and addressed by the Council of Chalcedon (AD 451), which stressed the 'mystery' of Jesus' Spirit / flesh engagement by defining the relationship of the divine and human natures as being unconfused, unchangeable, indivisible and inseparable. Chalcedon simultaneously emphasized that this union does not remove the distinctions.

But it must be stressed, for God to reveal himself in this very intimate manner (in human form), the specific engagement of the Spirit was indispensable to the process. In fact, in the incarnation of Christ, we have the clearest expression of the revelatory value of the Spirit's purposeful engagement with the material order. Without the direct and immediate engagement of the Holy Spirit with the material creature, the most explicit, clearest and superior revelation of God to humanity (Heb. 1:1–4), would not have been possible. The Spirit's intimate engagement in the material life of Jesus Christ does not stop at his incarnation. There is an ongoing teleological relationship between the Spirit and Jesus' earthly ministry.

In Luke's account we read, 'the Holy Spirit descended on him in bodily form like a dove. And a voice came from heaven: "You are my son, whom I love; with you I am well pleased"' (Luke 3:22). Accompanying the tangible *anointing* of the Spirit is a divine affirmation of royal kingship (Ps. 2:7), setting Jesus apart for his messianic ministry – a ministry intimately bound to God's eternal plan. Following this, the Spirit leads Jesus into the wilderness intentionally, to be tempted by Satan for forty days (Luke 4:1–3). Whereas God's previous 'son', Israel (Hos. 11:1), failed God's purposes by giving into the wilderness temptation, Jesus the ultimate 'Son of God' does not. Overcoming the temptation and validating his messianic credentials, Jesus proceeds in the power of the Spirit to proclaim the gospel to the 'lost sheep' of Israel: 'The Spirit of the Lord is on me, because he has anointed me to preach good news to the poor . . . to proclaim the year of the Lord's favour' (Luke 4:18–19).

The Spirit was, and remains, purposefully involved in Jesus' ministry. The Holy Spirit is actively empowering Jesus' proclamation and intimately involved in the commensurate role of pushing back the kingdom of darkness. In the context of being falsely accused of driving out demons under the authority of Beelzebub (the prince of demons), he responds with a revelation about the purpose behind these deliverances: 'But if I drive out demons by the Spirit of God, then the kingdom of God has come upon you' (Matt. 12:28). For Jesus, one of the key markers that the kingdom of God is being revealed is the Spirit's role in challenging and suppressing the forces of darkness.

The Holy Spirit is revealed in Scripture as the means of perpetuating the ministry of Jesus. In the opening verses of Acts 1, Luke's reflection on the last days of Jesus' ministry with his disciples sheds light on Jesus' ongoing presence through the Spirit following Pentecost. On an occasion after his resurrection, Jesus appeared to his disciples, who asked whether he was going to restore the kingdom to Israel. In response Jesus reminded them that such things are in the Father's grand design, and instructed them to patiently wait for the Spirit's coming, which would, in God's perfect time, make clear the ongoing purpose for their lives. In Jesus' understanding, the Spirit would provide the guidance and power to be his effective witnesses throughout every nation (Acts 1:8).

Subsequently, during Pentecost, the Spirit comes upon the group in power: 'All of them were filled with the Holy Spirit and began to speak in other tongues as the Spirit enabled them' (Acts 2:4). The event miraculously allowed many foreigners to hear God being praised in their own language, and to conclude that God had a special message for them. Peter, in response to the ensuing confusion, under the guidance of the Spirit, recognized this Spirit-event as being actually foreshadowed by the Spirit through the prophet Joel: 'In the last days, God says, I will pour out my Spirit on all people' (Acts 2:17). He then preached a message that instigated the salvation of thousands. Thus the New Testament church was born and the divine purpose of restoring 'all' of humanity through the gospel had formally begun; and this through the comprehensive and purposeful ministry of the Holy Spirit.

Not only in the life and ministry of Jesus does the wider New Testament reveal the ongoing teleological involvement of the Spirit. In Acts 5 the Spirit reveals that Ananias and Sapphira had deceived the church. In exposing this hypocrisy at this critical stage of the divine mission, the Spirit ensures that this particular sin would not cripple the embryo church's life: 'Great fear seized the whole church and all who heard about these events . . . Nevertheless, more and more men and women believed in the Lord and were added to their number' (Acts 5:11,14).

In Acts 10, we also read that the Holy Spirit engages an unwitting Peter in a landmark event: 'While Peter was still thinking about the vision, the Spirit said to him, "Simon, three men are looking for you. So get up and go downstairs. Do not hesitate to go with them, for I have sent them"' (Acts 10:19–20). Significantly, the resultant conversion of the first Gentile Christians through their encounter with Peter opened up the possibility for the mission to the Gentile world, a mission which would have been otherwise hindered by Jewish religious prejudice. In another account, to ensure the fulfilment of God's purposes in Paul's mission, the Spirit acted: 'When they came to the border of Mysia, they tried to enter Bithynia, but the Spirit of Jesus would not allow them to' (Acts 16:7). As we can see, the Spirit providentially orders specific local events, indirectly and directly, to the advantage of God's ultimate goal.

Not only does the Spirit have a teleological relation to salvation history, there is a strong eschatological dimension to this relationship as well. The Spirit works at establishing, guarding and thus preserving Christians with a view to the final salvation. In a number of his letters, the apostle Paul advocates that the abiding presence of the Spirit represents the *divine seal* of God's ownership, ensuring the eschatological blessing awaiting the faithful: 'He anointed us, set his seal of ownership on us, and put his Spirit in our hearts as a deposit, guaranteeing what is to come' (2 Cor. 1:21–2).

In appropriating this anointing, believers are admonished to be mindful of their ongoing moral condition, lest they sever the relationship with the Spirit, the abiding presence of God guaranteeing their future salvation: 'And do not grieve the Holy Spirit of God, with whom you were sealed for the day of redemption' (Eph. 4:30). Therefore, as an eschatological agent, the Spirit brings the certainty of the future into the present through an existential / moral engagement with the believer. This is not just instilling hope of a future redemption but, properly understood, represents an existential validation of a future reality, such that the believer 'in the Spirit' embraces the reality of that future – now!

However, the fullest eschatological import of the Spirit's teleological engagement with the material creation is clearly seen in Romans 8. This is Paul's great chapter of the Spirit, with the first sixteen verses specifically dedicated to the Spirit's role in guiding the Christian's moral life. For Paul, sharing in Christ's blessings means sharing in his sufferings, which, as far as Paul is concerned, is inconsequential in comparison to future glory awaiting the faithful (Rom. 8:18). Believers are caught in the tension between the eschatological 'now and not yet', and metaphorically speaking 'groan in travail' (like a woman in childbirth), awaiting final salvation (Rom. 8:23).

Moreover, Paul metaphorically suggests the created order is now 'groaning' in anticipation of its eschatological emancipation (Rom. 8:22). Not only so, but the forgiven sinners 'in Christ', together with the fallen world, aspire toward future deliverance, fully expressed in the new creation. But what empowers perseverance toward this future aspiration? For Paul, the solution is in a form of hope generated by the 'real' presence of the Spirit ('first-fruits': Rom. 8:23); hope which invariably helps the believers endure weakness (Rom. 8:24–6). In this regard, the Spirit intercedes on their behalf according to God's ultimate will. So it is that the Holy Spirit enables the tangible connection between the eschatological reality hoped for and the life of struggle and tension, presently experienced.

The Spirit, the Consecration of Nature, and Wisdom

If we believe that the Spirit of God is actively involved in the created order, and also believe that the Spirit's engagement is purposeful within that same order, then it should necessarily follow that we should *expect* to be able to identify the Spirit's working in 'our' world, in the process of revealing divine truth according to God's purposes. In this regard, we cannot claim that the Spirit's engagement will always be overt, rather it would be more accurate to claim that the Spirit can and does engage nature, in both primary (overt) and secondary (covert) manners.

In the capacity of primary causality, the Spirit engages the material dimension with the intent to directly reveal divine truths to God's people. For example, in Chronicles we read, 'He gave him the plans of all that the Spirit had put in his mind for the courts of the temple of the LORD and all the surrounding rooms, for the treasuries of the temple of God and for the treasuries for the dedicated things' (1 Chron. 28:12). The Spirit specifically inspired the temple designers / builders with the plans of its construction; an edifice designed to symbolically reflect the nature of the relationship between God and his people. Of course, the building itself does not 'directly' define the relationship between God and his people, insomuch as it describes what is at stake in the relationship – the necessity for purity. Without the Spirit-directed material representation of this temple form, the concepts of divine holiness, human sinfulness and the necessity for atonement, even if propositionally defined, would have lacked substantive clarity. In this example, we might then say that God's Spirit directly consecrates the material and/or the natural, to more adequately and fully reveal divine truth.

With respect to second-level causality, the more common of the Spirit's modes of interaction with the material, God's consecration of the natural is most evident in the story of Jonah. Given that the audience for the Jonah narratives are the Jewish people, and given that they are accustomed to having truth verified through signs (1 Cor. 1:22), we should find it rather unremarkable that God would miraculously engage nature in communicating truth. That said, all humans do exist in some material space, and given that we all learn through experience within that space, the fact that God should engage humanity through the material realm should appear quite 'natural'. Israel, like Jonah, were wilfully disobeying God's word, and needed something more powerful than the spoken word or written Scripture to get their attention. God employs the dramatic to do so; indeed a dramatic component is not abnormal in Old Testament prophecy, as W.D. Stacey argues, 'If a prophet resorts to dramatic action, it is much more likely to be because the word is not powerful enough, rather than not clear enough.'[21] God powerfully engages nature to reveal his truth to a people who have become complacent with the written or spoken word.

Jonah, then, is commissioned by God to proclaim the impending destruction of Nineveh. As soon as he received the charge, he fled on a ship bound for Tarshish – the opposite end of the earth. In challenging Jonah's flight: 'Then the LORD sent a great wind on the sea' (Jonah 1:4). The subsequent fear generated by the tempest drives the pagan sailors to cry out to their gods for help. Following desperate deliberation with Jonah, and at his own request, he is thrown overboard by the pagan sailors. The storm ceases with the following result: 'At this the men greatly feared the LORD, and they offered a sacrifice to the LORD and made vows to him' (Jonah 1:16). As we see this is not random event, as John Calvin observes, 'Jonah then meant that a tempest arose, not by chance, but by the certain purpose of God.'[22] This storm is deliberately manufactured by God to specifically reveal truths to the respective actors within the drama, exposing clearly the revelatory nature of God's power through the material order. This particular event is powerfully effective in proclaiming a message and evincing a result, that the cowardly Jonah was unable to do.

Though the text of Jonah does not explicitly state it, it can be assumed from the statement, 'But the LORD provided [a fish]' (Jonah 1:17), that the Spirit who powerfully created and shaped the world also has a hand in animating powerful natural phenomena in a purposeful way within it, for without the Spirit's dynamic power the actions of God in creation would not exist. The Spirit, by using the giant fish, creates a matrix within which Jonah is soberly able to re-theologize his view of reality, and by extension his view of mission. Had Jonah not experienced the distress of being three days in the belly of the giant fish, he would not have existentially come to terms with the gravity of salvation, and the necessity to share its divine message with the perishing.

Once the purposes of God have been fulfilled in Jonah's repentance, the Lord 'directs' the fish to vomit Jonah onto dry land. Just how the Lord commands the fish we are not told, but it can be confidently asserted that God's secret counsels are at work in this commanding, as Hugh Martin elaborates, 'He has arranged a series of causes and elements, and places them in various adaptations towards one another, but he supports, maintains, controls, and moves them at his own pleasure.'[23] Consequently, the unwitting actions of the giant fish are perfectly in step with God's purposes. Thus, we can conclude that the Spirit in enabling God's redemptive purposes of preparing, enabling and guiding his people, uses nature to this end.

Jonah's complaint, following Nineveh's repentance, represents one of the most explicit examples of the divine consecration of nature in Holy Scripture. In this account God employs no less than three aspects of the material world to communicate powerful truths to Jonah: flora, fauna and weather. Jonah is upset because he expected God to destroy the Ninevites, but in his mercy relents. Jonah then storms out of the city and begrudgingly watches and waits; expecting God to judge them anyway. Contrary to his wishes, God through the effective use of nature teaches Jonah powerful object lessons about the quality of his mercy. First, God provides a vine: 'Then the LORD God provided a vine and made it grow up over Jonah to give shade for his head to ease his discomfort, and Jonah was very happy about the vine' (Jonah 4:6). Jonah is delighted that the Lord would provide him with such a material comfort. However, to make his point, the Lord then 'provides' a worm to chew the vine, such that it begins to die. Furthermore, in concert with the worm, the Lord also provides a hot east wind to bring a complete end to the vine, and any comfort it might afford Jonah. The Lord then allows the weather to further stress Jonah. With the hot sun bearing down on him, he falls into despair and actually wants to die (Jonah 4:8).

In the wake of Jonah's despair over the vine's demise, the Lord makes the object lesson explicit through verbal revelation: 'You have been concerned about this vine, though you did not tend it or make it grow . . . Should I not be concerned about that great city?' (Jonah 4:10–11). Jonah actually had no appreciation of the depth of God's gracious love toward his enemies, until he experienced the loss of the shady vine. For Jonah, the truth of God's mercy was not fully apprehended until the consequences of its withdrawal were personally 'felt'. In this case, Jonah had to actually feel grief over the loss of a trivial plant, to more fully grasp the significance of God's grief over the potential loss of a city full of ignorant people – albeit pagans. I believe we may generally extrapolate, that any full appreciation of truth cannot be truly apprehended until the weight of it is felt through an engagement with material consequences. That is to say, we don't actually understand the gravity of some things until we tangibly or physically feel their consequences; we cannot fully understand sin until we feel its pain, and we cannot fully grasp the favour of God until we experience healing or material provision. Fully understanding divine truth is inextricably bound to human experience in the material world.

God the Spirit consecrates nature as a means of revealing his truth. In this process, the Spirit may animate material means in both primary and secondary senses. We saw how the Spirit, as a primary cause, orchestrated the design and construction of the Israelite temple. In this case, the Spirit had a direct role in engaging the material in order to reveal specific truths about God and how to relate to him. There are specific times and instances, albeit rare in human experience, where the Spirit will engage the material realm to directly communicate divine truth. Not only so, but the examples from the book of Jonah revealed where the Lord acted on nature, through secondary causality, to orchestrate factors that enabled a clearer understanding of the divine truth revealed. The events surrounding the storm, the fish that swallowed Jonah, and the growing and dying of the plant during Jonah's complaint were all indirectly orchestrated by God to augment the propositional revelation subsequently issued by him. Indeed, without these indirect natural interventions the spoken message would have lacked the full potency to drive the truth of the message home. From this example alone, and there are others in Scripture, we can assume that God's Spirit through the avenue of secondary causality works to orchestrate events, augmenting a deeper understanding of his spoken and/or written word.

Summary

Understanding the Spirit's engagement with the material world is not without its difficulties. As we have seen there is a predilection among thinkers to rely on reason, borrowing the common philosophical constructs of monism and dualism. Monism attempts to solve the Spirit / nature relationship by methodologically collapsing the Creator Spirit into the material dimension, such that all material reality is 'spiritually' constituted; in so doing the Spirit loses its divine transcendence. The other philosophical alternative, dualism, manufactures a clear separation of Spirit and nature. This approach sees nature as little more than a 'sign' that points toward higher realities, which are most fully apprehended through either abstract rational reflection or spiritual asceticism. Consequently, dualism sees little or no value in nature with respect to the Spirit's role in revealing truth. But, in setting these unhelpful ideologies aside, we concluded that a faith-based approach to Holy Scripture better serves the purpose of grasping the Spirit's *illogical engagement* with nature. The biblical portrayal of the Spirit is less concerned with the 'how' of abstract ontology and more concerned with 'what and why' of practical religion.

Further to adopting this faith-based Scripture position, we noted that the Spirit is actively engaged in the process of creation, specifically the *order* within that creation. While remaining ontologically distinct from the material world, the Spirit acts on and in it, instilling it with a divine order that humans can recognize. The human interpreter must approach this created order – not from a position of self-imposed objectivity, redefining the material order in terms of rational principles, but from a position of openness, willing to be the one 'interpreted by God' in the context of the gallery of God's natural artwork, a gallery designed by the Spirit. By setting aside hermeneutical autonomy, the truth-seeker is now open to the possibility of seeing what the Spirit is revealing through a dynamic engagement with the material world. From this faith-based position, those seeking truth expect God's Spirit to precondition the reality of life they experience in the world. Even if only covertly then, the Spirit plays a role in the disclosure and confirmation of the truth revealed through the design of the created order.

God's engagement with the created order and humanity within that order is also teleological and eschatological by nature. Simply translated, this means that the Holy Spirit's working in the world has a *purposeful and goal-oriented* focus. Under 'The Spirit, History and Divine Purpose', we observed, from various references to Scripture, that the divine Spirit deliberately acts within the particularities of history to execute, sustain and fulfil God's plan. This is never clearer than in the life and ministry of Jesus Christ; where the Spirit is presented as actively engaged at every stage – from his conception through to his ascension and the subsequent advent of the Spirit at Pentecost. The Spirit played a vital role not only in the messianic mission, but also in guiding the apostolic church and particular Christians within it, as they lived out their divinely ordained purpose, awaiting the conclusion of things. In this regard, the existential presence of the Spirit served, and continues to serve, as a deposit guaranteeing the receipt of the promise of eternal life offered to all who trust Christ and faithfully endure for him.

In the final section of the chapter, we considered the Spirit's consecration of the material in the process of divine revelation. We observed that God engages nature in two senses: primary and secondary. In the former, the Spirit directly intervenes in the process of revealing truth, as the example of the Spirit providing the design of the Old Testament temple shows. In this, the Spirit acts through secondary causality, prompting nature to conform to the specific purposes of God as they relate to a particular act of revelation, most notably illustrated by Jonah's experience with the vine. Indeed, there is a firm biblical precedent for the Spirit's consecration of the material order as it relates to the purpose of augmenting divine revelation.

The facts that the Spirit is intimately involved in the material realm, the Spirit has a creative role in establishing order and design within that realm, the Spirit acts purposefully and with ultimate intent within that created order, and the Spirit can and does consecrate material nature with a revelatory purpose enable us to draw some valuable conclusions. First, we can assume that the material realm is a real dimension of the Spirit's working, and as such should be considered as something more than static matter, but a dynamic reality. Second, the world we encounter, by virtue of its Spirit-design, is primed for human interpretation; it is a ready-to-use medium for the process of truth-seeking. Third, this dynamic reality is purposefully unfolding toward an ultimate goal and as such we should expect to see circumstances, acts and events in the world as having eternal relevance with reference to God. Finally, given that God uses nature, through the powerful interaction of his Spirit, to supplement the revelation and/or affirmation of truth, we should expect to see God working in and through this material dimension.

The Holy Spirit works through the material order to communicate divine revelation, if we are genuinely seeking the truth, God's truth. We only serve our ignorance by dismissing the value of the material world which is laid out before us.

4

The Spirit, Truth and the Church

Must we discover the truth ourselves? The quest for the truth in the West has largely been an individualistic one. The generally accepted notion that truth-seekers must act as self-sufficient intellectuals striving to gain a conception of the truth for themselves, and only in consultation with the academic or religious elite, fundamentally ignores the value of a shared dynamic offered by the spiritual community. Of course, the truth must be personally embraced, but this does not occur in isolation from others – especially other Christians. If the Christian church's goal in presenting divine truth is more than merely offering an appreciation of theoretical knowledge about God to individuals but, as the Scriptures suggest, to build one another up, then surely the communal dimension to perceiving truth must be taken more seriously. Indeed, if Christian truth has other-oriented ends, then surely understanding it must draw on other-oriented means: the means of the community of faith – the church. In the community, the Holy Spirit's presence serves to enable a delicate balance between individual interpretation and communal understanding. The Spirit, who established this unique spiritual communion, enables it to exist as both *organization and organism*, ensuring both the dynamic revelation of truth and its preservation. For the truth-seeker, the community of God's people is indispensable.

The Spirit and the Church

The Spirit's relationship to 'the church' vis-à-vis the revelation of truth has been the subject of long-standing discussion and debate. For some traditions, the Holy Spirit's engagement is little more than a formality, acting as the invisible divine agent that ratifies the church's institutional formulation of truth. In this view the Spirit works primarily through the ordained hierarchy. Then there is the polar-opposite view, which argues for the Spirit's authoritative engagement with the Christian community primarily through individual spiritual 'truth' experiences. In this view, any individual can claim knowledge from the Spirit that is then offered to the community, which itself is viewed as an 'organic' collection of individuals. In the former, individual spiritual conviction invariably gives way to the institutional agenda, with the hierarchy determining truth in spite of individual convictions. In the latter example, institutional structure is simply dismissed in favour of individual spiritual 'leading', with practically 'any' allegedly Spirit-filled individual having equal claims on truth for the church's guidance.

Perhaps the clearest example of the Holy Spirit working through ecclesiastical structures is seen within Roman Catholicism. In the Roman Catholic model, the epistemic relationship between any given individual believer and the Holy Spirit is functionally 'indirect'. That is to say, in the strictest sense any individual Catholic believer cannot 'formally' arrive at a valid understanding of truth that might be commonly accepted, without having it go through the conduit of the religious hierarchy. Hendrikus Berkhof notes of Catholicism, 'The Spirit's primary work is the creation and preservation of the sacramental and hierarchical structure and that the individual [believer] is fully dependent on that structure for his participation in the work of the Spirit.'[1] When the Spirit's guidance is mediated through the ecclesial leadership, the layperson is unable to arrive at any unmediated understanding of truth that might be contrary to that formally recognized by the church. As such, the Spirit is bound to the operations of the institutional church; in fact many would say that the Holy

Spirit's truth guidance is domesticated, vetoed by a greater ecclesiastical purpose.

But how could such a hierarchy-mediated view of the Spirit find validation? The answer, in fact, lies with the Roman Catholic Church's view of authority. Unlike Protestantism, at least superficially, which sees the Spirit's authority coming through the medium of the Spirit-inspired Holy Scriptures, Catholicism sees its authority channelled by way of apostolic succession. In Roman Catholic ecclesiology the authority of Christ is directly transmitted to the hierarchy of the church through the medium of Christ's apostles, Peter being the first pope of the church. Through this apostolic succession the church receives the power to teach and rule with the authority of Christ, as George Hendry indicates: 'in the exercise of these powers the church carries on the same mission and the same mandate which he [Jesus] had received from the Father. Its empowerment to fulfil this mission derives from the Holy Spirit, who proceeds from this doctrinaire and authoritarian Christ, and who, as such, is a Spirit of authority.'[2] Therefore, because the Holy Spirit's authority is bound to institutional authority, the individual believer has no direct legitimate access to the truth of God via the Holy Spirit outside the church authority structure.

The advantage of channelling the Holy Spirit's truth-validating capacity via the medium of ecclesiastical authority is that any deliberation of the truth is effectively 'peer-reviewed' and able to be measured against the 'time-honoured' traditions of the church and its collective wisdom. Indeed, it could be argued that the Jerusalem Council of the early church reflects this approach: 'God, who knows the heart, showed that he accepted them by giving the Holy Spirit to them, just as he did to us . . . It seemed good to the Holy Spirit and to us not to burden you with anything beyond the following requirements' (Acts 15:8,28). On the other hand, the disadvantage of such an approach is that it allows the institution to override any prophetic revelation that might originate from those outside the incumbent authority structure, effectively making the Holy Spirit's revelation conditional on the authenticity of the hierarchy – which may or may not be sound.

Also, institutions have the proclivity to resist change and are more often than not reticent to allow their systems to be critiqued, even if God can be proven to be the source of that critique, as responses to Jesus' ministry suggest: 'If we let him go on like this, everyone will believe in him, and then the Romans will come and take away both our place and our nation' (John 11:48).

In reaction to the Holy Spirit's key connection to ecclesiastical authority within Catholicism, the Protestant Reformers responded by 'technically' shifting the authority away from the ecclesiastical institution, by seeking out new ways of interpreting the triangular relationship between the Spirit, the church and the individual.[3] The Reformers picked up on the greater place of the individual, something that Catholicism was starting to place a greater emphasis on during the Middle Ages, with individual accountability before God being stressed.[4] They then proceeded to challenge the church's capacity to wield spiritual power and bind the consciences of these individuals, by placing an ever greater importance of the individual's personal responsibility before God, manifested in ideas such as the need for individual faith in Christ, the value of individual interpretation of Scripture, and the necessity for individual spiritual discernment.

As effective as this new approach was in breaking the bonds of ecclesiastical control over personal spirituality, it also sowed the seeds for 'spiritual individualism', so much so that later Protestants and their derivative movements found it difficult to see the value of the institution at all, as Berkhof suggests, 'The reason is that they [Protestants] have such an individualistic and spiritualistic or, at best, personalistic conception of the Spirit that they do not understand that God created structures as well as persons, that in his saving work he is also interested in structures in so far as they can serve his purposes.'[5]

Nevertheless, a greater capacity for the individual to discern the Spirit's authority came into being. Whereas Roman Catholicism channelled the Spirit's authority through ecclesiastical hierarchy, Protestantism routes it through the 'means' of grace – the sacraments of the Lord's Supper and baptism, and Holy Scripture. In as much as the Holy Spirit authoritatively directs the conscience toward truth, the Reformers created an inseparable link between the authority of the Holy Spirit and the authority of Holy Scripture. Most notable was the contribution of John Calvin.[6]

Calvin, popularly dubbed the theologian of the Holy Spirit, drew on Augustine's conjunctive relationship between letter and Spirit.[7] He argued that the Holy Spirit is not only responsible for the 'indirect authorship' of Scripture, but also the interpretation of it: 'we ought to seek our conviction in a higher place than human reasons, judgements or conjectures, that is, in the secret testimony of the Spirit . . . the testimony of the Spirit is more excellent than all reason.'[8] Note that, when Calvin speaks of the testimony of the Holy Spirit, he very much has in view an *inextricable link* with the Scriptures: 'God did not bring forth his Word among men for the sake of momentary display, intending at the coming of the Spirit to abolish it. Rather, he sent down the same Spirit by whose power he had dispensed the Word, to complete his work by efficacious confirmation of the Word.'[9] The authoritative word and authoritative Spirit are *necessarily* bound together.

However, although representing a significant shift from Catholicism, it may not be as radical as many suppose. Because Protestantism channels the authority of the Spirit through the means of grace (word and sacraments), means which are exclusively administered by the 'ordained clergy',[10] there remains an implicit dependency on ecclesiastical hierarchy in relation to the Spirit's revelation of truth into the church community. Within most Protestant denominations only the 'ordained clergy' are qualified to teach the Spirit-inspired word and administer the sacraments (baptism and the Lord's Supper). Despite a recognition that each 'individual' person is able to receive the conviction of the Spirit as they read the word and receive the sacraments, in reality the teaching elder / pastor (in association with a governing council) has the final power of veto vis-à-vis 'truth' as it comes to the community's general acceptance of it.

Therefore, given that clergy have the primary responsibility for the interpretation and teaching of Christian doctrine, it is implicitly acknowledged that laypersons are most benefited when they accept this interpretation with a submissive spirit, as John Calvin intimates: 'anyone who presents himself in a teachable spirit to the ministers ordained by God shall know by the result that with good reason this way of teaching was pleasing to God, and also that with good reason this yoke of moderation was imposed on believers.'[11] Even the spiritually gifted laity remains outside the 'inner circle' of truth-givers, as Michael Green writes: 'These gifts have no necessary link with holiness of life nor with power in service; they are gifts of the Spirit, not graces of character.'[12] So, even within Reformed Protestant ecclesiology, a movement which claims to make a radical break from the ecclesiastical binding of the Spirit, a strong dependency on institutional hierarchy for administration of the Spirit's truth remains.

This now brings us to the view that promotes the Spirit's engagement with the church as non-hierarchical. To appreciate how the Holy Spirit relates truth through 'individuals' into the Christian community, in the most direct and organic manner, we must briefly consider pietism. In contemporary terms we might deem this as the Pentecostal tradition, which has roots in movements such as the Anabaptists, the Quakers, and the Plymouth Brethren.

Broadly speaking, within this tradition, church is perceived as little more than an assembly of Spirit-filled individuals, who recognize in one another the authoritative working of the Spirit, through whom authoritative revelations of the Spirit are given to the church. The Spirit brings truth to the community via personal revelations or 'words of knowledge' from the Spirit, which are shared in a communal setting as if it was a direct message from God. Formal structure counts for little in settings such as this. As Millard Erickson suggests: 'In each of these groups there is a concerted effort to eliminate as much structural organization as possible. They rely upon the Holy Spirit to work in a direct fashion, to lead them to conviction of what he wants done.'[13]

However, this view is taken not without some justification. In Paul's correspondence to the Corinthians, he emphasizes to the Corinthians the necessity of the Spirit vis-à-vis truth: 'We have not received the spirit of the world but the Spirit who is from God, that we may understand what God has freely given us' (1 Cor. 2:12). He then goes on to outline how the Spirit works through individuals in the church:

> Now to each one the manifestation of the Spirit is given for the common good. To one there is given through the Spirit the message of wisdom, to another the message of knowledge by means of the same Spirit . . . to another prophecy, to another distinguishing between spirits, to another speaking in different kinds of tongues, and to still another the interpretation of tongues. All these are the work of one and the same Spirit, and he gives them to each one, just as he determines (1 Cor. 12:7–11).

Given that it is the Spirit that sovereignly determines who receives the gifts, and that these gifts are given for the edification of every believer, it does not take too much imagination to see how a model of church that effectively has no hierarchy and relies on the dynamic witness of the Spirit through the 'body' of gifted individuals, could be formed.

While this view has value in as much as it values an openness to the dynamic leading of the Holy Spirit, its fundamental weakness is its propensity to rely on allegedly 'spiritually gifted' individuals of questionable maturity. This was something Paul was patently aware of: 'Brothers and sisters, I could not address you as spiritual but as worldly – mere infants in Christ' (1 Cor. 3:1). In fact, many of the Corinthian believers, though claiming to be spiritual, were simply following along with the methods and priorities of the world they lived in, seizing on the Spirit's gifts as a means of self-promotion. The view that all members of the fellowship have an equal capacity to channel the Spirit's truth to the community represents a primary failing of this model, as Erikson verifies: 'the degree of sanctification and sensitivity to the Holy Spirit which they posit of the members of a congregation is an unrealistic ideal.'[14] Furthermore, from my own practical experience I have found that there are relatively few people within any given congregation whom the Spirit has gifted with the capacity to offer wise counsel for the whole church. However, to qualify this, I have also observed that these people may or may not be ordained clergy.

This brief survey has assisted us to see some of the background issues that affect our potential understanding of what is involved in this delicate matter of relating the Spirit's authority to the church's reception and understanding of truth. Quite rightly, it has left us with more questions than answers: Does the Spirit work through the institution of the church and by extension its ruling hierarchy exclusively, or does the Spirit guide the organic community of individuals through any allegedly gifted individual to reveal truth exclusively? Or is it that both can be true, and if so, how? So, the fundamental question before us is this: How does the Spirit relate to the church, and how does the Spirit reveal truth in and through the communion of saints that constitute it?

The Spirit-created Church

What is the nature of the Spirit's relationship to the church? The modern world is more interested in matters of empirical presence and pragmatic purpose than ontology.[15] Simply put, the modern world is far more pragmatic than in times past, and there seems to be a greater emphasis on how a thing appears or what it does, than what it is! This ideological trend carries into theological reflection as well, and the way theologians reflect on the nature of the Christian church. However, when the church is 'solely' considered from this pragmatic viewpoint, it is more open to being modified by the subtle exigencies of contemporary society, with its commitment to track along this empirical and/or pragmatic, trajectory. As such, it is easier than ever for the church to be subverted by phenomenon such as secular business models or entertainment agendas. Indeed, when the pragmatic nature of the church's organization and the role of that organization in human affairs becomes the primary focus, the 'essence' or essential nature of the church is naïvely assumed, casually dismissed or simply ignored. Once this occurs, the church devolves into nothing more than a human organization with a mere religious varnish; it becomes the world, because it uncritically 'does' what the world does.

However, what is required to understand the nature of the Spirit's work in the church is to take a step back from the exigencies of religious appearance and ecclesiastical practice and actually consider the church's true essence – what it is with reference to God. Unless we first consider the *essential nature* of this unique community, there is a real chance of missing the critical link between the church's spiritual / communal nature and its practical functioning. As Craig Van Gelder suggests, 'Defining the church functionally – in terms of what it does – can shift our perspective away from understanding the church as a unique community of God's people. In place of this, the church tends to become a series of ministry functions such as worship, education, service, and witness.'[16] Therefore, the first and most important question to answer in this whole endeavour of the Spirit's relationship to the church, is actually: What 'is' the church?

In formulating an answer, we must be careful not to closely draw analogies from other human institutions, lest in analogically defining its essence we distort its true nature, which may actually be inexplicable in human terms. Importantly, we must recognize that the church is something unique, and that this uniqueness stems from the church's special relationship to the Holy Spirit and God's purpose in the world through this relationship. The Spirit of God, as we shall see from the New Testament, not only takes the initiative in creating this unique community but also continues to empower, sustain and guide it in the ways of divine truth for the good of its members. Of course, a general appreciation of the church as the people of God has certain precursors related to God's dealings with the nation of Israel under a former administration of the Mosaic covenant. However, the event of Pentecost so radically modified the previous concept of 'the people of God' and the manner of it as a believing community, that it is most pertinent to use the events following Jesus' ascension as our primary point of departure for understanding the church's essential nature.

Significantly, the New Testament church was not founded on or created from human initiative. Following the resurrection, Jesus specifically instructs his disciples to do nothing, other than 'wait' for God: 'Do not leave Jerusalem, but wait for the gift my Father promised, which you have heard me speak about. For John baptised with water, but in a few days you will be baptised with the Holy Spirit' (Acts 1:4–5). Regardless of the disciples' questioning of Jesus vis-à-vis God's purposes for God's people (Israel), the Lord, rather, directs their focus *forward* toward a special event where the Holy Spirit will play a role in reinventing the 'people of God': 'It is not for you to know the times or dates the Father has set by his own authority. But you will receive power when the Holy Spirit comes on you; and you will be my witnesses in Jerusalem, and in all Judea and Samaria, and to the ends of the earth' (Acts 1:7–8). Based on this divine initiative, the disciples anticipate a special endowment of the Holy Spirit, the divine power to fulfil God's missionary will through the people of God.

This power is not drawn from any human contrivance, institution or resource. At the Jewish festival of Pentecost immediately following Jesus' ascension, the followers of Jesus were gathered. Suddenly, a sound like a violent wind instigated what appeared to be 'tongues' of fire that rested above each person – clearly symbolic of the Spirit's presence. The ensuing 'filling' of the Spirit was validated as each of these followers was enabled to praise God in foreign languages, languages that foreigners in the vicinity could clearly understand: 'Amazed and perplexed, they asked one another, "What does this mean?"' (Acts 2:12). Responding to the alleged confusion, the apostle Peter addressed the crowd and explained that this event represents the fulfilment of prophecy: 'In the last days, God says, I will pour out my Spirit on all people . . . Even on my servants, both men and women, I will pour out my Spirit in those days, and they will prophesy' (Acts 2:17–18). He further outlined that this dispensation of the Spirit was a direct consequence of the risen exalted Christ's promised endowment: 'God has raised this Jesus to life . . . Exalted to the right hand of God, he has received from the Father the promised Holy Spirit and has poured out what you now see and hear' (Acts 2:32–3).

The dynamic revelation of the Spirit and Peter's resultant address subsequently solicited from the crowd a desire to 'make right' their complicity with Jesus' crucifixion by willingly submitting to God's offer of salvation. At least three thousand people were added to the group of Jesus' followers that day. This newly formed 'community' of believers devoted themselves to the apostles' teaching, common fellowship and prayer. In fact, they lived together selflessly under the compulsion of the Holy Spirit and readily shared their possessions. So strong was their bond that every day they would meet in the temple courts to worship God and daily shared meals in their own homes.

Without doubt, the supernatural endowment of the Holy Spirit was at the heart of this transformative event; an event that not only signals the formation of the Christian church, but also represents the key to understanding the Spirit's ongoing relationship with the church. As Richard Gaffin argues: 'It is fair to say that everything said in the New Testament about the Spirit's work looks forward or traces back to Pentecost; everything pivots on Pentecost (along with the death and resurrection of Christ).'[17] Indeed, James Dunn goes as far as to argue that Pentecost is a primary watershed event connected to Jesus' ministry: 'What Jordan was to Jesus, Pentecost was to the disciples. As Jesus entered the new age and covenant by being baptized in the Spirit at Jordan, so the disciples followed him in a like manner at Pentecost.'[18]

Some have also effectively argued that Pentecost represents a new Sinai. Whereas the 'old' Sinai event constituted the people of God, founded on the written code of the Mosaic law, so Pentecost represents the 'reconstitution' of God's people for a new covenant age; an age in which the Spirit and not the written code determines the manner of their existence. Indeed this may actually be what Paul was arguing for in his letters to the Romans and Corinthians: 'But now, by dying to what once bound us, we have been released from the law so that we serve in the new way of the Spirit, and not in the old way of the written code' (Rom. 7:6), and 'You show that you are a letter from Christ, the result of our ministry, written not with ink but with the Spirit of the living God, not on tablets of stone but on tablets of human hearts' (2 Cor. 3:3). Furthermore, further extending his ideas from Paul's insights, Dunn describes it this way: 'In any New

Covenant theology, therefore, the Spirit is to be seen as the agent of the New Covenant and its supreme blessing – one who will write the law in their hearts.'[19]

So fundamental is the Spirit's coming at Pentecost that Dunn argues that even the notion of 'Christian' cannot be properly conceived before the full dispensation of the Spirit: 'In brief, then, the church properly conceived did not come into existence until Pentecost . . . And as one cannot say "Christian" without also saying "church", since Christian is by definition a member of the church . . . Nonexistence of the church prior to Pentecost means that there were no Christians (properly speaking) prior to Pentecost.'[20] If we might conceive of Israel as a people of the law (which they were), then we must then conceive of Christians as a people of the Spirit (which they should be), even though their immediate heritage draws on Israel's law tradition. Consequently, at Pentecost a new era began, a new way of living, serving and loving, a radically different existence from all that went before it. This is why Dunn, I believe rightly, affirms, 'There is no genuine Christianity on the wrong side of Pentecost.'[21]

Therefore, the events of Pentecost establish the fundamental credentials of the New Testament people of God's *state of being*. We must view the church as a divinely initiated, Spirit-formed community, a communion where the presence of the risen Christ is evident through the Spirit's empowering presence. This necessarily creates a culture where Christ's revelation expresses itself in the Christlike behaviour of the church's Spirit-filled members, who emulate Christ through loving charity one toward another as a direct consequence of their union with Jesus through the Spirit. The physical presence of Jesus is replaced by his 'spiritual' presence – the body of Christ. Without the Spirit, the notion of the body of Christ cannot practically exist.

The presence of the Holy Spirit is not to be viewed as something separate from the presence of the risen and exulted Christ. Any genuine Christian Pneumatology must acknowledge the necessary practical overlap between the two persons of the Trinity. Indeed, this overlap is most powerfully revealed in and through the church, where, as Gaffin notes, we witness: 'the absolute coalescence, the total congruence in the church between the work of the exulted Christ and the work of the Holy Spirit'. Gaffin adds: 'The work of the spirit is not some addendum to the work of Christ . . . By and in the Spirit, Christ reveals himself as present. The Spirit is the powerfully open secret; the revealed mystery of Christ's abiding presence in the church.'[22] The apostle Paul affirms this coalescence in his Corinthians correspondence when he functionally equates Christ with the Spirit: 'Now the Lord is the Spirit, and where the Spirit of the Lord is, there is freedom' (2 Cor. 3:17). It is this coalescence that enables the apostle to effectively talk about spiritual gifts with reference to the metaphor of *the body of Christ.*

The church is a Christlike, Christ-oriented spiritual community, founded by the Spirit with an inherent capacity to 'know' the truth of Christ, which, as the apostle John suggests, occurs through the Spirit who is the truth (1 John 5:6). That is to say, the Holy Spirit, as the presence of Christ within the community, confirms what is true with reference to Christ. John states that to remain in the community of Christ is to know and remain within the matrix of truth: 'They went out from us, but they did not really belong to us. For if they had belonged to us, they would have remained with us; but their going showed that none of them belonged to us. But you have an anointing from the Holy One, and all of you know the truth' (1 John 2:19–20). In John's estimation, then, to remain in the community of Christ (the church formed by the Spirit) is to remain in the 'environment' of truth, because the Spirit, which is the truth, has anointed those who belong to the community! Without this community the truth has no substance or authority, as Judith Lieu affirms: 'For 1 John, authority lies within the life and experience of the believing community; finding the way forward is a shared experience and examination of their present Christian life is done from within and not from outside.'[23]

However, 'truth' in the context of this Spirit-initiated Christ community cannot be reduced to a corporate affirmation of doctrinal maxims. There is a necessary practical and pastoral dimension to it; as Craig Van Gelder suggests, 'The church is a relational community because God is a relational God. Because believers have been reconciled with God, they must also be reconciled with one another.'[24] For John, to simply affirm theoretical truth without manifesting charity towards a fellow believer represents a contradiction: 'And we ought to lay down our lives for one another. If anyone of you has material possessions and sees a brother or sister in need but has no pity on them, how can the love of God be in you? Dear children, let us not love with words or tongue but with actions and in truth' (1 John 3:16–18). John views truth as something dynamic and practical, something more than propositions to be affirmed by the *doctrinally savvy* assembly, rather something manifested in actions toward those in need within the community through charitable acts of love. Love that is expressed in 'words alone' sits on the other side of the equation to love, which is demonstrated in actions – which, in John's estimation, proves itself to be truth!

This 'truth' is not only affirmed by charity toward fellow believers, but also by a universal concern for those on the outside of the church. The truth of salvation offered in Jesus was to be shared outside the Jewish community, with the Gentiles at Pentecost. In fact, was not the outpouring of the Spirit the very thing that enabled the phenomenon of 'tongues' to communicate God's praise to foreigners? It represents, as Gaffin suggests: 'The spirit now present is the universal Spirit; the Spirit is present in the New Covenant community, now no longer restricted to Israel, now expanded to include both Israel and the nations, Gentiles as well as Jews.'[25]

Robert Menzies would go so far as to suggest something more exclusive in this regard: 'If my exegesis is correct, the gift of the Spirit is principally an endowment of power for mission.'[26] Of course, the wider sweep of New Testament accounts suggest a more holistic application than Menzies alludes to here. However, it cannot be denied that the Spirit's endowment at Pentecost has an important role to play in revealing truth to a universal audience, and as such necessarily orientates the church with a missional posture. Of course, this suggests that the appropriation of divine truth can never stop at the intellectual appreciation of an exclusive elite, but must be something that is freely shared to a universal and diverse audience, as Paul's words imply: 'put on the new self, which is being *renewed in knowledge* in the image of its Creator. Here there is no Greek or Jew, circumcised or uncircumcised, barbarian, Scythian, slave or free, but Christ is all, and is in all' (Col. 3:10–11, author's italics).

What then 'is' the church? The church is a community formed by God's sovereign initiative through a specific endowment of the Holy Spirit at Pentecost. It is a community in which the risen and exulted Christ is present through this Spirit. Endowed by and having imbibed the Spirit, the church is 'necessarily' a community of truth, a dynamic organism where Jesus (the way, truth and life) is practically present in, among and through his people. This ongoing anointing of the Spirit necessarily creates an environment, a culture, of truth. But not truth as an abstract maxim or theoretical principle; but truth which is morally oriented, truth consistent with the nature of God – truth that manifests itself in love. This love is not only shared within the fellowship of the saints, but is also a love that compels Christians in the power of the Spirit to communicate and share the truth of the gospel to a universal audience; those who are, without discrimination or prejudice, to be included among God's people. God-initiated, Spirit-endowed, Christ-focused, neighbour-oriented; this community represents a matrix for God's truth, an environment in which the truth is known, loved, experienced, practised and shared – and this is only possible because of the Spirit.

The Spirit-gifted Church

Because of what the church 'is', understanding truth in any valid Christian sense necessarily requires a spiritual community. If the church is a community formed under the initiative of the Holy Spirit and, as we have seen from the witness of the New Testament, the Spirit effectively represents the truth through the abiding presence of Christ within this community, there must be some *means* by which the Holy Spirit tangibly enters into the community to dispense and clarify truth to its members.

So what mode of operation or means does the Spirit use to engage this community? The New Testament describes this means as 'spiritual gifting', that is the special endowment on believers by the Holy Spirit of particular abilities or talents used for the communicating, grasping and greater understanding and practice of God's truth. This Spirit-gifting enables divine capacities to operate through individuals to assist the whole community to grasp a 'holistic' appreciation of the divine will generally, and as it also applies in the particular personal situations of individual members. In much the same way that different members of an orchestra bring their differing talents to bear on the whole through variegated musical skills under the guidance of a conductor, so the Holy Spirit through specific supernatural endowments empowers and superintends a harmonious appreciation and practice of truth through these divine endowments within the church. Thus, the members of the community under the Spirit's anointing, through the use of their different divinely ordained talents, serve the body and organically reveal to the whole what is fundamentally true with reference to God. It is worth re-emphasizing that this revealed 'truth' is not just raw truth. Rather than revelation of what is parochially known among Christians as 'head knowledge', a mere technical appreciation of truth facts (which Paul clearly indicates does not serve divine purposes: 1 Cor. 8:1), it is truth as it is practically revealed within a community in which the Spirit moves to bless all concerned with revelation that correlates with God's will, a will that reveals human existence manifested as being in relational / moral harmony with God.

As such, the Spirit reveals truth in a dynamic manner, working through the body of Christ (the church) in a Christ-oriented ethos that does appeal to the mind, but more importantly edifies the other for the common good of becoming more like Christ *toward each other*, as Paul suggests, 'Now to each one the manifestation of the Spirit is given for the common good' (1 Cor. 12:7). When the Spirit distributes gifts, it is always for the good of the whole and never the personal advancement of the one gifted. Everyone is needed, because an essential tenet of Christian truth is that everyone is to be valued and everyone is loved. Moreover, in the church under the administration of the Spirit, no individual ever has the capacity for 'all' knowledge and wisdom, as Paul's statement suggests, 'To one there is given through the Spirit the message of wisdom, to another the message of knowledge by means of the same Spirit . . . to another miraculous powers, to another prophecy, to another distinguishing between spirits' (1 Cor. 12:8–10).

Even among the gifts that pertain to knowledge, there is a recognition that the dependency for a complete understanding of divine truth can never fall to any one person, or an elite group. In fact, even if 'one' person or a group of individuals may be chosen by a council, committee or ecclesial hierarchy to exercise wisdom-based leadership within such a community, the Spirit's gifting ultimately determines who may be qualified, and it may not be those that appeal to natural human sensibilities: 'All these are the work of one and the same Spirit, and he gives them to each one, just as he determines' (1 Cor. 12:11).

That said, although the Spirit reveals the truth though a multiplicity of gifted individuals, it is nevertheless true that there are some gifts that are of a more primary nature, more foundational in the process of empowering the 'truth community' to work toward the common good of building the character of Christ and edifying one another to the glory of God. Paul specifically makes note of these 'greater' gifts, in relation to purpose of the Spirit's gifting in his Ephesians letter:

> It was he who gave some to be apostles, some to be prophets, some to be evangelists, and some to be pastors and teachers, to prepare God's people for works of service, so that the body of Christ may be built up until we all reach unity in the faith and in the knowledge of the Son of God and become mature, attaining to the whole measure of the fulness of Christ (Eph. 4:11–13).

Apostleship, prophecy and evangelism are needed to establish the church, and pastors and teachers are foundational in maintaining the truths that the first three structure the church on – all five are commonly deemed 'knowledge' gifts.

For those accustomed to the more formal association of the Holy Spirit with church, it seems only natural to assume these 'primary' gifts are related to the ministries of an *elite few* set apart by the church hierarchy to prepare *the many* for works of service. Not only so, but these elite are also assumed to be privy to divine truth in a way that those with the lesser gifts simply are not.

However, the scriptural testimony in Ephesians 4 indicates these primary gifts are nothing more than the means of conveying the foundational truths of God to the people of God for their preparation, not a determining or validating this same truth. Those granted these foundational gifts are and remain agents of the Holy Spirit – always subject to the Spirit's authority.

It is important to realize that, although these individuals may have greater insight into doctrine and ability for conveying truths, they are never the source of, or hold a monopoly on, divine truth itself. The truths revealed through the gifted ministry of the few not only need to be validated by their own moral consistency, but also as they serve to equip the saints to practise the practical works of service, these prominent gifts are further validated as moral consistency and loving service is exercised in the whole church. The truth must flow down to practice.

The knowledge gifts are given to prepare the whole church to be mature, leading everyone, in various ways, into Christlike maturity. The practising of charitable service is just as valuable for appropriating divine truth as the revelation and teaching that encourage it. The practical gifts of the Spirit embody the truth that the knowledge gifts introduce. Although the charity gifts are contingent on the knowledge gifts they are not inferior to them, as Paul suggests:

> To one there is given through the Spirit the message of wisdom, to another the message of knowledge by means of the same Spirit, to another faith by the same Spirit, to another gifts of healing by that one Spirit, to another miraculous powers . . . All these are the work of one and the same Spirit, and he gives them to each one, just as he determines (1 Cor. 12:8–11).

While Paul emphasizes ontological equality, he also speaks of a functional hierarchy: 'And in the church God has appointed first of all apostles, second prophets, third teachers, then workers of miracles, also those having gifts of healing, those able to help others' (1 Cor. 12:28). Thus, all gifts are necessary to lead believers into the truth. Some have a primary role that the secondary gifts are contingent upon but, like a human body, no part is more valuable than the other.

What ensures the harmonious working of this body with its *egalitarian hierarchy* is a Spirit-infused ethos – the ethos of divine love. Simply knowing or doing things does not determine or validate truth; rather Christian knowing and doing must be characterized by a divine love to be authentic, as Paul states, 'If I have the gift of prophecy and can fathom all mysteries and all knowledge, and if I have a faith that can move mountains, but have not love, I am nothing. If I give all I possess to the poor and surrender my body to the flames, but have not love, I gain nothing' (1 Cor. 13:2–3). Selfless love is the highest virtue and ultimate proof of Christian truth. Only a Christian person who knows the truth of God is able to selflessly love like Christ. Knowing, doing and loving are all part of the truth equation, and all must be present for Christian truth to be valid, as John indicates, 'Dear children, let us not love with words or tongue but with actions and in truth. This then is how we know that we belong to the truth, and how we set our hearts at rest in his presence' (1 John 3:18–19).

Furthermore, Paul writes, 'Love never fails. But where there are prophecies, they will cease; where there are tongues, they will be stilled; where there is knowledge, it will pass away' (1 Cor. 13:8). Paul indicates here that love is a virtue of the divine nature that will never fade away, never lose its validity, whereas the things that the Corinthians deemed as essential are in the end simply transitory. If a Christian community believes that affirming certain doctrinal truths or upholding certain religious practices is the means of upholding truth, then they have missed Paul's primary point. Love, because of its eternal nature, is ultimate and the primary quality of truth.

David Garland observes, 'As an essential reflection of God's character, love can never end and is elevated to the highest good.'[27]

Love – being the highest good and the marker of conformity with God's nature – by extension becomes the means to knowing and ultimate proof of truth. Love in the Christian sense cannot be practised in isolation; it is not something someone necessarily attains through technical study or forms as a result of religious ritual (though these may be helpful in encouraging it); it is generated by the Spirit and proven as it bears fruit in ways that genuinely meet the needs of those inside and outside the fellowship of God's people. Knowledge, action and love work in a kind of hermeneutical spiral. To know truth leads to action which, if motivated by the Spirit, leads to love, which in turn leads to a deeper knowledge of God, and so on. Love is not only the ultimate proof of truth but the means to accessing it at ever-increasingly deep levels. If the Spirit is motivating the truth quest, then the more a person knows, the more they will do, and do motivated by love. The more they love the more they understand God and, by extension, the more they know the truth. Ultimately, without love divine truth will always be 'unknowable'.

In summary then, understanding truth in a 'truly' Christian sense cannot be reduced to a technical comprehension of doctrinal maxims, mere rational propositions divorced from a practical / moral life in conformity with God. Christian truth and its full appreciation is always practical, always moral, always relational, always charitable, always holy, always oriented toward a right engagement with God and neighbour, and always characterized by grounded love. Because of who God is (a morally pure relational being), truth to be consistent must manifest the character of God as it expresses itself in love toward the people God loves and holiness that conforms with the God who loves them. Truth must be embodied in the character of God's people and this embodiment finds its best expression within the community the Spirit created – the church. The church is a community the Spirit empowers, gifts and guides into true knowledge, true practice and true love. The Holy Spirit works personally but never individualistically; it seeks to work for the good of the whole so that the individual can appreciate divine truth in the fullest possible sense. The Spirit-endowed gifts ensure that everyone is included, everyone is needed and everyone can know truth fully.

The Spirit-ordered Church

As we move toward addressing more directly the questions posed at the beginning of the chapter, it is helpful to review what we have discussed so far. First, we observed that the church is a creation of the Spirit, brought into being by divine initiative and not the will of any human governing body. Second, not only does the Spirit create the church but it also provides the *means* of leading this community into the truth, through the endowment of spiritual gifts to members of the church body – the whole body. In this supernatural endowment, the Spirit differentiates between primary and secondary gifts: those that equip for service and those that do the practical serving. Of course, this indicates a kind of functional hierarchy, which appears to operate alongside an ontological parity, in which all the gifts, either primary or secondary, are of equal value in the 'body of Christ'. Not only so, but the Spirit, as the dynamic agent of God, endows every believer with an ethos of love; which, when manifested, becomes the ultimate proof that the church is walking the truth.

Thus, the Spirit endows gifts on the church for Christlike maturity and the glory of God, and the Spirit introduces the truth to the community through the knowledge gifts, validating it through practical gifts, and further verifying it through demonstrated love. How we might grasp the relationship of all these things is the subject of our present discussion.

Hendrikus Berkhof rightly affirmed: 'The church as a creation of the Spirit is both an institution and a community.'[28] But how does the Spirit simultaneously work through the institution (the hierarchical structure) and the organism (the body of Christ)? The latter is easier to come to terms with than the former, but both need to be properly addressed; for the structured organization is equally determined by the work of the Spirit as impromptu acts of service generated from the Spirit's leading. In fact, the apostle Paul suggests as much when reproving the Corinthian believers: 'Therefore, my brothers and sisters, be eager to prophesy, and do not forbid speaking in tongues. But everything should be done in a fitting and orderly way' (1 Cor. 14:39–40). Order and structure are just as much the work of the Spirit as prophecy.

It is interesting when Paul outlines the fruit of the Spirit (the indicators of the Spirit's guiding presence) to the Galatians, that the first virtue on his list is love and the last is self-control (Gal. 5:22–3). The Spirit animates the community of faith with the ethos of love, and does so through the medium of gifts. However, if it is truly the Spirit's work it will always be characterized by self-control, being done in a fitting, orderly and restrained manner – a way that leads to peace (also the fruit of the Spirit). Even the most fluid of organisms needs structure and order. The question is, how does the Spirit bring these?

Some have suggested that structure in the church is merely of an artificial nature, an often lifeless though necessary structure upon which the organism depends. In this view church administration, programmes, liturgies, etc. are viewed as human structures that are necessary to enable the functioning of the church's more 'spiritual' ministries – discipleship, etc. Colin Marshall and Tony Payne, in the book *The Trellis and the Vine*, draw out this dichotomy between technical administration and spiritual ministry. Using the trellis and vine as a metaphor for the relation between institution and organism, the sense is given that the institution is an artificial structure that is necessary for 'real' ministry to grow on: 'Vine work is personal and requires much prayer. It requires us to depend on God.'[29] It seems institutional work does not! In these authors' view the Spirit is actively at work in the vine (organism) but not necessarily in the trellis (organization). On the surface, this appears to be an attempt at navigating around a flawed ecclesiology, by creating a false dichotomy so that the practical exigencies of an antiquated religious system can be accommodated with church revitalization. However, Paul sees no such dichotomy. He sets 'all' the gifts on the same 'spiritual' plane: teaching, healing, helping and, yes, even administration (1 Cor. 12:28)! For the apostle, even the administrative component of the church is dynamic and living, something that not only augments the Spirit's ministry but is also an equally vital part of it.

Furthermore, the New Testament's use of the temple metaphor suggests no such divide between organism and organization: 'Don't you know that you yourselves are God's temple and that God's Spirit lives in you? (1 Cor. 3:16–17) and 'you also, like living stones, are being built into a spiritual house to be a holy priesthood, offering spiritual sacrifices acceptable to God through Jesus Christ' (1 Pet. 2:5). Nothing is more structured in religious life than a temple, especially in Jewish religious life, where the temple provided the means for communicating the fitting manner of approaching and relating to God. The Spirit even endowed gifts on the original builders: 'So Bezalel, Oholiab and every skilled person to whom the LORD has given skill and ability to know how to carry out all the work of constructing the sanctuary are to do the work just as the LORD has commanded' (Exod. 36:1). Following Pentecost, the Spirit is involved in building and maintaining God's 'new' temple, the church: 'In him the whole building is joined together and rises to become a holy temple in the Lord. And in him you too are being built together to become a dwelling in which God lives by his Spirit' (Eph. 2:21–2). The temple represents structure and order, and the Spirit is clearly involved in this structure and order.

However, the New Testament's most effective metaphor in communicating the Spirit's role in revealing the complementary relationship of organism and organization vis-à-vis the church is *the body*. We have already considered this in our discussion on spiritual gifts, how Paul compared the church to a human body in which every member plays a part in accomplishing God's goal through the Spirit's gifting. Most people think of the human body as an organism free from the rigours of any rigid structure – a 'soft' organic thing. But this is far from true. The 'hard' skeletal system provides structure to the body, an ordered framework of bones that enables the softer organs to be truly effective. Indeed bones, which are often considered lifeless and hard, are organs. Although they appear inflexible, solid, static things, bones are nevertheless living, growing, flexible organs that give structure to flesh, even aiding in the production of blood that gives life to every organ. It seems the body then is a perfect model for revealing how the Spirit can dynamically animate both structured institution and fluid organism. With this metaphor we can see that the lifeblood of the Spirit can flow through the entire *body of Christ*; whether the organ it nourishes is 'hard' or 'soft' it matters not, the Spirit enables all to function and accomplish its God-given purpose – together.

It seems the problem relates to attempting to meld human institutions with divine ones, and then ignoring or placing a human interpretation on the Spirit's work, instead of actually letting the Spirit work! However, as we have seen, Paul's metaphor of the body is able to accommodate these potential dichotomies in a way that enables them to complement each other without compromising the Spirit's organic working or organizational leading and the egalitarian nature of true religious life in the Spirit-created community. The Spirit orders and gifts the church in everything from administrative structure to ministries of miraculous healing, ensuring that all work together to fulfil God's purposes and reveal his truth, not only to the members, but also to an onlooking world that so desperately needs to see truth in a tangible way through acts of love and service to 'the other'.

Summary

Coming to terms with truth, certainly divine truth, requires far more than individual reflection. The Holy Spirit leads people into the truth with the assistance of the medium of the church – the communion of Christ's people. Of course, the church is far more than a human organization or religious establishment, but a unique phenomenon created by the Spirit to fulfil God's divine purposes in revealing divine truth for the edification of his people. The church is uniquely the creation of the Spirit, and the truth that the Spirit reveals is communicated into and within the fellowship by means of the Spirit's methods, principally the 'gifting' of *every believer.* There are primary gifts that equip the *body of Christ* for service, and secondary gifts that actually perform this service within the *body*; no matter which, each has a valuable role to play in revealing, confirming and validating truth.

Not only so, but the Spirit engenders an ethos of love within this community, ensuring this *egalitarian hierarchy* is harmoniously maintained. In doing so, the Holy Spirit ensures those with the more prominent knowledge gifts don't ignore the contribution of those with the apparently 'lesser' service gifts, and that those with the less prominent gifts don't despise the wisdom offered by the former; all work together for the common good – the edification of the community toward Christ-likeness.

The Spirit created the church as a unique organization, not the kind that has a top-heavy hierarchy. The Spirit created organic ministry within the church, but not the kind that appears as a loose amalgam of charismatic individuals. Through Paul's simple metaphor of the 'body', we are able to appreciate how structure and service work hand-in-hand as a living organism. We can see how the former (organization) supports the latter (organism), even as the latter nourishes the former. Such a dynamic is only possible through the Holy Spirit's living presence, which enables the truth to be recognized, believed, practised and loved among God's unique community of people. As such, without the Spirit working in and through the church, the grasping of divine truth, in its fullest sense, would simply be impossible.

5

The Spirit, Truth and Personal Experience

Experience is fundamental to human understanding. Yet, whenever experience is suggested as a valid source of truth for Christian understanding, one of two reactions typically arise. Either, the experience is logically *rationalized* to the degree that any derivative truth is subjugated to pre-existing reason, or it is emotively *spiritualized* to a degree that existential feelings are made to equate with truth content. In either case, the substance of experience is modified to suit the 'I' (the human self). As such, any experience necessarily becomes something 'I' contrive, with embedded truth something 'I' manufacture. However, authentic experience is of great value to knowing and if properly understood is robust enough to withstand the distortions that 'I'-oriented reason and emotion present to it. In fact, when derived from the Holy Spirit's powerful influence, a form of interpretation and understanding of experience emerges that overrides the inquirer's inherent biases. It does so by convincingly challenging the hard-wired prejudices that naturally resist divine truth, penetrating the self-oriented human nature to reveal the truth in spite of the 'I'. The Holy Spirit reveals truth that genuinely originates outside *the self*, even as it is encountered within it and by it. Holy Spirit-generated experience is a source of truth that boldly confronts and forcefully liberates the 'I', providing a valid form of experience that is life-transforming.

Human-oriented Spiritual Experience

Experience is common to all humans; but it is the spiritual form of experience that occupies our focus here. It may *seem* normal for those saturated by Western rationalism to assume that spiritual experience is something purely introspective or intuitive, perhaps even free from the influences of formal ideas, but this is not entirely correct. We must appreciate that the human truth-seeker is a holistic being, and Christian experiences cannot be unrelated or disconnected from thoughts – whether formal or informal. Consciously or unconsciously, we all draw from a bank of ideas that form the way we frame our thinking about the things experienced, in fact many of these ideas influence how our *experience is experienced*. Occasionally experiences that we have no formal frame of reference to interpret do take us by surprise, but more often than not our 'learned' logic plays a subconscious role in convincing us that most experiences must be self-generated, bound to what the 'I' wants them to be, with little room left for truth revelation through genuine surprise experience.

Of course, this notion of a human-generated view of experience usually begins when the focus of experience falls on the *interior life* of the experiencing person, either rational or sensual. Notwithstanding the apostle Paul's reflections on the moral 'self', for example in Romans 7, it is generally accepted that the forefather of 'inner' religious understanding is the early church father, St Augustine. Augustine pioneered what we now understand as reflection on the inner life, with his seminal text, *The Confessions*. In this work Augustine outlines in detail the inner struggles that led to his coming to faith in Christ and subsequent experiences that flowed from it. *The Confessions* represented an entirely new genre with respect to reflecting on one's relationship with God, as John Peter Kenny suggests: '*The Confessions* is an account of contemplations in which the soul discovers transcendence of the lower world and comes to know directly the existence of God.'[1] Indeed, Augustine's notion of experience instigated a significant 'inward' turn in religious contemplation, unwittingly laying the foundation for everything from medieval mysticism to modern psychology. Jason Byassee makes this bold claim: 'If the confessions feel familiar to us, it is because Augustine has so deeply affected the ways we think about the world – and more importantly, about God.'[2]

Augustine's introspective reflections in *The Confessions* are best understood against the backdrop of his musings over his own moral shortfalls. His reflective process is particularly evident as he discusses the nature of the sinful 'self'. Augustine is not content to merely admit he was a sinner who needed forgiveness, but reveals an acute awareness of the very anatomy of sin itself; exposing the deep causes of his guilt-inducing power. Through marrow-dividing reflection on his personal moral struggles, Augustine discovers that what makes sin pleasurable in the very first instance, and consequently sinful, is the inherent pleasure it gives to the rebellious soul.

He argues that 'actual' disobedience itself is a greater motivator for sin than the short-term material gain or sensual pleasure that the sinful act appears to yield. This is powerfully illustrated by his autobiographical reflections on a particular petty theft of fruit. He writes:

> Those pears were truly pleasant to the sight, but it was not for them that my miserable soul lusted . . . I stole those simply that I might steal, for having stolen I threw them away. My sole gratification in them was my own sin, which I was pleased to enjoy . . . the only good flavour in it was my sin in eating it.[3]

For Augustine the essence of sin's pleasure lay not in the lust for the material object itself, but in the desire to break the rules and act autonomously in the face of truth. In short, it is the delight in moral rebellion and the attending feeling of partaking in the forbidden that animates all sinful 'acts'.

But Augustine's most penetrating reflections on the inner human self come from his reflections on his own conversion experience. In examining the depravity resident within the soul, Augustine describes his nature as that of a captured wild beast: 'Thus I was sick and tormented, reproaching myself more bitterly than ever, rolling and writhing in my chain till it should be utterly broken.'[4] Holding nothing in reserve he adds, 'Now when deep reflection had drawn up out of the secret depths of my soul or my misery, and had heaped it up before the side of my heart, there arose a mighty storm, accompanied by mighty rain of tears.'[5] Having dredged up the blackness of his moral self from deep within, he now encounters God's revelation breaking in, issuing forth a light of hope and creating a new existential reality:

> I was saying these things and weeping in the most bitter contrition of my heart, when suddenly I heard the voice of the boy or a girl – I know not which – coming from the neighbouring house, chanting over and over again, "pick it up, read it; pick it up, read it." Immediately I ceased my weeping and began most earnestly to think whether it was usual for children in some kind of game to sing such a song, but I could not remember ever having heard the like. So, damning the tide of my tears, I got to my feet, for I could not but think that it was a divine command to open the Bible and read the first passage I should light upon . . . I wanted to read no further, nor do I need to. For instantly, as a sentence ended, there was infused in my heart something like the light of full certainty and all the gloom of doubt vanished away.[6]

For Augustine, the inner life is more than complex mental impressions or innate ideas of philosophical contemplation (something he was not unaccustomed to prior to becoming a Christian); rather it represents the previously unexplored regions of the soul in relation to God, as John Peter Kenny argues: 'a deeper reality – beyond body, mind, and time – a self grounded in the eternal and the divine.'[7] The influence of this seminal thinker was and is profound, as Augustine's legacy of reflecting on the inner life is methodologically echoed within the writings of medieval mysticism, the Reformers such as Luther, the Puritans such as John Bunyan, and a myriad of modern authors. Before Augustine's time, this level of critical self-reflection was unimagined; following his time, it has become virtually impossible to understand the interior religious life in any other way!

While Augustine may have been influential in laying the foundation for introspective reflection, it was the contribution of rationalist philosophers, such as Rene Descartes, that provided the logic to fully separate experience (as it related to the religious / thinking 'I') from the external world. Descartes emphasized the notion of the thinking 'self' as self-contained and independent from the physical body. For Descartes, the incorporeal self (the thinking consciousness) represented the true essence of humanity, while the body was only secondary: 'First of all, I perceive that there is a big difference between the mind and the body in so far as the body, by its nature, is always divisible where the mind is evidently indivisible.'[8] The mind is unified and unchanging and able to exist beyond death, whereas the body is in a constant state of flux and degradation. Moreover, he not only advocated a dualism between body and mind, he also differentiated between the *experiencing subject* and the *perceived object*.

For the first time, the experiencing subject (the thinking 'I') was clearly and distinctly differentiated from the objects of perception in the outside world. Consequently, with the inner self presented as the true self and experience primarily related with reference to this subject, the notion of *experience* as 'subjectively' defined begins to emerge. If Augustine pioneered the association of experience with the *internal*, and Descartes categorized it as a *subjective* phenomenon, then Immanuel Kant would ensure that the notion of experience in the Western consciousness would fully become *a construct* of the inner human self.

Kant introduced his transcendental aesthetic: the pure intuition of time and space. For Kant, intuitions without concepts to give them form were simply blind; the mind cannot think unless it has sense data to work with. Consequently, the perceptions from the senses are presented to the mind (intuitively conditioned by time and space), and rationally organized into concepts. To get from perceptual sensations to abstract ideas, the mind must rely on structural principles to think about things. In this regard, Kant introduced Newton's categories. These categories of understanding synthesize the data of sensation, and make all thought (concepts) possible. Consequently, the active human mind then organizes sense data according to innate rules, which make the *order of experience* necessary and irreversible – fashioned by the human mind.

As such, all human experience represents a 'formed' sense of experience. Kant's *world as it is for us* is 'effectively' a reality *made by the mould of the human mind*. We humans structure the world according to our categories (which are universal and necessarily a priori). Indeed, the mind is no longer passive in the realm of experience; rather it is an active contributor in 'creating' the reality we then experience. Consequently, ideas drawn from experience are not simply remembered (Plato), or discovered (Descartes) but, according to Kant they are actually created!

For Kant then, what we experience are always things *for me*. What actually 'is' remains something that can only be known about, but never 'truly' known. Why? Because this *thing itself* remains outside the scope of 'my' experience, and has its own existence independent of me; thus what it is 'to me' will always be a construct of 'my' experience. As such, Kant created a world-view that presents all empirical data 'exclusively' through our 'subjective' experience. Kant's ubiquitous influence on Western thought-culture has subtly influenced the way most Western thinkers perceive human experience.

On the opposite site of the rationalist school, experience has been interpreted by those favouring existential feelings as a primary source of authority with reference to the emotional / spiritual 'I'. The work of the late-eighteenth- to early nineteenth-century theologian, Friedrich Schleiermacher, is of particular interest here. Schleiermacher was raised among the Moravian brethren, but his inquiring mind took him in a more 'liberal' direction, allowing his pietistic heritage to be philosophically modified. A disciple of Kant, Schleiermacher's brand of epistemology fundamentally accepts Kant's premise that understanding is related to human experience. However, Schleiermacher rejected Kant's rigid dualism in favour of a model of understanding that suggests all knowledge appears as either *concept* or *judgement*. Effectively, knowledge of an object can be seen through both modes alternatively; when the conceptual form predominates speculative theory abounds, while when the judgemental form predominates empirical science occurs. The two forms are in a distinct but constant organic relationship.

But Schleiermacher's greatest contribution to the value of human experience comes from his theology of *the ego*, and how human *feelings* provide the ground of certainty and the basis for truth. Schleiermacher saw 'the conscious self' as the individuation of universal divine reason. This is because he appropriated the philosopher Spinoza's monism, which in turn forms the basis for his own organic monism (all things are organically united).[9] On this monistic platform, the human self-consciousness represents an existential 'marriage' of universal reason with incarnated human reason – the latter being a representation of the former, not a part of the whole, as Julia Lamm suggests, 'Schleiermacher thus agrees with Spinoza that finite things are not individual substances; rather than deny the very concept of individuality, however, he redefines it in terms of relationality.'[10] In his scheme the subject / object division is removed, and it is replaced by the notion that the human ego is a representation of the greater whole of the created order, enabling unity of thought with all things, *based on feeling*. For Schleiermacher, the basic foundation of the truth grasped through experience is not Descartes's *thinking self*, but the *feeling self* – that deep inner consciousness that connects with ultimate truth from God.

Furthermore, Schleiermacher believes that every person has an innate sense or 'feeling' of divine dependence, which enables him or her to connect to a higher divine consciousness and a corresponding feeling of freedom: 'all those determinations of self-consciousness which predominantly express our receptivity, affected from some outside quarter [relate to] the feeling of dependence. On the other hand, the common element in all those determinations which predominantly express spontaneous movement and activity is the feeling of freedom.'[11] The feeling of dependence is essential to human nature, and by extension human attempts at understanding truth: 'If the feeling of absolute dependence, expressing itself as consciousness of God, is the highest grade of immediate self-consciousness, it is also an essential element of human nature.'[12]

This *feeling of absolute dependence*, which is 'really' a feeling of dependence on God, represents an ever-present, 'direct', albeit subconscious, connection with the divine, and is not dependent on any other media: 'The higher self-consciousness is in no way dependent on outwardly given objects which may affect us at one moment and not at another. As a consciousness of absolute dependence it is quite simple, and remains self identical while all other states are changing.'[13] This being the case, Schleiermacher can effectively advocate that understanding truth begins with our *felt sense* of divine dependency.

In short, our 'feelings' become the primary mode for coming to terms with what is sure or true. Even if we might progress to rational reflection on external data such as the Holy Scriptures, the feelings always serve to confirm whatever we may think!

However, as much as Schleiermacher might suggest that religiously based God-dependency lies at the basis of all human attempts at truth understanding, his monism disallows him from seeing God's truth as a form of divine revelation that comes *over and against human sinfulness*, corrupted as it is. Moreover, he fails to fully appreciate the Spirit's challenging and convicting power through this mode of divine revelation. Rather, because of his monist tendencies, Schleiermacher concludes that the divine Spirit is simply manifest in humanity as the highest enhancement of their own reason.[14] In fact, the Holy Spirit is viewed as being 'united' to the human nature: 'the Holy Spirit is not something that, although divine, is not united with the human nature, but only somehow influences it [the human nature] from without.'[15] This union, consistent with Schleiermacher's monism, is extended to include a wider scope, as he suggests:

> All that remains to explain is the fact that this union is realised in the form of a common spirit. Now everything (even in human nature viewed apart from redemption) that has spiritual power is absolutely the same in all individuals of a race and is incapable of any individualising modification, and above all, reason, we regard as something not varied according to the individual, but is in all and in each the same.[16]

Schleiermacher believed that to discover truth, we must 'get in touch' with those deep feelings of *divine dependence* and allow them to instigate a search for truth in which the Holy Spirit will correlate and confirm those feeling-based notions through our reason.

As such, the truth ultimately may be whatever we feel it to be, even as it correlates with our human reason; reason, of which the Spirit is the highest enhancement and expression. Of course, it may be fair to argue that all humans do have a sense of divine dependency, but to make that the foundation of a way of conceiving truth opens the way to all kinds of errors that emanate from human nature's inherent fallibility. In conceptualizing experience in this way, people can never ascertain whether the truth they come to know is based on something their feeling-animated imagination has created, or is actually God's inner revelation through a genuine work of the Holy Spirit.

In summary then, when we take Augustinian introspective experiential religion, filter it through the logic of Descartes and Kant, psychologize it through a myriad of 'modern' influences, and then disseminate it into the popular consciousness with all its inherent 'peer pressure', it is not difficult to see how the prevailing view of *experience* largely remains defined in terms of the 'I' (something I create). This is the case where *rational bias* takes over.

On the other hand, if we infuse the *popular religious consciousness* (also unavoidably influenced by these rationalist ideologies) with Schleiermacher's feeling-based methodology, either as separate from rationalism, or in concert with it, it is difficult to avoid the conclusion that all religious experience and the truth it allegedly yields must originate with and from within the human self. Therefore, if experience is considered in such a manner, then the conclusion will invariably be that *experience* 'must' be something manufactured by the experiencing subject – something 'I' create!

Practically, this leads to two outcomes in the contemporary religious mindset: either a rationalistic scepticism, in which the rational 'I' disparages the value of sense experience as a basis for authority; or a feeling-based emotivism that uncritically embraces any experience as a potential direct revelation from God, and the sole basis of truth for 'me', irrespective of what is true beyond 'my' existential senses.

But what if experience was not something humans create, manufacture or contrive with their own natural biases? What if it was something substantial that actually engaged them from the outside? If this is so, is there a more adequate way of embracing the value of such experience, that augments our understanding of truth?

Divine Initiative and the Conditions for Experience

The positions of rationalism and spiritualism adumbrated within the previous section fail to adequately represent the nature of true experience, especially the divine experience that most sincere Christians encounter. Nor do they do justice to a plain, precritical reading of Holy Scripture – the testimony by which all Christian experience should be tested. These human-oriented interpretations of experience invariably derive from uncritically allowing the non-regenerate or carnally conditioned *rational or sensual 'I'* to take precedence within the truth quest. That is to say, if we approach the task of truth-seeking as something the natural 'I' must think or 'I' must feel, then human nature will always become the primary reference point – truth will always be truth with reference to 'me' and for 'me'.

Indeed, Helmet Theilicke correctly identified this flaw: 'The conditions in the "I" for the possibility of faith and religious understanding always develop surreptitiously . . . into normative factors exercising dictatorial control.'[17] He further suggests these positions will necessarily require anything that cannot be integrated into 'my' concerns being treated with suspicion. Thus, when it comes to truth claims, the 'I' – being the dominant controlling force – will always hijack the quest if it is not identified for what it is: an anthropocentric means of determining truth, where what 'I' think or 'I' feel becomes the final arbiter, irrespective of external factors.

Of course a consciousness of the human 'I' always exists in any knowledge endeavour, but should it be allowed to 'take over' the truth endeavour? I believe not. Rather, Christians must redirect their conscious attention toward another primary reference point outside themselves; not the human 'I', but the divine 'I am'.

When the apostle Paul said, 'It's no longer I who live' he was suggesting that the human 'I' was no longer the dominant force in controlling his thinking, motives and actions. God's sovereignty had powerfully broken into Paul's life through his encounter with the risen Christ, and now through the indwelling presence of God's Spirit, resident by virtue of divinely endowed saving faith, the Spirit governed his perspective on all things. Indeed, when such a believer is fully yielded to God, the Holy Spirit does not simply modify the human self – it subjugates it! Theilicke puts it this way: 'The spiritual Word, as we have shown, is not just an imparting and instructing Word which builds on our [natural] epistemological presuppositions, which is limited by them, which makes contact with them, and which fits into their framework. Instead it is an active and creative Word. It ploughs up the old and fashions the new creature.'[18]

Consequently, the Spirit does not merely alter the 'flesh', but: 'Through coming from the outside, the Spirit takes us up into himself.'[19] As such the 'I' that once controlled the truth-seeking endeavour, the 'I' that sought to make all knowledge *sensual or rational* conforming to its own 'fleshly' agenda, is now the 'I' transformed and taken over by the indwelling Christ through the Spirit. This Holy Spirit-subjugated 'I' has access to the mind of God; the mind that has the capacity to know and experience all things as God would have humans see them: '"For who has known the mind of the Lord so as to instruct him?" But we have the mind of Christ' (1 Cor. 2:16).

In such a state of being, *spiritual experience* is not to be construed as something the 'I' creates, but is recognized as something that God enables, even specifically creates; something that does not correlate with our natural self – it may even be offensive to it in the initial stages.

Allow me to illustrate. Imagine receiving the news of the unexpected loss of a loved one, or that you had been diagnosed with terminal cancer, or indeed that you had been falsely accused of a crime. No one thrown into such circumstances willingly manufactures that experience for himself or herself. If there is any manufacturing involved, it is generally toward the denial of the painful experience. Even a vain attempt at denial does not and cannot negate the power of the experience thrust upon the person. In this case, as in nearly every case, the validity of the experience 'itself' is not the problem. The problem is the validity of the human interpretation of it.

To arrive at a valid interpretation of any given experience, the Christian interpreter must be prepared to resist the comfort that either their rational or sensual selves might offer (which have a proclivity to fashion the experience to conform to natural prejudices), and extend their trust to the God who really does know the interpretation of the experience: 'Trust in the LORD with all your heart and lean not on your own understanding' (Prov. 3:5). As disarming as this might seem, the experiencing human is not the centre of all interpretative reality, and does not have the capacity to simply create all experiences and arbitrarily fashion truth from them.

There is a greater divine force at work, shaping events and the inevitable human experiences associated with them – events and experiences which can and do originate outside the *human self*. These experiences *from the outside* are not only unmanufactured by the self, but are commonly shared by many and consequently can be defined independently from what particular individuals may think or feel about them. Individual experience may be emotively felt and rationally perceived by *the self*, but the divinely initiated experience 'itself' does not originate from this inner source.

Interpretation may be created, but not the experience itself; as ultimately there is a Creator of experience that stands over and above the human 'I'. This Creator acts either directly with primary sources in some miraculous way or indirectly through secondary causes in an ordinary way, to reveal truth within the realm in which human experience plays out. This Creator of experience is God (Father, Son and Holy Spirit) whose acts are independent of and unconditioned by the human 'I'. Through the experiences that humans sense and perceive, God reveals truth that becomes only clearer as those people abandon a reliance on their natural reason and feeling, and entrust themselves to God in faith. Indeed, this way of faith is a radical departure from the 'natural' way humans perceive truth. Of course, to embrace truth revealed through experience by faith, there must be an acknowledgement that God has created the material conditions from which all human experience is derived, and by extension the capacity and necessity to learn through it.

If we accept the account of Holy Scripture, then we must believe that without God's creative hand the capability for any human experience would be non-existent. God created the heavens and earth (Gen. 1:1), which were initially formless and void; a reality which only God could experience. Then came a sequence of purposeful creative acts: the formation of light, land, water, vegetation of all types, the planets to govern the seasons, the animals that inhabit the earth, and lastly humankind created in God's own image. God established an order that conscious existence inhabits. Moreover, he created a highly complex environment in which human experience flourishes, being eagerly embraced by a humanity shaped with the rational, sensual and emotional capacities to extract sense data from this environment. *In short, God created the conditions for experience and the human being with the capability to experience all things within this conditioned environment.*

As such, humans are primed to learn from experience. In fact, humans invariably find themselves *experiencing* before cognizing any rational thought, or indeed speaking any language to categorize what is reasoned. The very physiological make-up of the human creature shows us that we have been specifically designed to learn from experience. God creating the human being with the multiple senses of sight, hearing, taste, touch and smell, all of which are employed to extract sense data, in concert with a rational mind, hard-wired with certain cognitive and moral capacities. But before that mind is employed in an orderly manner for the task of understanding, it is used to process the data we gain from our senses in a raw, intuitive way.

God has created us to experience so that we may learn. We are made to experience, made to learn, and made to see God and his truth in and through experiences. Therefore, against Descartes's notion 'I think, therefore I am', understanding in the most fundamental sense is more accurately represented in this way: *I am, therefore I think*. Existence and the experiences offered as a consequence precede *conscious* rational reflection.

Along similar lines, Martin Heidegger argues that one's being-in-the-world (*Dasein*) precedes rational reflection, and the act of experiencing represents our first level of understanding. He writes, 'In interpreting, we do not, so to speak, throw a "signification" over some naked thing which is present-at-hand, we do not stick a value on it; but when something within-the-world is encountered as such, the thing in question already had an involvement which is disclosed in our understanding of the world, and this involvement is one which gets laid out by the interpretation.'[20] In his oft-cited example of the worker hammering, Heidegger infers that the worker using the hammer does not understand the complexity of the physics that make the hammer useful; he or she only understands its purpose through practical use. Therefore, before any conscious understanding of the hammer's value is known, it is known through the experience of using it.

Implicit understanding through tangible experience necessarily precedes rational interpretation. Humans created in God's image, created to learn from experience, are placed in the world conditioned for understanding by God's creative hand. In effect, the conditions for understanding are plainly laid out in this reality in which we are *thrown into* from birth, hard-wired to learn from the experiences encountered, coming to understand this created order through our first and most basic experiences of it. This world is created by God, and created specifically to be an environment in which humanity can analogically learn about God through the phenomena he created. It is laid out like a giant work of art, an intricate tapestry communicating fundamental truths to those who chose to seek them, as the psalmist reflects, 'The heavens declare the glory of God; the skies proclaim the work of his hands. Day after day they pour forth speech; night after night they display knowledge. There is no speech or language where their voice is not heard. Their voice goes out into all the earth, their words to the ends of the world' (Ps. 19:1–4).

Therefore, when we experience things through our created existence we are reacting and responding to God's revelatory initiative. Regrettably, the unconverted sinful nature is blind with delusional self-interest, and readily bends its thoughts away from any notion of the divine provenance behind divinely revealed experience. The apostle Paul insightfully points out this fact in his Romans letter: 'For although they knew God, they neither glorified him as God nor gave thanks to him, but their thinking became futile and their foolish hearts were darkened. Although they claimed to be wise, they became fools' (Rom. 1:21–2). Further to this he writes, 'They exchanged the truth of God for a lie, and worshipped and served created things rather than the Creator' (Rom. 1:25).

The human nature, corrupted as it is, can never see the world aright, no matter how hard it tries. It can never see with the relative purity it once had prior to 'the fall', and never see the truth as God intended it to be seen; in this regard all its experience is corrupted. But does this mean that humanity is irreparably blinded to the truth through experience, lost to wander in its fallenness, perpetually numb to the revelation of God though the dynamic medium of experience? By no means. God has not left humanity without the means to engage him through the mode of experience; in this regard the Holy Spirit plays a key role!

The Power of God's Direct Engagement through Experience

God has preconditioned the world for understanding through experience, and this preconditioning opens the way for God's revelation through human experiences encountered within this same world. If God took the initiative to create the world as a means for human experience, then it follows he also intends to 'directly' engage human senses through this medium, to powerfully reveal himself and his truth to them. Regrettably, most humans shut out God to avoid the possibility of such an encounter, with its convicting power. Yet, over and against this general rejection of God and his revealed truth, there are those who are open to God's benevolence and humbly recognizing that it is God who actually initiates the experiential engagement.

Far from searching for and editing God's revelation according to learned rationalities or emotionally comfortable sensibilities, these people acknowledge God's truth as coming to them *from the outside*. Indeed, the author of Psalm 139 expresses such a sentiment: 'O LORD, you have searched me and you know me' (Ps. 139:1). The person truly open to God recognizes that the initiative in searching for truth does not *actually* reside with the human seeker, but the divine seeker (God).

In fact, the person truly open to God has a sense of awareness that God is ever-present in the movements of their life: 'You know when I sit and when I rise; you perceive my thoughts from afar. You discern my going out and my lying down; you are familiar with all my ways' (Ps. 139:2–3). They also have an acute sense of God's interaction with them within the spiritual dimension: 'Where can I go from your Spirit? Where can I flee from your presence?' (Ps. 139:7). They acknowledge God is working to guide them through the tangible experiences of life; whether they come or go, there is a sober appreciation of God's abiding and guiding presence: 'If I rise on the wings of the dawn, if I settle on the far side of the sea, even there your hand will guide me' (Ps. 139:10). Not only so, but there is a very real expectation that God will personally engage with them to reveal his specific will, as they navigate the vagaries of life's circumstances seeking divine guidance: 'Search me, O God, and know my heart; test me and know my anxious thoughts' (Ps. 139:23).

It seems then, that the Lord, who has created the conditions for human experience, readily employs human sensibilities to personally interact with his beloved people; those who have responded to his divine initiative, to his free offer of the gospel in Christ, and who are open to the leading of his Spirit and willing to acknowledge God's guiding presence in the circumstances of their life (even if they may initially resist that presence, because it threatens the self-oriented human 'I'). For such as these, the experience of God is no fantasy, but a tangible, life-altering reality. However, to add some weight to these assertions let us now direct our attention to the saints, recorded in the pages of Holy Scripture, who have powerfully encountered God's truth through raw experience. What we shall see is that divinely initiated experience countered their deeply held dogmatic assumptions to reveal a new and fresh level of understanding and its life-changing consequences.

God's revelation of truth through experience was certainly powerful in the case of Abraham (or Abram). Abraham was God's chosen, the forefather of the Jewish people. From Abraham, not only would the Jewish nation arise, but also a messiah, who would offer the hope of deliverance to the whole world would emerge. God wanted Abraham to grasp this truth, but was such a weighty revelation possible to grasp? How could God communicate to Abraham the wondrous truths about his future plans through him? In answering such hypothetical scepticism, God uses the powerful medium of experience to accomplish his intended goal. In Genesis 15, the word of the Lord 'comes to' Abraham in a vision (v. 1). Now, in the experience of that vision, God offers Abraham consolation by revealing and affirming his purposes for him. He states that despite Abraham's age, he will have a son, through whom God's grand plan to grow a nation of descendants would come to pass. To validate this promise, God exposes him to a powerful sensual experience: 'He took him outside and said, "Look up at the heavens and count the stars – if indeed you can count them." Then he said to him, "So shall your offspring be."' On this account, 'Abram believed the LORD, and he credited it to him as righteousness' (Gen. 15:5–6). Thus, on the basis of this 'experience', Abraham genuinely believed the content of the revelation, formally confirmed by God's affirmation: 'he credited it to him as righteousness'.

Although this particular revelation impacted Abraham's consciousness, he sought a further guarantee from God that this was no fantasy or dream: 'But Abram said, "O Sovereign LORD, how can I know that I shall gain possession of it?"' (Gen. 15:8). So, in a ceremony (in which Abraham supplied the animals involved), God causes a deep sleep to come over Abraham, and in this entranced state reveals to him that his future offspring will be enslaved for four hundred years (later revealed as the slavery under the Egyptians) and that following this enslavement, they will return with great wealth to this land (Canaan) – taking possession of it in fulfilment of this promise. To verify this prophecy, a specific sign is given: 'When the sun had set and darkness had fallen, a smoking brazier with a blazing torch appeared and passed between the pieces' (Gen. 15:17). Thus, through these powerful experiences and signs, God reveals and establishes his covenant with Abraham, the covenant that the Jews would subsequently deem as foundational to their faith.

The impact of these experiences stayed with Abraham, forming his understanding of God, enabling greater steps of faith. Later on, God appeared to Abraham in order to ratify the former covenant, further establishing it with a tangible religious rite: 'You are to undergo circumcision, and it will be the sign of the covenant between me and you' (Gen. 17:11). In offering this ritual, God further validates divine truth with religious experience. Then, later still, Abraham is exposed to what many believe to be the greatest test a human would be likely to face. God required him to offer his son as a sacrifice to God, the boy being chosen heir of the promise formally made, ratified with various signs.

Against all natural reasoning, Abraham embraces the experience and proves himself true to God. This tangible step of faith becomes the catalyst for his future blessing: 'I swear by myself, declares the LORD that because you have done this and have not withheld your son, your only son, I will surely bless you' (Gen. 22:16–17). Surely it is not out of order to suggest that the impact of his previous experiential engagements with God shaped Abraham's capacity for the incredible step of faith. If not, why else would he conclude the following: 'Abraham reasoned that God could raise the dead, and figuratively speaking, he did receive Isaac back from death' (Heb. 11:19)? So it seems that divinely initiated experience played a foundational role in revealing, establishing and confirming truth to Abraham, truth that not only changed his personal life, but all posterity who follow God in the same manner of faith.

Moving forward to God's actions in the New Testament era, the Spirit's power challenges human prejudice, revealing divine truth to an avowed hater of God's 'new ways': Saul of Tarsus (later Paul). Paul afterwards describes his state prior to conversion as: 'circumcised on the eighth day, of the people of Israel, of the tribe of Benjamin, a Hebrew of Hebrews; in regard to the law, a Pharisee; as for zeal, persecuting the church; as for legalistic righteousness, faultless' (Phil. 3:5–6). Indeed, if there was ever a person with pre-conceived prejudices against the 'novelty' of Christianity and its spiritual tenor it was Saul.

Yet, through an 'experiential encounter' with the risen Christ and subsequent anointing of the Holy Spirit, Saul's stringent views are radically transformed. The account of these events is set out in Acts 9. On his journey to Damascus, where Saul intended to persecute the Christian church, a 'light from heaven' suddenly appears and a divine voice challenges him, halting his passage. In this encounter Saul is commanded by Jesus to go into the city and wait; he is then immediately struck with blindness. While waiting in the city, Saul is granted a vision of a certain man named Ananias, who is also visited by the risen Christ and commanded to seek out Saul. In a divinely co-ordinated encounter between the two, and the resultant visitation of the Holy Spirit, Saul receives his sight back, a powerful metaphor of his transformation into a follower of Christ. Saul is radically and completely changed by a sequence of powerful experiences.

The power of the experiential encounter wrought a dramatic change in a way that no rational argument or 'subjective' feeling could achieve. According to the account, Saul did not actively seek out the experience, nor did he internally manufacture it; in fact he did not 'actively' participate in the experiential events until his own baptism. Saul's personal relationship with God was transformed, as was his approach to serving God.

Paul later intimates that such 'power encounters' were authenticating proof of his own apostolic ministry: 'My message and my preaching were not with wise and persuasive words, but with a demonstration of the Spirit's power, so that your faith might not rest on human wisdom, but on God's power' (1 Cor. 2:4–5). Moreover, his hermeneutics was reconditioned by this new appreciation of the Spirit: 'We have not received the spirit of the world but the Spirit who is from God, that we may understand what God has freely given us (1 Cor. 2:12). Saul (now Paul) came to see that understanding truth no longer relies on a mere rational interpretation of the law, or a dependency on human philosophy; rather it must be founded on a dynamic engagement with God through the Spirit, and the truth that the Spirit reveals must be experienced to be known!

Not only Paul, but also the apostle Peter encountered the truth through experience. Peter's vision in Acts 10 represents one of the clearest examples of how an experiential engagement with God can challenge deeply held human prejudices. This event coincides with an angelic visitation to a Roman centurion, named Cornelius, and the angel's subsequent command to send men to Joppa to fetch Peter. As Cornelius' men are on their way, Peter ascends to the rooftop to pray and wait for a meal to be prepared for him. As he waited and prayed, he fell into a trance and encountered a vision of a sheet being let down from heaven by its four corners. Within this sheet were different kinds of animals and reptiles, which many of Jewish heritage considered ceremonially unclean. During the vision, a voice from heaven issued a command: 'Get up, Peter. Kill and eat' (Acts 10:13). Instinctively, Peter resists the command, stating, 'Surely not, Lord! . . . I have never eaten anything impure or unclean' (v. 14). The voice then commanded him not to declare unclean what God considers clean. The same vision occurred three times.

While Peter was pondering the meaning of the vision, the men coming from Cornelius arrived, and the Holy Spirit said to Peter, 'Simon . . . do not hesitate to go with them, for I have sent them' (v. 20). On arriving at Cornelius' house the following day, the meaning of the heavenly revelation is made clear to Peter: 'I now realise how true it is that God does not show favouritism, but accepts those from every nation who fear him and do what is right' (Acts 10:34–5). Without question, this divinely initiated sequence of experiences transformed Peter's deeply held prejudices, opening up a new vista on divine truth for him. As in the case of Paul, Peter did not initiate the experiences, he did not seek them or manufacture them in any way and, as we can see from the account, at least initially, he vehemently resists the assertions of the verbal revelation associated with the vision. Indeed, Peter continued to entertain scepticism regarding the miraculous experiences, right up until the point where he hears Cornelius' testimony, and how his divinely initiated experiences coincided with that of Peter's (Acts 10:34).

Peter was not alone in this matter of enlightenment. Those believers of Jewish extraction who accompanied Peter to Cornelius' house, who had known of Peter's prior experiences, were also challenged. Their Jewish prejudices were transformed when the Holy Spirit manifested on those Gentiles as it had at Pentecost (Acts 10:45–6). Indeed, the account suggests that the purpose of these experiences had a wider application than Peter and his few friends. As these events were related to the larger group of Jewish Christians, who disbelieved God had a plan for the Gentiles, a change came about. At the hearing of this collective testimony, they too became convinced of the veracity of this divine revelation and its application: 'When they heard this, they had no further objections and praised God, saying, "So then, God has granted even the Gentiles repentance unto life"' (Acts 11:18).

As we can see, a significant transformation in truth understanding took place regarding the formerly deep prejudices against the Gentiles' inclusion in God's favour. This transformation was grounded on the revelation through the experience and the active role of the Holy Spirit in that experience. In these examples, and a multitude like them, the key to the veracity of experience in an attainment of truth is a genuine role of the Holy Spirit; implicit in the case of Abraham, clearly explicit in the cases of Paul and Peter. The Spirit's active role in generating, co-ordinating and interpreting divine revelation enables the truth to become clear to those whom God wants to challenge. In this regard, the words of the apostle John offer the most succinct summation: 'And it is the Spirit who testifies, because the Spirit is the truth' (1 John 5:6).

Summary

We observed there is a natural proclivity among Christians to interpret experience along either rational or sensual lines; refashioning or even creating the experience to suit whatever bias they might favour. We also learned how these views of experience became reified in the popular religious consciousness, but suggested that such self-oriented interpretations of experience fail to do justice to the reality of experience as it is encountered. We also observed how God created the conditions for human experience and that the very nature of creation and the human being within it suggest that experience must be a valid medium through which humans come to know truth. However, as most humans choose to reject God's revelation and embrace their own interpretations, it should come as no surprise that such a view of experience encounters widespread rejection.

Yet God did not leave humans in ignorance. The Lord God can and does powerfully break into the 'hardened reality' of the human 'I' to reveal his truth and, as we have seen, this is most powerfully achieved through divinely initiated experience. In the examples of Abraham, Paul and Peter, the initiative in the experience was solely God's, evidenced by the manner that the experience was initially rejected. Through the Spirit's power, the truth broke through and in the experience the recipients encountered something life-changing. Genuine truth comes from the outside but is internally impacting and emotionally powerful. But, to be embraced as a truly valid form of experience, it must be measured against another external source, a source that is less corruptible than human feelings – Holy Scripture.

6

The Spirit, Truth and Holy Scripture

How can we know the truth is not just 'our' truth? Until this point, we have been considering truth from the point of view of a person seeking truth within the material realm of divinely created revelation, one who also acknowledges the value of truth-seeking within the matrix of community, and consciously or unconsciously draws on the medium of human experience in this process. But how can this person be sure they are not simply aligning their perception of truth with their own 'natural' prejudices? How can they know they are not making up their own version of truth, verified by their own experiences? Of course, Christians legitimately argue that Holy Scripture provides the *regulating standard* in this regard. However, not all agree as to where Scripture 'itself' derives its authority to actually regulate. Some suggest its authority is proven by reason, others argue its veracity is vindicated by history, while still others seem to find reassurance in the collective wisdom of religious tradition. Yet in each case, the 'real' *final authorization* for Holy Scripture's authority is drawn from human methods, means external to Scripture *itself*, and is actually relying on human adjudication to provide the validation for Holy Scripture's authority. Is there a way of upholding the final authority of Holy Scripture, a way that is not corrupted by human means? Indeed, could Holy Scripture's source, the Holy Spirit, supernaturally enable Scripture's interpreter to affirm Scripture's truth in such a way that does not compromise its primary authority to challenge 'individual' perceptions of truth?

What is Truth?

Truth is not to be interpreted in the same way in any and every context. In order to investigate the claim that Holy Scripture might be the ultimate regulating authority in matters of truth, we must first establish the 'type' of truth Scripture seeks to validate. Christians all too readily, and often uncritically, bring to a reading of the Bible expectations about truth that are foreign to its content and commission. In placing an interpretative grid over the Bible that belongs to other domains of logical reflection, an expectation is placed on Holy Scripture that demands it validate any form of truth, even to the point of supporting things like scientific theories or mathematical facts.

While some biblical references might offer oblique support to aspects of these other intellectual domains, should the reader really expect Scripture to do the heavy lifting in validating such things? Should we expect it, for instance, to accurately validate the earth's geological age? I suggest not! It is therefore critical for the interpreter to actually grasp the *manner or type* of truth Holy Scripture reveals and upholds, lest they unwittingly discredit the Bible's authority by asking of it more than its divine author intended. As such, the seeker of divine truth must first address this fundamental question: 'What is the *nature* of the truth revealed in and validated by Holy Scripture?'

Truth, as is presented in Holy Scripture, cannot simply be defined in terms of an abstract concept, a measure of technical precision or a timeless philosophical maxim. It is important to understand that truth as Scripture reveals it is not simply 'a thing' that a person might objectify and place under a microscope to measure, observe and debate. Of course, many interpreters view Holy Scripture as merely documentary evidence that needs external methodologies to be authenticated; consequently they apply to Holy Scripture philosophical and/or scientific criteria to determine if its assertions are true.

If they then conclude these assertions are true, according to these methods, they classify the veracity of these assertions by the terms of the criteria applied within the methodology. For example, if logic determines Scripture is true, the truth of Scripture is then conditioned by that logic – and its truth is now rationally framed. This is seen in certain presentations of the doctrine of *scriptural inspiration*, which advocate that every single word of Scripture is seen as dictated divine truth, to be interpreted literally, and that anyone who does not ascribe to this narrow view is heretical. Not only does this approach undermine the 'actual' authority of Scripture by reconditioning 'how' truth might be verified, but also it invariably leads to a construction of truth foreign to the *relational content* of Scripture.

Furthermore, of even greater concern than the damaging effects of these various methods of framing truth within Scripture is the deeper issue of epistemic corruption. By this I mean that the interpreter unwittingly enables human rational capacities to be placed above the simple assertions of Scripture and God's divine revelation within it. Unwittingly interpreters stand in judgement over Holy Scripture, even as they presume to use it to validate what they consider to be true. Invariably, the truth they have arrived at by subjecting God's revelation to such methods, represents little more than the 'kind' of truth they want to affirm; a type of truth manufactured by their deep rational consciousness to bring assurance to their rationally conditioned minds; a truth consistent with their own limited and fallible logic, that has only been filtered through the medium of Holy Scripture to give it some kind of legitimacy.

Although appearing to be 'biblical' this method produces a *form of truth* that can be objectified, placed on a 'dogmatic' pedestal and tenaciously defended, and all the while remains remote from the supreme subject of Holy Scripture itself, God. This objectified form of rationally conditioned truth maintains an existence in the minds of many well-meaning Christians simply because they have *not yet* come to terms with the epistemic posture required to approach Holy Scripture, that is, the posture of simple faith.

The words of Scripture speak clearly of this posture: 'Trust in the LORD with all your heart and lean not on your own understanding' (Prov. 3:5). Rather than coming to Holy Scripture with a subconscious mindset of rational 'control', with all its attending desires to establish logical certitude independent of obedient intimacy with

God, the readers / interpreters are required to come with genuine humility and a faith-based sense of vulnerability; they must come to these sacred words with a sober abandonment of human rationalism and sensualism; trusting that God does actually speak truth and that his word 'is true' – even if it doesn't naturally make sense.

But to reach the point of engagement with God's revealed truth in Scripture, there must be an implicit understanding that such faith requires a vibrant relationship with God – not merely an engagement with an idea, a rational construct, or even a belief in a remote deity. It requires a relationship with a living person – the person of God himself!

Truth as it is revealed and upheld in Scripture is not measured in relation to some objective or remote 'thing'; it is actually measured in relation to someone. This is part of the reason Jesus Christ said to his disciples: 'I am the way and the truth and the life. No-one comes to the Father except through me' (John 14:6). In Jesus' estimation, coming into an appreciation of truth involves far more than abstract reflection on an idea about God or emotional feelings of him. For Jesus there must be a 'coming toward' in terms of relationship, a coming into a living relationship with the heavenly Father – and this by way of a personal trust relationship with Jesus himself. Therefore, to know the truth is to come into a trust relationship with Jesus, which in turn leads to an intimate relationship with God the Father, and by necessary extension this implies that one has come into an appreciation of what is truth in terms of divine intimacy, not in terms of calculating reason or felt sensuality.

Consequently, the nature or 'type' of truth, as it is revealed in Holy Scripture, is fundamentally relational and moral. That is to say, truth, as God wants us to know it, is never an observable 'thing' remote from our personal existence before the divine personhood of God. If we accept that God created us, and that we were created in his image, created for relational intimacy with him, then surely to align ourselves in intimate relation to this Creator God in the appropriate posture of worship, holiness and service is to align ourselves with the source of truth itself. Thus, we may rightly assert that truth represents a state of being, a state of being relative to God and his existence as a personal being. The more a person understands this, the closer they are to the truth – that is, God himself!

Because God is a relational being within himself (Father, Son and Holy Spirit), to enter into an appreciation of his truth necessitates an entry into a Trinitarian relational experience with him. In fact, the roles of the respective members of the Godhead, in engaging humanity in revelation, reflect this necessary relational nature:

> But when he, the Spirit of truth, comes, he will guide you into all truth. He will not speak on his own; he will speak only what he hears, and he will tell you what is yet to come. He will bring glory to me by taking from what is mine and making it known to you. All that belongs to the Father is mine. That is why I said the Spirit will take from what is mine and make it known to you (John 16:13–15).

The Father reveals truth to the Son and, in the material absence of the Son, the Spirit reveals the same truth, through the Son, to Jesus' own followers as if the Son were present with them. If this passage reveals anything, it reveals that a person cannot 'really' know truth without knowing God intimately. So it is that truth, as Holy Scripture reveals it, is intrinsically relational.

But if truth is relational and knowing it involves intimacy with the divine, then surely other aspects of the divine nature must have a bearing on the nature of truth as well? Coming to an appreciation of truth represents more than an intimate knowledge of God's personal make-up – his ontology. Given that God is also a moral being, it must follow that truth is also conditioned by his morality in a relational way. When the aforementioned considerations are taken into account, morality and truth are necessarily bound. Indeed, it is most likely that human moral failure is at the heart of all ignorance of truth, because in reality people don't lack the potential to grasp the truth because they lack intelligence, they fail to grasp it because their own selfish natures blind them from seeing God's true nature and the demands it makes upon them. In short, human pride mutes an appreciation of the divine attribute of moral purity, and consequently mutes personal moral accountability.

In the Old Testament, entering into truth meant entering into a form of practical wisdom that empowered a person to walk in moral conformity to God, and an appreciation that God's truth is the heart of the 'best life possible': 'I guide you in the way of wisdom and lead you along straight paths. When you walk, your steps will not be hampered; when you run, you will not stumble. Hold on to instruction; do not let it go; guard it well, for it is your life. Do not set foot on the path of the wicked or walk in the way of evildoers' (Prov. 4:11–14).

Knowing truth and living morally were intimately related. As such, knowing truth is related to knowing God, and knowing God is directly related to morality, then it must follow that an individual's own morality is a component part in discerning truth. After all is not 'personal sin' the thing that separates humanity from God, and the thing that muted truth in the first place? The apostle Paul's assessment is valid in this regard, 'For although they knew God, they neither glorified him as God nor gave thanks to him, but their thinking became futile and their foolish hearts were darkened' (Rom. 1:21). Yes, even Christians who acknowledge their need for forgiveness may have their capacity for understanding truth marred by unrepented personal sin. Jesus also suggests the way toward clarity is moral: 'Blessed are the pure in heart, for they will see God' (Matt. 5:8). He is implying that perception of God is dulled by moral impurity, and conversely stating that clear knowledge of him is advanced by moral purity. The challenge for the truth-seeker, then, with God's gracious empowerment, is to pursue the purity of heart that enables the clarity of God's life-giving truth to be revealed.

So, if relationality necessitates morality, then morality necessitates an authority that demands a response. Once truth-seekers realize that the nature of 'truth' in Holy Scripture is relational and moral, they must confront the fact of personal accountability to God – the source of that morality. A person cannot know truth about God and remain distant from the fact. Coming to terms with divine truth implies coming to terms with God's lordship – his personal authority over one's life.

After reflecting on every manner of human wisdom, the author of Ecclesiastes concluded, 'Now all has been heard; here is the conclusion of the matter: Fear God and keep his commandments, for this is the whole *duty* of every human being. For God will bring every deed into judgment, including every hidden thing, whether it is good or evil' (Eccl. 12:13–14, author's italics). According to this text, to know the truth necessitates that the knower shape their life with reference to that which is known, and this knowledge requires certain moral actions and a life of moral conformity to the subject known; because the person who knows these things, to whatever degree, will be called to account by God. Donald Bloesch sums it up well, 'Truth in the Bible is indissolubly related to concrete life and obedience.'[1]

The nature of biblical truth is authoritative, because it is moral and relational, which now leads us to the last significant quality of truth for discussion: the non-relativity of biblical truth. Once it is determined that truth is authoritative, and that this authority has exclusive reference to God (the ultimate Being), then it must follow that truth, as it is revealed in the Holy Scriptures, must also be absolute. As such, we may assert that in Holy Scripture there is no 'his' truth, 'her' truth, or 'my' truth; truth is 'the truth' on the basis of relativity to God alone – which makes it absolute.

Truth as it is presented in Holy Scripture may be discussed, debated and reflected upon, but is never negotiable with reference to its fundamental content. For example, you may discuss the moral complexities regarding 'on demand' abortion, but no matter what self-oriented justifications for its action may be offered up, in terms of the Holy Scriptures, its essential moral content stands – murdering another human is fundamentally wrong (Exod. 20:13). At the risk of sounding overly simplistic, in the Bible, truth is true because God, the source of truth, declares it to be so. While many attempt to water it down, relativize it or modify it to suit their own agendas because it is too confronting, that does not change what it is: relational, moral, authoritative and absolute, exclusively with reference to God.

So, when it comes to the manner of truth we are dealing with in Holy Scripture, the interpreter must not presume to be dealing with a 'some-thing' akin to a mathematical equation, a scientific formula or a philosophical principle, something that can be remotely observed and clinically discussed. This truth is not 'a thing' that can be engaged without having a personal impact on the one engaging it. The truth is inherently personal, as Bloesch affirms:

> In the deep sense truth is identified with God himself, and the stamp of truth therefore characterises both his words and his works. Truth is not so much an idea as a person, not so much a formulation as an act. This note is especially evident in the Johannine writings: 'I am the way, and the truth, and the life; no one comes to the Father, but by me' (John 14:6 [RSV]).[2]

To come to the truth, then, involves coming to God through Christ, and remaining in the truth necessitates living in conformity with Christ: 'If we claim to have fellowship with him yet walk in the darkness, we lie and do not live by the truth' (1 John 1:6). Truth in the Bible may be informative about God and life as it relates to him, but it is also necessarily transformative, as a person cannot meaningfully engage it without being personally impacted by it. It is confronting, you either submit to it or reject it. This is so, because of its inherent morality, its inherent absolute authority. As far as truth in Holy Scripture is concerned, to know *the truth* is to know God, and to know God is to order the most intimate dimensions of your personal moral life around his divine will.

What Gives Holy Scripture Its Authority?

Holy Scripture has the divine imprimatur upon it, but simply affirming this alleged fact in a quasi-fideistic way does not solidly confirm the grounds of its divine authority. Ultimately the authority of Scripture exists by virtue of its connection to God and, like faith in God, it must be embraced by faith. What is important is having faith in the right means of that affirmation, lest the authority affirmed be undermined by the method of affirmation. As discussed in the previous section, if we conclude that the nature of truth as presented in Holy Scripture is personal and moral, it must necessarily follow that it is also personally and morally authoritative. Everyone who acknowledges this (and ultimately those that don't) will find themselves accountable to the truth-giver by virtue of the power of this inherent authority. This being the case, it is necessary to work this through to appreciate it more fully, and that we might understand the implications for embracing or not embracing the correct source of Holy Scripture's authority.

In reality, not many truth-seekers believe the Bible has authority on the grounds of faith alone, even though they may claim so. Throughout the centuries multitudes of well-meaning religious thinkers have felt the need to validate the authority of Holy Scripture in a way that primarily appeals to human reason and, of course, in order to make sense to the non-believers whom they are trying to convert. Many have also sought to do justice to the practical material processes of the Holy Scriptures' formulation and transmission, in order to demonstrate the rational credibility of the process. Now there is nothing wrong with this unless, as we have mentioned, the divine authority is undermined by wrong methods of verification. That is why it is important to follow a proper process in affirming Scripture's source of authority.

How, then, may we know what gives Holy Scripture its capacity to be the final regulating authority in truth deliberations or, more precisely, what angle might be taken to arrive at this conclusion without corrupting that conclusion? To do this we will consider some of the traditional approaches.

Canonicity

The issue of affirming the primacy of the authority of Holy Scripture was foremost in the minds of the early Christian community. During and immediately following the apostolic era, a multitude of religious documents came to the fore that laid claim to the divine imprimatur – some valid, many not. Because of the potential to confuse and distort the gospel and the truths that surrounded it, the early Christians were faced with the daunting task of deciding which documents were to be included in the canon (the standard for orthodoxy) and which are apocryphal (false representations of truth). In this regard, Bruce Metzger suggests the early fathers applied three standards to canonicity: 'three criterion (orthodoxy, apostolicity, and consensus among the churches) . . . came to be generally adopted during the course of the second century, never modified thereafter.'[3] Given the significance of these criteria, some attention should be given to considering their validity with reference to Scripture's authority.

First, let us briefly discuss orthodoxy. Orthodoxy suggests that there is a commonly held 'right' standard by which the veracity of any doctrine, idea or writing might be measured. In the early church they called it the 'rule of faith', which incidentally was inferred in the New Testament: 'Dear friends, although I was very eager to write to you about the salvation we share, I felt I had to write and urge you to contend for the faith that was once for all entrusted to the saints' (Jude 3). Yes, even as the New Testament is being written, a tradition developed among Christians that served to affirm a common orthodoxy among the wider church that affirmed *the faith*. Metzger also indicates that a number of terms were used for this standard: 'Besides "the rule of faith" other terms with more or less the same meaning do occur. "The Canon of Truth" and "the rule of truth" were used apparently by Dionysius of Corinth.'[4] So, this commonly held orthodoxy assisted the early fathers to proceed in the task of affirming canonical writings with a degree of confidence.

Second, for an alleged holy writing to have validity for inclusion in the canon, it needed to have distinct apostolic derivation. That is, the document needed to be authored by an apostle or, at least, by a close member of the apostolic party (e.g. Luke). If a document compared in style, content and doctrinal consistency to a known and accepted epistle, such as authored by Paul, then the chances of inclusion in the canon were high. If the document's style and content were unknown, or if the doctrine seemed askew to the previous mentioned 'rule of faith', then its chances of being attributed as apostolic were low (e.g. the Gospel of Thomas). The early Marcionite Canon (AD 130–40) included predominately Pauline letters while the later Muratorian Canon (AD *c.*170) recognized an acceptance of a greater number of known New Testament writings. From this we can gather that the process of acceptance of canonical works was happening relatively quickly following the apostolic era, and that the first-hand 'sense' of what was apostolic was still alive in a community only one or two generations removed from the actual authors, thus determining apostolicity may not have been as difficult as we might think.

Third, the notion of consensus among the churches served as a means of validating canonical writings. This is the notion, simply put, that if enough people believe or practise the same things for long enough, it must be right. With respect to canonicity, Metzger puts it like this, 'This was, of course, based on the principle that a book that had enjoyed acceptance by many churches over a long period of time, was in a stronger position than one accepted by few churches, and then only recently.'[5] On one level this method falls over, in as much as a heretical work could be upheld by a number of churches for a long period of time, which is what the Protestants would argue about some books that Roman Catholicism endorses. Yet, on the other hand, if the works are endorsed by a wide enough spread of churches / individual Christians of differing traditions or unconnected in any institutional sense, and this happened consistently for long enough, then the principle of consensus carries more weight.

Interestingly, the early church fathers didn't overtly discuss the criteria of *divine inspiration* in their deliberations over canonicity; rather they assumed the other criteria simply validated it. Bruce Metzger suggests that the notion of *inspiration* was only a background consideration that was assumed, 'In short, the scriptures, according to the early fathers, are indeed inspired, but that is not the reason they are authoritative. They are authoritative, and hence canonical, because they are the extant literary deposit of the direct and indirect apostolic witness on which the later witness of the church depends.'[6]

However, employing the means of orthodoxy, apostolicity and consensus to confirm what is canonical is useful by way of confirming the authority of Scripture, but not useful in establishing it in the first place. As such, it is necessary to ask, 'How do we know what is orthodox and apostolic, and why did the churches continue to affirm certain books and not others?' The following criteria have been applied in this regard.

Historicity

There is an argument to make, that the fathers were on the right track by not relying on inspiration 'alone' as being adequate to establish canonicity. In fact, C.H. Dodd also implies that inspiration is too readily assumed as the only valid means: 'The authority of the Bible is in fact often treated as a simple correlate of its inspiration.'[7] In addition, Dodd argues that the historicity of Scripture also adds weight to its authority. For him, the Holy Scriptures represent a solid historical record: 'The Bible is indeed not only a history of the revelation of truth, but it is the record of a history which itself, in Christian belief, was a divine revelation.'[8] What he is, in effect, saying is that all history is divinely created and purposeful, and that God's redemptive acts are played out in history, and are recorded in Scripture to validate this history. If history is valid, so are the historical Scriptures. Now, it is helpful to understand that C.H. Dodd was more than likely countering ideologies which were suggesting the Bible was heavily influenced by mythology: 'In studying the Bible, then, we are dealing with actual history, disclosing a meaning which reaches beyond history, and not with a myth whose factual content is negligible.'[9] In this view the Bible represents historical events, a grounded revelation of truth.

However, it is not simply the historical groundedness of Holy Scripture that gives it authenticity, but the process of this holy revelation's tangible development also lends weight to this authenticity. With sixty-six separate books with around forty different human authors, over a considerable period of time, and with a definite progression toward a goal (the advent of Christ) and a climax (the return of Christ), there is a case to make that God's revelation not only describes history but defines it! The revelation of God enables history to be interpreted in an ultimate sense, to make sense of events as having a greater purpose than serving human ends, as Dodd again affirms:

> For the Christian, things and events are a sacramental manifestation of God. He finds God in historical events and in the things about him, and sets out to deal with events and things that fall within his range of activity in such a way as to make them a clearer manifestation of the divine. Thus the Bible as a historical record of events possesses a truly religious value.[10]

God owns history, and the truth revealed by him through Holy Scripture enables the reader to interpret all history as a purposeful progression, toward a distinct goal.

Thematic unity

Having touched upon the idea of progression of divine revelation through history, and having made reference to a highpoint of that revelation, it most naturally follows that we should consider the thematic unity of Scripture. Given the multitude of different books and different human authors, and that written over a significant period of time, should we expect to see a thematic unity? If there is a truth within Holy Scripture that binds this extensive revelation together it is most commonly affirmed as Jesus Christ – his person and work. The Bible seems to reveal the complementary themes of creation and redemption; God creates a perfect work; humanity ruins it; God graciously intervenes to restore it and, primarily through the work of Jesus Christ, re-establishes an even better eternal created order. And at the core of these dual themes is God's grace manifest in Jesus Christ; this, as Bryan Chapell suggests, may be overt or covert:

All scriptural texts give us a way of interpreting our world and of understanding our God from a redemptive perspective. Some predict the coming of Christ; some prepare us to understand aspects of his nature and ministry; some reflect the human predicament that requires rescue; and some encourage a grateful and obedient response as a result of God's redemption.[11]

Of even sharper focus than the evangelical interpretation of the centrality of grace manifest in the historical revelation of Jesus Christ's person and works is the more concentrated notion that Jesus Christ is supremely and overtly central in the entire creation / redemption framework. Karl Barth promoted the centrality of Christ in a more comprehensive sense than former presentations. For Barth, Christ is not merely the subject matter of revelation, he is revelation; God's word is self-witness, and cannot be reduced to historical formulations or logical provable assertions. Indeed, to prove God via scientific methodologies would be to corrupt the witness with human agendas. As such, Scripture is not 'about' the text, the authors or the method of transmission; it is really about Jesus Christ – the revealed Word of God. In essence, the centrality of Christ, as revelation, simply makes redundant any technical arguments around the veracity of the text of Scripture.

Barth does not diminish the testimony of Holy Scripture; rather he orientates it in such a way as to show Christ as always central, as Brandon Smith suggests: 'His method is, in a sense, a hyper-Christological hybrid of theological and hermeneutical methods. He saw Christ as the key to seeing Scripture as a whole. He was less concerned with the text and its unique peculiarities, and more concerned with encountering and contacting the divine reality.'[12] In fact, this is most clearly seen in Barth's treatment of the Old Testament, as Roger Keller indicates: 'Although OT time was quite different from the fulfilled time of Christ, it was coordinated with it. As it was coordinated with Jesus, it became a witness of him in expectation, thereby being revelation in expectation.'[13] For Barth, the Old Testament is not merely pre-Christ revelation anticipating his messianic office; it is thematically integrated with the New Testament witness to him. The Bible, and the Old Testament in particular, is interpreted so christologically that it has no substantive meaning otherwise.

As compelling as it might seem, in the final analysis thematic unity, like the canonicity and historicity we discussed before it, does necessarily establish the authority of the truth set forth in the Bible. In reality, these are human 'means' of verification, and do little more than affirm the authority of Holy Scripture to those who already believe it. They are merely human attempts to establish its credibility before a sceptical audience. In fact, these same methods could be 'generally' applied to any collection of written works to establish their integrity and credibility. As such, canonicity, historicity and thematic unity do not 'establish' Holy Scripture as truth, or confer upon it divine authority. At best, they are only *secondary ways* of confirming what is also known or assumed to be authoritative, in the first place.

In fact, only when carefully considering these means is the inquirer forced to dig deeper and seek out the 'source' of the authority that these *means* actually seek to affirm. For example, in establishing canonicity the early church fathers applied criteria such as apostolicity to authenticate a particular writing. Yet we are compelled to ask, 'Where did the apostles get their authority?' Or, 'What enables an apostle to produce a work of divine authority whereas an ordinary Christian is unable to do so?' Invariably, the inquirer is driven back to the source of revealed truth, to a point where the *dynamic intersection* between divine authority and human writing occurs – a juncture where the Holy Spirit dwells in dynamic interaction.

What 'Really' Gives Holy Scripture Its Truth and Authority?

Truth, authority and power are intrinsic to God's word, and these qualities demand a response. The words of God are not vain utterings, meaningless assertions or empty discourse; rather, when God speaks he reveals truth that demands action, truth that powerfully engages and necessarily transforms. We see this in the account of Ezekiel 37 and the prophetic vision, where the prophet is instructed by God to communicate God's truth to people who were considered spiritually dead: 'Then he said to me, "Prophesy to these bones and say to them, 'Dry bones, hear the word of the LORD!'"' (Ezek. 37:4). In response Ezekiel states, 'So I prophesied as he commanded me, and breath entered them; they came to life and stood up on their feet – a vast army' (Ezek. 37:10). The vision illustrated to Ezekiel the power of God's prophetic word, a word that had both the power and authority to restore what was lost and bring hope to a hopeless situation – bringing the dead back to life.

However, God's word is an authoritative truth even before it is revealed to human subjects, and in the written form that engages them, it is authoritative because of its originator's authority, as Timothy Ward affirms: 'The authority of Scripture is dependant entirely on the authority of God, and comes about only because of what God has chosen to do in the way he authors scripture.'[14] Now regarding the 'way' God authors Scripture, there is a fundamental question that needs to be asked: How does this authoritative word of divine truth come to humanity in written form, and how does it do it in a way that its intrinsic divine authority and consequent transformative power is not compromised?

The starting point for apprehending the transmission of God's authoritative word into written text is recognition of the *divine initiative*. It is important to understand that Holy Scripture is not a human invention and does not originate in the human imagination, as the apostle Peter affirms, 'For prophecy never had its origin in the human will' (2 Pet. 1:21). God does not 'contract out' the task of manufacturing the authoritative content of Holy Scripture to human authors, even though they write 'in their own' words. Todd Billings acknowledges that there are human and divine elements in the transmission of Scripture, but both are not equal in authoritative value: 'in the production of Scripture, divine and human agency are both active, though divine agency takes the initiative and deserves credit as a primary author of these "God breathed" words.'[15] The power of the divine word is its capacity to challenge the sinful human will, which 'naturally' resists it, as Billings intimates, the word: 'emerges scandalously from God's revelation in the historical moments'.[16]

Inspiration

At the coalface of Holy Scripture's production is a fallible human author, who exists in a particular time and place, who is addressing particular people with particular issues. Consider this extract from Paul's letter: 'When you come, bring the cloak that I left with Carpus at Troas, and my scrolls, especially the parchments. Alexander the metalworker did me a great deal of harm. The Lord will repay him for what he has done. You too should be on your guard against him, because he strongly opposed our message' (2 Tim. 4:13–15). Paul is offering instructions that seem to have no greater extended application than his immediate needs, and also issues a warning about an individual who was causing trouble to the Christian cause in a particular ancient location. It might be easy to dismiss this 'humanness' as something incidental or even counterproductive to divine revelation. But we must remember that God is not conveying abstract philosophical principles; rather he is communicating a message of grace to real people in a grounded way. Rather than suggesting that the humanness of Scripture counters its authority, it might be argued that it upholds God's methodology – to graciously engage the lost where they are. However, we are still left with the question: What is stopping fallible humanness from corrupting the authority of divine revelation, in the process of transmission? It is at this point we enter into reflection of the Spirit's role in inspiration – the act of spiritually transmitting the word of God into written form.

First, it is important to understand that the Holy Spirit's engagement with humanity is a power encounter. God overcomes human limitations through powerful supernatural intervention: '"Not by might nor by power, but by my Spirit," says the Lord Almighty' (Zech. 4:6). The Spirit represents a divine force that is able to overcome both the overt and covert power of human 'flesh', with its inherent weaknesses and fallibilities, to accomplish God's purposes; in this case, to reveal truth in an uncorrupted manner. This power aspect of the Spirit in human engagement is most simply illustrated by the anointing of Samson, the Old Testament judge: 'The Spirit of the LORD came upon him in power so that he tore the lion apart with his bare hands as he might have torn a young goat' (Judg. 14:6). Samson, like many of the Old Testament prophets, was able to do supernatural things through the Spirit's 'power' anointing.

Likewise, Paul references the power of the Spirit as key to his communication of the gospel: 'My message and my preaching were not with wise and persuasive words, but with a demonstration of the Spirit's power, so that your faith might not rest on human wisdom, but on God's power' (1 Cor. 2:4–5). The same spiritual power is present when the Spirit engages a human author (fallible, corruptible and weak) as a medium to communicate the word of God (infallible, incorruptible and strong).

The act of 'inspiration' that enables the human authors of Holy Scripture to produce the holy writ may not be a dramatic power encounter (as with Samson), but the principle still applies. The Spirit that enabled Samson to overcome human limitations is the same Spirit that enabled Peter, Paul, John and the other apostolic authors to overcome the fallibilities of 'the human nature weak and corruptible' to produce an authoritative message of truth, human in form, but divine in authority. When encountered by the Spirit of power, the malevolent power of the flesh gives way; the divine power overcomes the fallible to reveal the infallible.

Before we briefly address the mechanics of inspiration and its role in divine revelation through the production of Holy Scripture, it is worth clearly differentiating inspiration from revelation in this process. In this regard, Donald Bloesch's explanation offers the best summary:

> Inspiration depends on revelation and serves revelation . . . Inspiration is not the ground of revelation but an element in revelation . . . Inspiration

concerns the reliability of the scriptural witness; revelation refers to the self-disclosure of Jesus Christ in the biblical witness. Inspiration signifies the election of the biblical witness; revelation, the uniting of the biblical witness with God's self witness. Inspiration is the overseeing and directing of the biblical writing; revelation is a rendering of the biblical testimony transparent to its divine content. Inspiration means that the Bible is penetrated and filled with the Holy Spirit; revelation occurs when the Bible transmits the word of God by the action of the Spirit. Inspiration has to do mainly with the form of the Bible; revelation with its content. Inspiration concerns primarily the sign; revelation, the thing signified. Revelation is the shining light of God through the prism of Scripture; inspiration is ensuring that Scripture can be a prism for God's light. Inspiration reaches its goal in revelation; revelation finds its springboard in inspiration.[17]

Basically, 'revelation' is the *truth revealed*; 'inspiration' enables that truth revelation to be presented in a reliable written form that enables the truth to be continually applicable.

To ensure this reliability, some have suggested that God engages in a form of dictation or direct transmission. This theory advocates that the divine takes over the human author such that the human author contributes little to the process, and what is written is purely the 'word of God'. However, a simple reading of Holy Scripture and its inherent humanness soon reveals that this dictation idea falls flat. Scripture contains the account of God engaging real people, in real world situations, through the medium of real, flawed and fallible people through people who are equally flawed and fallible.

On the other end of the scale, some suggest Scripture represents 'inspired human' thoughts, the musings of individuals and their personal reflections on the divine and divine interactions – like a work of art, literature or poetry. Yet the consistency of unified witness, the power of Holy Scripture to influence the lives of believers through millennia, and the capacity for the same to 'speak with' authority in guiding and confirming in a multitude of situations suggest there is more to this book than inspired human sentiments.

How then are we to understand this difficult issue of divine inspiration through the means of a human author; a process that produces a grounded human document with divine authority?

The fact is, Holy Scripture itself reveals the answer to this question. The text of Scripture suggests that the Spirit speaks through the human authors: 'Brothers and sisters, the Scripture had to be fulfilled which the Holy Spirit spoke long ago through the mouth of David concerning Judas' (Acts 1:16); 'You spoke by the Holy Spirit through the mouth of your servant, our father David' (Acts 4:25); and 'The Holy Spirit spoke the truth to your ancestors when he said through Isaiah the prophet' (Acts 28:25). Now when these verses suggest the Holy Spirit 'spoke through', it is suggesting that the Holy Spirit powerfully influenced them to the point that the words 'they' spoke, which later became Scripture, were so inspired by the Holy Spirit that they may be described as the Spirit speaking. However, it is the text of 2 Peter 1 that gives us the greatest clue of the Spirit's modus operandi during the process of inspiration. Peter wrote, 'For prophecy never had its origin in the human will, but prophets, though human, spoke from God as they were carried along by the Holy Spirit' (2 Pet. 1:21).

For Peter, prophecy (the divine word) was never carried along by the human will, but rather carried along by the Holy Spirit's impetus. He uses the word *fero, menoi*, which is the passive form of the present participle of the verb *fero* (to carry) to portray the manner in which the Spirit engages with the human author in the process of inscripturation. Like so much of Holy Scripture, metaphors are employed to communicate truth, and in this case it is a sailing metaphor: a symbol suggesting that, as the wind powers and influences a sailboat in its direction of travel, so too the Spirit of God powerfully influences the direction of the human author / prophet and the message communicated.

Although the metaphor suggests that human authors are involved in the process (as the helmsman of a ship), it also fundamentally implies they are passive as to the spiritual forces acting on them. Yes, human writers play a part in the communication process, but without the supreme power of the Spirit acting on them, the communication would go nowhere, have no power and influence no one. This manner of inspiration is not deistic dictation, or mystical human inspiration, but the intentional and direct action of the Spirit on the divinely appointed human author to render the word of God as Holy Scripture, authoritative and powerful for all who encounter it under the Spirit's leading – a timeless divine message through a historic, concrete and manifestly human setting.

Illumination

However, the Holy Spirit inspiring the authorship of Holy Scripture is only part of the equation; no one can grasp divinely inscripturated truth without the concomitant working of the Spirit through divine illumination. The Spirit-inspired truth, resident in Scripture, can be interpreted and understood as truth only when the Spirit 'quickens' the mind of the reader to actually grasp the divine logic in what is written. Without the Holy Spirit's intervention, the interpretation of the word would remain an enigma, even seeming foolish, as Paul intimates, 'The person without the Spirit does not accept the things that come from the Spirit of God but considers them foolishness, and cannot understand them because they are spiritually discerned' (1 Cor. 2:14). Or, if not interpreted as foolishness, it is at least relegated to some form of ancient history, with no present application, as Paul Achtemeier suggests, 'Unless inspiration continues to the reading and hearing of Scripture, Scripture remains a museum piece, of interest to antiquarians who want to affirm that at one time the Spirit of God inspired a collection of writings, but its present utility is no greater than any other object from the remote past.'[18]

Coming to terms with truth as we have defined it is not something humans can do under their own power; it is not a matter of 'willing to know' and then coming into a place where the mind brings itself in conformity with objective truth, such as Plato might suggest in his theory of education. Rather, it is as Donald Bloesch suggests: 'the refocusing of the mind by the Spirit of God, who breaks into our reality from beyond'.[19] Divine truth is so contrary to the natural 'unspiritual' logic of the human nature that it cannot be accepted by such a mind, that is why Paul calls it 'foolishness to the Greeks'. But when God sovereignly acts on the human nature in power the scales of human blindness fall off, and the Spirit-influenced mind is able to make sense of this enigmatic divine revelation, because the source of interpretation and source of inscripturation are one and the same. But there are certain prerequisites for this illumination; it simply cannot be conjured up at will, it is itself subject to the divine initiative.

The primary precondition for an illuminated mind is the human response to the divine initiative, through faith. That is, to respond to the gospel of grace. This is clearly illustrated through Paul's challenge to the Athenian philosophers in Acts 17. After referencing an inscription on an object of worship, stating 'to an unknown god', Paul suggests who this unknown God might be, the God and Father of Jesus Christ, and that he could be found if he was sought. However, rather than appealing to human reason, he argues that finding God involves responding to his offer of salvation: 'In the past God overlooked such ignorance, but now he commands all people everywhere to repent' (Acts 17:30). Now, at this allegedly outrageous claim, many mocked him and indignantly departed when they heard him talking about the resurrection of the dead, 'but' those who responded to the Spirit's prompting through the gospel proclamation embraced this message in faith: 'Some of the people became followers of Paul and believed' (Acts 17:34).

Yes, there was a prevenient working of the Spirit on those who believed, but this belief was in concert with embracing the gospel and submitting in faith to Jesus Christ. Understanding the message of the gospel, therefore, is integral to the condition of divine illumination, for once having believed and being indwelt by the Spirit, the believing person can perceive Holy Scripture with clarity, and even if it is not understood in its entirety, it is understood truly. Therefore, divine illumination is a facility only available to those who have responded to the gospel of Jesus Christ, and concomitantly have received the indwelling presence of the Holy Spirit, the regenerating Spirit that not only changes the disposition of the heart to one of obedience to the divine will, but changes the capacity of the mind to comprehend divine logic, something mysterious for those who have not embraced the gospel.

In fact, the existential presence of the Spirit is so fundamental to grasping divine truth that the author of the Johannine epistles suggests that it actually equates to truth itself. In defending the validity of the incarnation of Christ against proto-gnostics, John indicates that the inner testimony of the Spirit actually represents a primary authentication of truth: 'And it is the Spirit who testifies, because the Spirit is the truth' (1 John 5:6). John is suggesting that the inner testimony of the Spirit, with respect to discerning truth from error, is actually to be equated with an innate capacity to know truth – in this case truth as opposed to error. This is something also elucidated in his fourth gospel: 'But when he, the Spirit of truth, comes, he will guide you into all truth. He will not speak on his own; he will speak only what he hears, and he will tell you what is yet to come. He will bring glory to me by taking from what is mine and making it known to you' (John 16:13–14). In John's account, Jesus' sending of the Holy Spirit is explicitly for revealing truth; whether bringing into mind former revelation or granting discernment in a current situation, the Spirit is the ever-present agent of truth to the Christian disciple.

What gives Holy Scripture its authority? The answer is quite simply God's Spirit, under the impetus of God's initiative, powerfully acting on human authors and in human readers to establish and confirm divine truth. A truth that is repeatable because it is transmitted in written form, but a truth that is continually and dynamically applicable in varying contexts because of its 'spiritual' nature. In and through the Spirit, Holy Scripture is the most powerful form of truth in existence; nothing has and does transform like it!

Why Does God Give Us Holy Scripture?

If the Holy Spirit represents the primary agent of truth, then why would a Christian person need the Holy Scriptures at all? Why not simply rely on the Spirit and the resultant power of internal conviction and guidance; after all, isn't that what the apostle John was implying in 1 John 5:6?

When we read in Romans: 'But now, by dying to what once bound us, we have been released from the law so that we serve in the new way of the Spirit, and not in the old way of the written code' (Rom. 7:6), surely Paul is suggesting that the 'way of the Spirit' supersedes the necessity to appeal to written Scripture as a means of guidance? Indeed, as much as traditional commentators might suggest that Paul is simply referring to a new hermeneutics, that is, a new way of interpreting the law via the Spirit, the whole tenor of Paul's argument is implying something much more comprehensive: a moving away from an old-covenant, letter-based religion to a new-covenant Spirit-based religion, more along the lines that Sigurd Grindheim argues: 'The role the Mosaic Covenant as such had to play in redemptive history is now over. The new covenant is not described as in continuity with the old, as if the new covenant by giving the spirit brought the old covenant to fulfillment.'[20] For Paul the 'new way' of the Spirit represents a new approach with a heavy reliance on the Spirit.

But just because the 'literal' Mosaic law has been displaced, does that mean that 'all' Scripture has also been superseded? What is obvious from a reading of the Pauline epistles is that Paul not only sees a continuing role for the authority of Holy Scripture, but also implies that its role is pre-eminent in validating truth. Galatians is arguably Paul's strongest polemic against law- or letter-based religion: 'Now that faith has come, we are no longer under the supervision of the law' (Gal. 3:25), yet the same letter is replete with examples where he authoritatively quotes the law-oriented Old Testament in support for his 'new' Spirit-oriented religion. Is Paul contradicting himself in this matter? I believe not. In advocating the superseding of the Mosaic law- or letter-dependent form of religion, he also clearly sees a continuing role for the authority of the Spirit-inspired Holy Scripture because, as we shall soon see, Holy Scripture represents the perennially valid material testimony of the Spirit. So, even though its application might be significantly different in the new covenant era, for

Paul, Holy Scripture's essential authority remains unchanged as the God-breathed word; retaining the primary means of authority for the validation of true doctrine.

Notwithstanding these preliminary discussions about the continuing necessity of Scripture's testimony, there are two texts of Holy Scripture that specifically deal with the subject of Holy Scripture's authoritative primacy: 2 Peter 1, and 2 Timothy 3.

What is most powerful about Peter's affirmation of Scripture's authority in his second epistle is the testimony that precedes his special reference to the nature of Scripture's authority. In this Peter affirms he was a close follower of Jesus (an apostle) and that he was an eye-witness to the divine experience of Jesus' transfiguration on the mount: 'We ourselves heard this voice that came from heaven when we were with him on the sacred mountain' (2 Pet. 1:18). Yet, above and beyond these existential authenticating factors of eyewitness and apostle, etc. he then goes on to affirm a greater authority: 'And we have the word of the prophets made more certain, and you will do well to pay attention to it, as to a light shining in a dark place, until the day dawns and the morning star rises in your hearts' (2 Peter 1:19).

Interestingly, the rendering of 'And we have the word of the prophets made more certain' is not precise. The Greek text literally says: 'and we have a more certain prophetic word.' The adjective 'more reliable' is a comparative accusative that connects with 'prophetic word', which in effect renders the translation: 'we have a more reliable prophetic word'. This 'more reliable' prophetic word to which Peter refers is the word of the prophets as set down in Holy Scripture. It is a truth that he considers, comparatively, to be more reliable than even an eye-witness account of a genuine religious experience in the presence of Jesus!

In effect, Peter is encouraging his readers to see that even the most genuine 'spiritual' experience given by God still does not carry the same weight of reliability as the testimony of Holy Scripture; which, he goes on to add, gains its authority from the Holy Spirit: 'For prophecy never had its origin in the human will, but prophets, though human, spoke from God as they were carried along by the Holy Spirit' (2 Pet. 1:21).

In effect, Peter is stating that the Scripture's reliability and dependability are so, because of its divine provenance; that is Holy Scripture is reliable because its content does not originate in the flawed will of humanity; rather it originates in the imperfect will of God, revealed as this will powerfully animates the human authors through the Holy Spirit's power. Thus, in Peter's estimation, when comparing an authentic spiritual experience with the Spirit-inspired revelation of God in Scripture, it must be affirmed that Scripture is to be considered the more reliable of the two testimonies, even though both may be considered valid. In this regard the Spirit's testimony is not set over and against the testimony of Scripture, but complements it by providing an enduring material witness of the Spirit's divinely revealed truth.

We now consider the second of these key texts, from Paul's second letter to Timothy: 'All Scripture is God-breathed and is useful for teaching, rebuking, correcting and training in righteousness, so that God's servant may be thoroughly equipped for every good work' (2 Tim. 3:16–17). In this statement Paul is explicitly affirming the practical value of Holy Scripture, and he does so by first stating the basis of Scripture's authority. He refers to 'all' Scripture, principally to the Old Testament writings, but implicit in that statement would be a realization that what he was writing would also become authoritative Scripture. The key to this affirmation is the word 'God-breathed'.

Implicit in this notion is the presence of God's Spirit in its creative, life-giving capacity. In the Old Testament the notion of Spirit (Heb. *ruach*) is derived from the root concept of 'wind / breath'. It is found no fewer than 387 times in the Hebrew Bible; it reveals truth about God's dynamic, powerful and intangible essence. The correlative term (Heb. *neshamah*) conveys the idea of 'Spirit' as the life-giving breath of God. The creative Spirit of God is metaphorically represented as 'the breath' of God, and conceptually connects God's Spirit to his powerful, life-giving word; the Spirit-empowered word that shaped the material world and breathed inner life into the first human, Adam (Gen. 2:7).

The breath of God in this context is a metaphor for the authoritative Spirit-inspired word of God. What Paul is suggesting, then, is that Holy Scripture originates from God himself, with the very ideas of God 'breathing into' the human author and influencing the content of what is written, which is then communicated in written form as the authoritative 'word of God'.

Because the Spirit-originated word has authority it is considered practically useful in the following ways:

1. *Teaching*: Personal spiritual experiences do not have universal application, so to communicate truth that may be applied to anyone in any context, Holy Scripture is used as a far more effective means for communicating doctrine. The base content may be referred to again and again, in its material form, and as this teaching is repeated and reapplied, the foundational truth can be referred to repeatedly and reapplied in fresh and meaningful ways.
2. *Rebuking and correcting*: Without an 'objective' reference, rebuking and correcting can be interpreted as a personal attack. But firmly based on the testimony of Holy Scripture, these admonishments not only give the person offering the challenge confidence, but also the person receiving it the assurance that the truth being offered comes from a higher source; and if the Spirit is present in the conviction then it will become self-evident that this is actually a message from God.
3. *Training in righteousness*: If Christians are to receive the training in righteousness commensurate to their faith (Rom. 6:22; 2 Cor. 7:1; 1 Tim. 2:2; 2 Tim. 2:22; Heb. 12:14), then there needs to be a concrete source that enables consistency of training across the board. Yes, a Spirit-led believer may offer advice, direction and example about a godly life and the disciple may lean on the convicting presence of the Spirit, but without the concrete witness of Holy Scripture to confirm, support and consistently remind, given the vicissitudes of the human condition, the teaching may become inconsistent.

Scripture, therefore, provides a concrete, repeatable, consistent and universal means of teaching truth that prevents that truth from being modified and drifting with circumstances, which could occur with even the best-intentioned teachers and disciples.

Of course, from Paul's point of view this Scripture-based instruction has a purpose – practical obedience. The goal of Spirit-inspired Scripture is to instruct a Spirit-guided life – a life lived in conformity with Christ, for the glory of God the Father.

So why does God give us Holy Scripture in concert with the Spirit's guidance, not relying on the presence of the Spirit alone? Simply because the fallibility of the human condition cannot allow for a *consistent* reception of God's truth. Without the Spirit working through inspiration and illumination the sinful human person would never grasp the divine logic of God, either in Holy Scripture or any other kind of revelation. Alternatively, without the concrete, material witness of Holy Scripture the internal convictions of the Spirit would be susceptible to the vagaries of the natural human condition. No humans, no matter how spiritual, are capable of maintaining a consistent, infallible walk with God without some external regulating authority to offer them guidance. The Spirit working through the word provides the instruction, the corrective and the guidance needed for the Christian to maintain a consistent walk of obedience with God; it provides a regulating influence to counter the vicissitudes of the human experience.

Summary

To embark on the quest to validate Holy Scripture as the primary regulating authority in matters of truth, we needed to discuss the nature of truth. We asserted that the 'type' of truth validated by Scripture was and is not scientific or philosophical in nature. Rather, the truth presented in and validated by Holy Scripture is relational; this primarily with reference to God. Because it is relational it is also moral, and by necessary extension is authoritative over a person's moral / practical life. We also considered what gave Holy Scripture and its truth claims this authority. It was advanced that perhaps canonicity, historicity and thematic unity might do so. But, as helpful as they might be in offering reassurance to the person defending the authority of the Bible, they do not actually endow authority on Holy Scripture; they merely affirm what is so.

What 'really' gives Holy Scripture its authority and moral power is from another place than human affirmation. It comes from the divine presence of God, through both the authorship of Holy Scripture and its divinely empowered interpretive processes. Such a powerful presence is only possible through the direct agency of the Holy Spirit, who powerfully influenced the human authors of Scripture by overcoming the fallibilities of their human natures, to reveal divine truth through them, in a grounded human form. Indeed, the same Spirit that inspired these authors also serves to illuminate the hearts and minds of the interpreter, by giving divine insight into what was written and then dynamically applying it in real, practical and relevant ways.

The Holy Spirit is the authoritative source of Holy Scripture, and has supervised the production of a work that is consistently reliable. Its message is repeatable in a multitude of different contexts. Because human nature is fickle, the reliability of the Spirit's capacity to regulate truth in any individual is often contingent on that individual living in conformity with God's will. It is all too easy for individuals to drift away in their relationship with God and start to rely on what they interpret as spiritual leading, which may be little more than their own inclinations. Holy Scripture remains a consistent witness to the Spirit's leading, a regulating means of divine truth for fallible Christians who desire to live in a consistent relationship with God. Without it, Christian faith is like a ship without a rudder on a stormy ocean. Without its stabilizing influence, it would only be a matter of time before that faith would become shipwrecked by the guidance of inconsistent means.

7

The Spirit, Truth and Practical Obedience

God's truth is beyond rational comprehension. The mind's striving to attain knowledge of God's truth always reaches its limit short of its goal, because authentic knowledge of the truth involves more than engaging the intellect. To know God's truth as fully as it might be known, the truth-seeker must practise what is known in the power of the Spirit. But this is not as straightforward as it might seem; the Spirit faces extreme opposition from a phenomenon the Bible calls *the flesh*. The flesh represents the *human self*, animated by all its natural powers and faculties – physical, mental, emotional and spiritual. Not only so, but the flesh is energized by *sin* – a self-oriented disposition hard-wired into the human consciousness, that is fundamentally antagonistic toward God. The flesh under the influence of sin (known as *the sinful nature*) animates every desire and action that resists God's truth, being just as potent as *the world* or *the devil*, which also conspire against God's truth. Even as liberating as the gospel of Jesus Christ is, believers remain incapable of subjugating the flesh's stultifying power without divine assistance. They 'need' the Spirit's power, in full measure, to effectively live what they acknowledge as true and by extension grasp it as true. To 'know' the truth fully, believers must be free from the sinful nature's controlling influence by ceding primary influence over their thoughts and actions to the Holy Spirit. But this influence must arise from more than a sentimental attachment to past 'spiritual encounters'; it must originate from an ongoing vital relationship with Jesus Christ, in the power of the Spirit.

Such a relationship empowers a life beyond *knowing about* the truth, to a life of obediently *living in* it.

Doing and Knowing

To know the truth fully a person must tangibly experience it. For example, a priori rational reflection cannot ultimately enable a person to come to terms with the data gained from the senses of taste, smell or touch. Even if rationality could attempt to define what was experienced, it must do so by drawing on experience at some point. To suggest something tastes like chicken, one must have prior experience of the taste of chicken! There is always a dimension to knowing that extends beyond the rational and enters the experiential. What is valid for the natural is even more so for the supernatural. Coming to terms with divine reality, a 'reality' that extends beyond the boundary of human rationality, involves an engagement with transcendent experience and the mysterious elements of truth it reveals. Indeed, unless a person leaves a *reliance* on the flesh's rationality, they can never come to a true understanding of divine truth. They could never comprehend 'fully' something like 'the peace of God that passes all understanding' – a state of being that embraces God beyond head knowledge. To know God's truth in such a way, then, requires an abandonment of the flesh and its deceptive desire to lay hold of lesser forms of truth.

Examples of this kind of 'practical knowing' are replete in Holy Scripture. In his letter to the Philippians, Paul writes, 'And this is my prayer: that your love may abound more and more in knowledge and depth of insight, so that you may be able to discern what is best and may be pure and blameless until the day of Christ' (Phil. 1:9–11). Paul is intimating here that knowledge and depth of insight are the product of *love abounding*, and that through this a deeper insight arises. Insight, in this case, is the product of practically applying love; with the practitioners only able to 'truly' discern what is best for their lives as they grow in knowledge as a result of practising. Consequently, in Paul's logic, true knowledge pertains to a life of holiness and conformity to the image of Christ. In this sense, knowing transcends rational and speculative endeavours and enters into the domain of faith-based life of practical obedience to Christ; which, in Paul's estimation, leads to a clearer understanding of truth, as known and experienced through the eyes of God. Becoming like God in practising godliness is to become more like God in understanding – to enter into the reality of his truth.

Paul's most poignant affirmation of experience-based knowledge, however, is built on his own personal relationship with Christ; he writes, 'I want to know Christ and the power of his resurrection and the fellowship of sharing in his sufferings, becoming like him in his death, and so, somehow, to attain to the resurrection from the dead' (Phil. 3:10–11). Paul is not asserting that he wants a clearer appreciation of the accuracy of Jesus' historical life, or a more profound definition of his relationship to the Trinity, or even a more precise understanding of any other technical point of doctrine. Paul is affirming a desire to intimately experience Christ in practice, and so become more like him. However, this is even more than a bald-faced imitation of Jesus, where one might understand Jesus by 'walking a mile in his shoes'; it is that, but there is something deeper. Paul is also referring to a sense of experiencing the mystical presence of Christ, as he lives out the life of Christ, such that it is Christ's presence that controls his very existence: 'I have been crucified with Christ and I no longer live, but Christ lives in me' (Gal. 2:20).

Implicit in Paul's understanding is the secret working of the Spirit. To know in this way is to allow the Spirit to instil the 'mind of Christ', such as to animate one's motives and desires, so that the reality of Christ's presence becomes one with the believer. Consequently, truth is not a 'thing' that is simply intellectually grasped, but a dynamic power that embraces the knower and draws them into the reality of God. No longer is the flesh the controlling influence over the person's logic, no longer do false forms of truth animate a person's view of reality, but the truth of God, via the presence of God, takes over that person's life – they become the embodiment of what is true by entering into a realm free from sin's all-controlling influence. Free from the deceit of sin's inward-looking orientation and free from the flesh's self-oriented power, the recipient of the Spirit's power is able to see clearly, to view their existence in relation to God's ultimate reality through the eyes of God – to know as God does (as truly, but not as comprehensively).

In fact, this freedom is what Jesus was alluding to when he addressed the Pharisees on the subject of truth. The Pharisees were people who had allowed their sin-guided human natures to fashion their view of God, to the point that they believed falsehood was actually truth. In John's Gospel we read the account: 'To the Jews who had believed him, Jesus said, "If you hold to my teaching, you are really my disciples. Then you will know the truth, and the truth will set you free"' (John 8:31–2). Jesus is suggesting here that those that 'hold' to his teaching – that is those that not only intellectually agree with his ideas, but abandon their 'fleshly natures' to whole-heartedly follow what he teaches – actually practise it by, for example, loving their neighbour. These people enter into an understanding of truth that sets them free from sin's control.

A perfect example of this 'holding to Jesus' teaching' is the penitent tax collector Zacchaeus. Zacchaeus responds to Jesus' teaching, not merely with a rational acknowledgement of technical truth, but whole-heartedly embracing his understanding of truth in faith-based actions. His faith in Christ leads him to embrace truth that leads to a real-life transformation: 'But Zacchaeus stood up and said to the Lord, "Look, Lord! Here and now I give half of my possessions to the poor, and if I have cheated anybody out of anything, I will pay back four times the amount." Jesus said to him, "Today salvation has come to this house, because this man, too, is a son of Abraham' (Luke 19:8–9). The truth set Zacchaeus free because he whole-heartedly embraced it!

In contrast, the Pharisees who claimed a heritage to Abraham and the orthodox religion that flowed from this heritage 'practically' remained slaves to sin because their knowledge of God was conditioned by their self-oriented religious natures (the flesh): 'They answered him, "We are Abraham's descendants and have never been slaves of anyone. How can you say that we shall be set free?" Jesus replied, "I tell you the truth, everyone who sins is a slave to sin'" (John 8:33–4). Jesus was suggesting that even though they intellectually claimed to know the truth, their lives were full of defective moral practices and, as such, revealed that they remained slaves of sin, continuing in ignorance of divine truth. How then does Jesus respond to their self-righteous claims? 'I know you are Abraham's descendants. Yet you are ready to kill me, because you have no room for my word' (John 8:37). Jesus could see through their veneer of religion, he could see that they claimed to walk in the truth, but in reality violated it at the deepest level, by harbouring murderous intentions toward him.

The Pharisees' technical affirmation of religious credentials meant little to Jesus. What mattered to him, what truly verified a claim on truth, was how consistent a 'believer's' actions were with the Father's will. Yet, they actually respond as if they are in step with the Father's will: '"The only Father we have is God himself." Jesus said to them, "If God were your Father, you would love me, for I came from God and now am here. I have not come on my own; but he sent me. Why is my language not clear to you?"' (John 8:41–3). It seems sin has so clouded their logic that they could actually hold to a technical view of truth and God that suited their form of religion, while morally denying it in practice. Jesus, seeing their hypocrisy, bluntly states the facts: 'You belong to your father, the devil, and you want to carry out your father's desire. He was a murderer from the beginning, not holding to the truth, for there is no truth in him. When he lies, he speaks his native language, for he is a liar and the father of lies' (John 8:44). In effect, their perception of truth, albeit religiously justifiable, was actually a lie.

In claiming to be proponents of orthodox truth, and having an intellectual appreciation of doctrine with a strong Jewish heritage, the Pharisees in actuality, had no appreciation of truth. Why? Because their 'fleshly natures', animated by the controlling power of sin, deceived them into thinking they were practising truth when all the while they were embracing nothing more than a thinly veiled falsehood. They remained blind to truth because they remained captive to sin's deceitfulness, made even more deceptive by a form of religion that never challenged them to 'truly' practise what they preached. So dark was their sinfulness that they were not only blind to truth, but also they actively resisted it, as Jesus states: 'Yet because I tell the truth, you do not believe me!' (John 8:45). Jesus does not say, 'You don't believe me, in spite of me telling you the truth.' He actually says it's 'because' he tells the truth they don't believe! As we can see, the flesh nature animated by sin is so resistant to truth that it will actively oppose it. Sin-motivated human nature hates the truth, and will do all it can to resist it. As such, until these inner powers of the flesh and sin are overcome, no amount of intellectual knowledge can lead a person into the truth of God.

The power of God to bring 'real' transformation is required to set people free from the power of sin. The Pharisees in their self-righteous blindness could never know truth, even though they had an intellectual appreciation of its principles. Paradoxically, Zacchaeus, a 'sinful' tax-collector without a shred of religious credibility, entered into a true understanding of divine truth because he whole-heartedly surrendered his will to God through faith in Jesus. His faith necessarily translated into a practical grace, emulating his 'new' Lord, and thus proving that the 'old' power of the flesh and sin had been broken in his life. Truth for Zacchaeus was all-encompassing. It was not something to intellectually know, alone; it was something total, something holistically transformative. We know Zacchaeus knew the truth because he embraced it fully and proved that God had transformed his life through practical generosity. What his mind perceived, and what his heart believed, he practically manifested in his love for others – salvation had transformed him and the truth had found him. Zacchaeus had come to experience truth in its fullest sense and, as a consequence, he was now free.

Humility: Breaking the Power of Human Pride

The biggest hurdle to being set free from the controlling influence of the flesh / sin phenomenon is human pride. The inherent pride of the self will not allow a person to willingly embrace God's truth; for fear that the ingrained falsehood will be exposed. In fact, this is Jesus' *actual assessment* of the human status, 'This is the verdict: Light has come into the world, but people loved darkness instead of light because their deeds were evil. All those who do evil hate the light, and will not come into the light for fear that their deeds will be exposed' (John 3:19–20). The truth always exposes the unholy condition of the human self. For a person to actually come into 'the light' of the truth, there must be a 'breaking of the will', an inner contrition of heart, a state in which guilt is acknowledged and the shame of the sinful self and its actions is truly experienced. Yet, because of the embarrassment that is perceived to result from this contrition, there is always a resistance to *the light of the truth*. People, instinctively, either run from truth or resolutely resist it. For an inner transformation that could break the power of the flesh to occur, there must be a prior work of God's grace in the human heart, a prevenient working of the Holy Spirit to convict the sinful self of guilt and convince it to admit its shortcomings.

In James's epistle we read, 'But he gives us more grace. That is why Scripture says: "God opposes the proud but gives grace to the humble"' (Jas 4:6). This theme of God opposing the proud and bestowing grace on those who humbly trust him is replete throughout Holy Scripture. Given that pride is the fundamental cause of Satan's fall from grace, which in turn led to the subsequent temptation of humanity and their fall, it should not surprise us that this subject is high on God's agenda. The flesh nature, animated by the power of sin, strongly resists God's grace; it resists it because its fundamental will is for absolute self-sufficiency, a fool's errand and goal that is impossible to gain – by virtue of being human. The challenge of the Holy Spirit through the testimony of Scripture, in concert with its prevenient 'inner' convictions, is to stop resisting God and submit to him. Scripture does not seek to placate the flesh in any way, or encourage 'self-worth' on the pathway to overcoming the flesh and sin; rather it goads the recalcitrant person to stand against their 'natural' disposition and humble themselves and submit: 'Submit yourselves, then, to God. Resist the devil, and he will flee from you. Come near to God and he will come near to you' (Jas 4:7–8a).

What James is assuming in God's grace is the secret working of the Spirit. This powerful prevenient working of the Spirit is somewhat like a computer program that is always running in the background. The rebellious human nature is so predisposed with its own agendas that it scarcely, if ever, notices the Spirit's subtle 'background' workings. But James's challenge is clear: when the temptation to sin confronts us, we must resist it, and in so doing unconsciously employ that background power of the Spirit to liberate us from sin's addictive pull. In this disposition of submission, the Spirit's background power comes to the fore, enabling the power of Satan to tempt and distract to be broken – in James's words he will flee!

James's next challenge is often overlooked, but it represents one of the keys to overcoming the power of the flesh. James issues a challenge that also comes with a promise: 'Come near to God, and he will come near to you' (Jas 4:8a). What, in effect, James is suggesting is this: the closer a person moves to God in humble moral conformity, away from the temptations of Satan; the closer God will draw near to that person, in truth. Once a person begins to respond to the subtle promptings of the Spirit, the power of God to resist and overcome the power of the flesh becomes greater – the Spirit increasingly animates the human motives rather than the flesh. Thus, the closer one is to God, the easier it is to resist the pull of the flesh.

But this humble drawing near to God should not be deemed as something merely formulaic, a 'one-step' means of getting an inside track with God. Rather, dispelling pride through humility requires deeply felt repentance that involves both external and internal transformation. James writes: 'Wash your hands, you sinners, and purify your hearts, you double-minded. Grieve, mourn and wail. Change your laughter to mourning and your joy to gloom' (Jas 4:8b–9). The washing of hands refers to the removal of external sin; the dispensing of habits, practices and actions that reveal the flesh is controlling a person's life. The purifying of hearts refers to inner cleansing, to address the motives and desires by addressing one's thought life, such that the believer would be single-minded in their divine pursuit, not simply saying they want to serve God, while acting as if they don't.

Sin must be considered with such gravity that it draws a person to lament, feeling sorrow over how it grieves God. The Christian should not seek to lift themselves up with any positive consolation, rather in pursuing abject humility they will trust God to lift them up, granting the power to walk in victory: 'Humble yourselves before the Lord, and he will lift you up' (Jas 4:10).

At the very heart of humility and contrition, there must be something called 'surrender'. That is, a full relinquishing of the power of the 'old' fleshly control over to God. Paul writes, 'For we know that our old self was crucified with him so that the body of sin might be done away with, that we should no longer be slaves to sin – because anyone who has died has been freed from sin' (Rom. 6:6–7). Through a spiritual 'union with Christ' the believer is able to lay claim to the reality that their old nature has been crucified with Christ. That is to say, sin's power has been broken, that it may no longer automatically control the believer's moral desires. Paul's logic regarding the broken power of sin would suggest the following: if Christ died to vanquish the power of sin and death, and if the believer is united to Christ; then by virtue of faith in Christ and a spiritual union with his 'reality', the believer can now claim power over sin and death as being 'actually' valid for them. On the basis of this indicative, therefore, Paul issues a strong imperative: 'Therefore do not let sin reign in your mortal body so that you obey its evil desires' (Rom. 6:12). If sin reigns, the truth is suppressed, but if through the Spirit's power it is nullified then the truth comes to light, and God's reality becomes clearer.

However, the Christian must not be hasty in coming to terms with this 'surrender', lest they miss the most crucial element of it. Paul says, 'Do not offer the parts of your body to sin, as instruments of wickedness, but rather offer yourselves to God, as those who have been brought from death to life; and offer the parts of your body to him as instruments of righteousness' (Rom. 6:13). This is not simply a two-step process where the Christian, first, stops yielding their bodies as instruments of wickedness and then, second, starts yielding their bodies as instruments of righteousness. Simply put, it is not 'stop' surrendering to sin and 'start' surrendering to righteousness; rather

Paul is emphasizing that the Christian must first surrender their will to God – alone. That is, the human self-will must be completely subjected or surrendered to the will of God (in much the same way as Jesus did in Gethsemane). After, and only after, surrendering the will to God is the offer of one's 'members' as instruments of righteousness valid; an offering uncontaminated by the flawed human self-will.

In order to break the power of the sin / flesh, it is not enough to stop doing bad things and start doing good things, because it is only a matter of time until the flesh will distort the good things toward bad – turning righteousness into self-righteousness. The Christian's moral conduct, and subsequent understanding, 'correctly' comes from being submissive to God's will (based on faith) and not merely enacting of the human will, in God's name. What is required of believers is full submission, a full yielding of their will to God's; to absolutely surrender to his Lordship to and in the power of the Spirit. When this occurs, the offering of their *bodies as instruments of righteousness* will have no recourse toward 'self-righteousness' but instead will only lead to an expression of the true righteousness, which reflects the heart of one yielded to God's lordship; righteousness empowered by the Spirit that reflects the true nature of God – a righteousness enabling a clear vision of divine truth. 'Blessed are the pure in heart, for they will see God' (Matt. 5:8).

Therefore, to know the truth as it manifests as God's righteousness in lived experience, the flesh must fully surrender to God in the power of the Spirit. Perhaps a fitting metaphor for this is the situation of the ancient Israelite leader Gideon. The Lord challenged him to turn men away from the battle with the Midianites, lest the Israelites seek the glory: 'The LORD said to Gideon, "You have too many men for me to deliver Midian into their hands. In order that Israel may not boast against me that her own strength has saved her"' (Judg. 7:2). This would be the Lord's victory and it would be the Lord's power that would deliver them. As a consequence the Israelites would have no reason to be filled with pride in their own achievements. So it is with 'the flesh' and doing the will of God. Only by surrendering 'first' to God and his all-sufficiency can the power of the flesh be overcome such that God's strength can bring about victory over sin and lead the person into an experience of God's truth – free from the subtle distortions of human pride. Indeed, the message the prophet Zechariah received from the Lord captures the heart of this truth: '"Not by might nor by power, but by my Spirit," says the LORD Almighty' (Zech. 4:6).

Self-control: Maintaining the Spirit's Power over the Flesh

The flesh is the Spirit's greatest adversary and is not easily overcome. In fact, the Spirit's vanquishing of the flesh is not a 'once-for-all-time' phenomenon. As long as believers live, the flesh and its capacity to lead them away from God's truth will endure. Yes, the Spirit is able to suppress the power of the flesh and subjugate its capacity to control the self, but it must do so on a continual basis to enable the Christian to continue in the truth. In much the same way that a person who has been diagnosed with cancer lives with the continuing threat that the disease will return with destructive power if unchecked, so Christians live with the knowledge that the power of the flesh will return with a vengeance, if unrestrained by the Spirit's continual empowerment. Although believers are passive with respect to the 'actual' capacity to suppress the flesh and its sinful desires, they do have an active role to play in setting the conditions for the Spirit's power to operate in an unhindered manner. Believers are responsible for actively participating in the ordering of their own lives, such that the Spirit might continue to suppress the flesh's negative influence, and empower lives of joyful service to God.

Believers are called by God to exercise self-control, applying disciplined restraint under the Spirit's prompting. Of course, the Spirit is absolutely necessary if forms of human-empowered restraint are attempted. They usually manifest as self-righteous religiosity, rigorous stoicism or bizarre asceticism. In fact, all of these are merely alternative expressions of the 'fleshly' life, and are ineffectual in what they purport to achieve, as Paul states: 'Such regulations indeed have an appearance of wisdom, with their self-imposed worship, their false humility and their harsh treatment of the body, but they lack any value in restraining sensual indulgence' (Col. 2:23). The power to actively exercise self-control comes from the Spirit alone; Paul again:

> So I say, live by the Spirit, and you will not gratify the desires of the sinful nature. For the sinful nature desires what is contrary to the Spirit, and the Spirit what is contrary to the sinful nature. They are in conflict with each other, so that you do not do what you want. But if you are led by the Spirit, you are not under law (Gal. 5:16–18).

Without the Spirit, there is no self-control! Spirit-empowered self-control is the capacity to exercise moral restraint; the ability to restrict the flesh's nefarious desires from having their way over the self. The power to exercise this self-control comes through 'gifting'. The Spirit does not simply *give* the believer this capacity as an attribute, but God gives the Spirit as the primary gift. The Spirit itself *is the gift* that enables this virtue, and indeed other virtues, to become manifest in the believer's life. These virtues (sub-gifts) demonstrate that the person is controlled by the Spirit. Paul speaks of them in the following way: 'But the fruit of the Spirit is love, joy, peace, patience, kindness, goodness, faithfulness, gentleness and self-control' (Gal. 5:22–3). The Spirit supernaturally bestows on the genuine believer the capacity to unconditionally love like God, to experience joy in all circumstances, to know peace when conflict abounds, to experience patience in the sternest trials, and to express kindness, goodness and faithfulness when it is unnatural to do so. Finally, the Spirit engenders the believer with, perhaps, the most useful of all qualities – self-control. Self-control offers the capacity to subjugate the 'beast within'; to suppress the sinful nature that craves rebellion against God through the manifestation of every kind of sinful practice – practices that are abominable in his eyes.

As the gatekeeper of truth, the Holy Spirit holds the flesh captive to its bonds, restraining that which would destroy the truth if given its way. It is the Spirit's empowering presence that enables the Christian person to spontaneously resist the temptations of the flesh, and the Spirit that enables this resistance to become a constant reality. In constantly restraining the flesh, the Spirit enables the practice of daily self-denial, a quality that Jesus deemed as essential for anyone who would wish to follow him: 'Then he said to them all: "Those who would come after me must deny themselves and take up their cross daily and follow me"' (Luke 9:23). The disposition of self-denial extends beyond the capacity to resist spontaneous temptation toward sinful 'acts'. It also enables the believer to overcome the innocuous natural qualities of the flesh that hold a person back from fully 'following' Jesus. For example, Spirit-empowered self-denial enables the Christian to rise early to pray, to give generously to those in need, or to minister to another at their own inconvenience; it enables them to overcome the natural laziness of the flesh and the hindrances it brings to the service of God.

However, for spontaneous self-control and daily self-denial to be fully effective, there are certain spiritual disciplines that the Spirit uses to strengthen the believer's capacity to overcome the power of the flesh. Examples of such disciplines might be solitude, personal prayer, alms-giving (to the poor), ministering to the needy, and Sabbath-keeping, all of which serve as habitual practices of restraining the capacity for the flesh through self-denial. But chief among such disciplines is fasting. Fasting is not something many modern Christians are accustomed to, although it is something spoken about in Scripture in general and by Jesus in particular, as part and parcel of a 'normal' Christian life. Fasting, as it is represented in Scripture, involves the deliberate withholding of food, either total or partial, for a set period of time. Fasting challenges the flesh at its most obvious and vulnerable point – the bodily appetites. It brings into sharp relief the issue of human dependency on God, and the value of the spiritual realm in the sustaining of life, above and beyond a mere material existence.

Fasting represents a primary means of suppressing the power of the flesh and the opportunity to enhance the power of the Spirit. It is not a practice for the 'extra' devoted – prophets, priests, and such. Rather, fasting is represented in Scripture as being as common in practice as prayer. Immediately following his teaching on prayer, Jesus teaches his disciples about fasting: 'When you fast, do not look sombre as the hypocrites do, for they disfigure their faces to show men they are fasting. I tell you the truth; they have received their reward in full' (Matt. 6:16). Rather than a formal religious activity, Jesus is suggesting that fasting is about inner devotion to God; it should not be for drawing attention to oneself, as some were in the habit of doing. Rather, fasting, was designed to direct attention away from 'the self'. For Jesus, the fast was to be directed toward the Father, with the express purpose of denying 'the self'; that one might see the true source of human nourishment is actually Father God. In this most fundamental sense then, fasting puts practising subjects in a posture of openness to the source of divine truth; it places them in direct intimacy with the heavenly Father and out of the clutches of their 'fleshly desires'. Such a posture is truly pleasing to him: 'and your Father, who sees what is done in secret, will reward you' (Matt. 6:18).

The matter of divine dependency is brought into sharp relief by the practice of fasting. Nowhere is this more clearly illustrated than in the temptations of Jesus. Having been led by the Spirit into the wilderness, Jesus fasts for forty days and nights and, doubtless, at the end of the time is extremely hungry. At this 'moment of weakness', Satan attempts to mislead him: 'The devil said to him, "If you are the Son of God, tell this stone to become bread"' (Luke 4:3). Satan, mistakenly, is working on the assumption that Jesus, like any human controlled by the 'flesh', is predisposed to give into natural bodily appetites; in this case use his 'powers' to obtain for himself the thing that might satiate the bodily desires. But Jesus, through the clarity of mind and clearness of focus gained from forty days of denying the flesh, is able to counter the temptation of Satan and his appeal to the flesh with the following answer, quoted directly from Deuteronomy 8: 'It is written: "People do not live on bread alone, but on every word that comes from the mouth of God"' (Matt. 4:4). Humanity is not simply an animal driven by animal desires, as the flesh would have us believe; rather as beings created in the image of God, who should see that life comes from God's creative word. Through fasting, the ultimate 'truth' about the nature of humanity's relationship to God comes clearly into focus.

Consequently, fasting highlights that the flesh does not have to 'control' the entirety of human existence, and that there is more to life than the body. Furthermore, the example of Jesus reveals that when a believer resists giving into the temptations of the flesh in order to honour God, then God honours them with his provision: 'Then the devil left him, and angels came and attended him' (Matt. 4:11). When a person denies the flesh for the sake of God and his kingdom, God will meet their every bodily need. Moreover, having subjugated the power of the flesh to control 'the self', that person has opened up the reality of the Spirit's presence in their lives, such that they are able to walk in the power of the Spirit, accomplishing the will of God in their lives, as Jesus did following his victory over Satan's temptations: 'Jesus returned to Galilee in the power of the Spirit, and news about him spread through the whole countryside' (Luke 4:14). Fasting, through the wilful denial of the self, subjugates the power of the flesh, enabling the believer to resist the temptations of Satan and the draw of the world. Fasting is instrumental in allowing the power of the Spirit to become a reality in the lives of believers, giving them the capacity to live victoriously in God's 'reality'.

With the breaking of the power of the flesh through the practice of fasting, the power of the Spirit is activated in believers, granting them the capacity to perceive divine truth in practically applicable ways. The apostle Paul, in challenging the Corinthian Christians about the necessity to live consistently to the faith they allegedly confessed, wrote: '"Everything is permissible for me" – but not everything is beneficial. "Everything is permissible for me" – but I will not be mastered by anything' (1 Cor. 6:12). The Corinthian believers, although claiming to follow Jesus, allowed their moral values to be conditioned by the surrounding libertarian culture, asserting that 'all' behaviours were permissible. Of course they were 'free' in Christ, but Paul wanted to assert that 'that freedom' must be exercised with divine restraint; restraint that ensures the flesh will not lead them to become slaves again to its desires. Paul not only spoke of the Spirit's power over the flesh, but he also lived it out. He knew the destructive power of the flesh and personally knew the incapacity of the Mosaic law to 'master' it. For Paul, the Spirit offered the only solution: 'So I say, live by the Spirit, and you will not gratify the desires of the sinful nature' (Gal. 5:16). For the apostle, living by the Spirit was *the* way of mastering the flesh and gaining a clear perception of God's reality. Knowing the truth and walking in the truth were one and the same!

Through the Spirit-empowered discipline of self-control, believers are able to be free from the appetites of the flesh that would deceive them into thinking that life in the material world was all there is – that is, life exclusively as material reality. Through Spirit-directed restraint, the mastery of the flesh is broken and believers are able to perceive another reality – God's. Through the Spirit the veil of the flesh is torn down, and the vista of the divine truth is opened up. They can now see things as they 'really are'. Therefore, revelation of truth and the Spirit's working in the moral life of a Christian person are directly related. Practically living in moral conformity to God's will enables the believer to perceive a reality previously hidden – hidden from all without the Spirit. But living in moral conformity to God's will fundamentally requires a disposition that desires moral complicity – the disposition of obedience.

Obedience: The Mindset of the Spirit

Many Christians are resistant to the notion of obedience being a 'necessary' aspect of the Christian life, and by extension the practical dimension of knowing the truth. In Protestant circles, more often than not, this arises from the notion that salvation equates with personal justification by faith alone. Spiritual formation, moral obedience and practical service – being outside of the scope of justification – are by logical necessity, outside the scope of salvation. This in turn leads to an ignorance of practical moral necessity, and a devaluing of a habitual life of conformity to God's will. While purporting to have 'genuine' Christianity, many actually practise a form of 'nominal'

Christianity that is Christianity in theory but not in action. I believe this theoretical divorce of faith and obedience is at the heart of the malaise that exists within first-world expressions of Christianity. It also explains why many of these Christians are so easily captivated by 'worldly' ideologies, and remain ignorant of vital divine truths – such as obedience.

But obedience *is* a necessary part of salvation. Of course, moral obedience is not 'causally' necessary, that is it doesn't make a person right with God. In fact in no way can 'doing' good things ever be good enough to win favour with God. However, obedience is 'consequentially' necessary. That is to say, obedience proves a person is right with God, and that the faith they claim is genuine faith in God. In short, moral obedience is the fruit that validates the root of authentic faith. Indeed, the reader does not have to look very hard at all in Holy Scripture to find a plethora of references advocating the necessity of moral obedience. Notwithstanding the multitude of commands in the Old Testament about obedience being a necessary condition of covenant blessing, the New Testament gospels also issue a number of challenges in this regard. Jesus said, 'If you love me, you will obey what I command' (John 14:15). The Great Commission of Jesus explicitly states that obedience is to be taught: 'Therefore go and make disciples of all nations, baptising them in the name of the Father and of the Son and of the Holy Spirit, and teaching them to obey everything I have commanded you' (Matt. 28:19–20).

Furthermore, the New Testament epistles explicitly reference the necessity of obedience in the Christian life. The apostle Peter wrote: 'To God's elect, strangers in the world . . . who have been chosen according to the foreknowledge of God the Father, through the sanctifying work of the Spirit, for obedience to Jesus Christ' (1 Pet. 1:1–2). The apostle John also wrote, 'And this is love: that we walk in obedience to his commands' (2 John 1:6). Paul, the primary advocate of justification by faith alone, explicitly goes out of his way to state the value and necessity of obedience in relation to the gospel: 'Through him and for his name's sake, we received grace and apostleship to call people from among all the Gentiles to the obedience that comes from faith' (Rom. 1:5); 'I will not venture to speak of anything except what Christ has accomplished through me in leading the Gentiles to obey God by what I have said and done' (Rom. 15:18); and 'but now revealed and made known through the prophetic writings by the command of the eternal God, so that all nations might believe and obey him' (Rom. 16:26). We must conclude that obedience, then, is a necessary part of the Christian life, not an option!

Obedience is part and parcel of the Christian life. But I am not simply arguing for the necessity of obedience alone, but that obedience is linked with the Spirit's capacity to reveal truth. Moral conformity to God's will does have a significant role to play in drawing a person into a closer orbit to God's presence, and by extension God's truth. James writes, 'Come near to God and he will come near to you. Wash your hands, you sinners, and purify your hearts, you double-minded' (Jas 4:8). When James says 'come near to God', he is really challenging his readers to live more closely to Gods' will – to obey him! Now, this obedience should not be practised in some blind, slavish or legalistic manner; this would be simply ceding control of the moral life to the flesh, negating any 'real' benefit obedience might bring. Rather, when the New Testament speaks of the necessity of obedience it does so with some qualifications.

First, obedience is motivated by love. Perhaps it might be more accurate to assert that love acted out represents genuine obedience to God. For the Christian Jew, who conceptualized obedience to God in terms of 'the law', Paul offered this particular challenge: 'The commandments, "Do not commit adultery," "Do not murder," "Do not steal," "Do not covet," and whatever other commandment there may be, are summed up in this one rule: "Love your neighbour as yourself." Love does no harm to its neighbour. Therefore love is the fulfilment of the law' (Rom. 13:9–10). Allegedly, practically conforming to God's will involves acting in love toward 'the other'; whether that 'other' is God or one's neighbour. If love is the fulfilment of 'the law' (God's codified will) then it must surely follow that genuine practical charity comes from a willingness to please God, and not merely a grudging disposition of legalism toward a set of laws. In the New

Testament ethic, to love God is to obey him; this kind of obedience is motivated by love. In short, authentic obedience is inseparable from love.

Second, obedience is based on faith. When a person seeks to please God, they must do so by abandoning all self-oriented agendas. This kind of abandonment requires 'real' faith. Consider the example of Abraham. He was asked by God to sacrifice his 'one and only' legitimate heir, the son through whom the divine covenant promise would be fulfilled. Constrained by human limitations Abraham was caught in the most extreme conundrum – to let his son live and disobey God or kill his son and nullify God's promise. The only way that Abraham could approach this kind of obedience was through the matrix of faith: 'By faith Abraham, when God tested him, offered Isaac as a sacrifice. He who had received the promises was about to sacrifice his one and only son, even though God had said to him, "It is through Isaac that your offspring will be reckoned." Abraham reasoned that God could raise the dead, and figuratively speaking, he did receive Isaac back from death' (Heb. 11:17–19). Abraham's obedience required trusting God at the expense of human reason and powers. This kind of obedience effectively represented faith in practice; to act in any other manner would have been disobedient. Because of Abraham's faith he was greatly blessed by God.

Finally, obedience is animated by the Spirit. Only the Holy Spirit could empower faith beyond the bounds of human reason, and engender love beyond the limits of human charity. Genuine obedience will always be associated with the Spirit, as these scriptural references affirm: 'We are witnesses of these things, and so is the Holy Spirit, whom God has given to those who obey him' (Acts 5:32); 'Those who obey his commands live in him, and he in them. And this is how we know that he lives in us: We know it by the Spirit he gave us' (1 John 3:24); and 'who have been chosen according to the foreknowledge of God the Father, through the sanctifying work of the Spirit, for obedience to Jesus Christ and sprinkling by his blood' (1 Pet. 1:2). The power to genuinely obey God, the power to move closer to God through obedience, and the power to know the truth of God all come from the Holy Spirit. The flesh, no matter how far it tries to remove itself from the influence of sin, can never attain the kind of moral conformity that God desires. Only through divine empowerment and the abandonment of the flesh through surrendering to the Spirit can a Christian believer enter into a position of divine intimacy. For it is only through divine intimacy, made possible through the Spirit's empowerment, that the truth can truly be encountered. In summary, true obedience (the kind that pleases God) comes from God's initiative alone; through the Holy Spirit's empowerment it is motivated by love and guided by faith.

Yet many Christians find it difficult to exercise this kind of obedience. Yes, they may affirm all the things previously mentioned but somehow 'lack the motivation' to perform. The reality is that the world is full of distractions and Satan's temptations, which are so overwhelming that even the most devoted Christians find it hard to resist them. What is required, more often than not, is to practically respond to the Spirit's *still small voice* and just 'do it' – just obey. If a Christian has allowed the Spirit's power of self-discipline any sway over their life, then they have the capacity to overcome the malaise that the surrounding culture saturates them in. They learn to 'just obey' even if they don't feel any positive impulse to do so. Indeed, what such people invariably find is that they 'act themselves' into wanting to obey, and subsequently feel the desire for obedience rising as the act plays out. I have lost track of how many times Christians have said to me, 'I didn't feel like getting up and coming to that early morning prayer meeting, church service or Bible study; but when I made the effort to come, despite my feelings, I was so glad I did!' In such cases moral obedience is the fruit of the self-discipline previously engendered by the Spirit. Obedience simply requires grit.

Coming to knowledge of the truth really isn't, as they say in colloquial speech, 'rocket science'. All it requires is simple obedience; not legal obedience. Legalistic rule-keeping leads people away from the truth into a burdensome religion that weighs them down with fear and guilt – it never leads to the truth. But an obedience that is truly engendered by the empowering presence of God's Spirit motivates service through love and fills the heart with courage to step out in faith, facing the impossible. This kind of obedience always leads to the truth because it comes from God and leads back to God; its source and destination are truth. This kind of obedience leads truth-seekers into the presence of God, into personal intimacy, and when they arrive there; their quest for knowing is consumed by the wonder of God, by his beautiful presence.

Summary

Truth is not simply a 'thing' that people attain through knowledge. The Spirit leads people toward the truth but, as we have seen, the biggest hindrance to the truth is the flesh, the human nature under the influence of sin. Entering into the truth necessitates being free from the constraints of the flesh. Through the Spirit's power human pride can be subdued, genuine self-control can be established, and the true motivations and practices of obedience established. Ultimately, entering into the truth requires being free from the flesh to walk in the Spirit. To encounter the Spirit is to enter the realm of truth, because the Spirit is the truth. This truth is not a list of facts, a set of principles or table of commandments; it is an existence of conformity with God in the Spirit, in the intimate presence of God himself. So, as you can see, if a person truly finds God, they find the truth. Now here is the irony, when a person finds God in this manner, they realize that all that is 'really' worth knowing is only ever found in him. The truth they thought they were seeking has fallen away; what they thought was the truth was really only 'signposts' leading to the one who is truth – leading to God. So what is the truth? Knowing God through intimate conformity with him in Jesus Christ, through the empowering presence of the Spirit!

Conclusion: Two Ways to Truth

By now the astute reader would have reached the conclusion that this book has been about two alternative ways to the truth. The first way originates with human nature: *the flesh*. It is a way that follows the pathway of independent reason, drawing on the self-sufficient human capacities that attend it. The second way follows the pathway of faith in Christ. It draws on divine power to animate its progress, and puts no faith in the human flesh. Rather, it humbly draws its energy from a divine source – *the Spirit*. The Spirit not only provides the means to reach a goal of understanding, but provides a new understanding of the nature of truth itself, that what was originally thought to be the goal was something quite different. But are there really two methods to find the one truth?

Which method of truth-seeking is adopted is largely dependent on the 'ultimate reality' the truth-seeker embraces at the beginning of the quest. If the seeker is concerned only with the 'here and now', with truth relating to a good life within a temporal existence, then the pathway of reason and human self-sufficiency is adequate. Indeed, if the destination is a health, wealth and wisdom for the duration of one's natural life, the pathway of the flesh serves the purpose adequately; not without serious inconsistencies though.

On the other hand, if the destination is eternal glory, an existence that transcends this present life, an existence based on an intimate relationship with a personal God within his eternal kingdom, then the pathway of faith in Christ, and only this pathway can reach the destination, as Jesus said, 'I am the way, the truth, and the life, no one comes to the Father except through me' (John 14:6).

As you can see, there are not 'really' two ways to the one destination, at all. Rather there is only one 'false' way, and one 'true' way. But the quest for truth is far more than defining two methods of reaching a destination, whether that destination is temporal or eternal; true or false. It involves coming to terms with the nature of truth itself!

If the destination of the truth quest is the 'best life possible' here and now, the truth will always 'be' a set of principles, maxims or laws; ideas associated with a philosophical system – truth is little more than an abstract theory. If, however, the truth quest seeks out a destination beyond the 'here and now', an eternal reality with God, then the truth should no longer be seen simply in terms of a definable theory. From God's perspective, truth represents relational intimacy, moral conformity and active devotion to his being. Truth, morality and obedience are all related. In the first method, truth is an idea that animates an existence, in which the human actor is central. In the second method, truth represents a holistic engagement with God; a relationship expressed in terms of moral and relational conformity.

The second definition of truth, the second way of grasping it, the second view of life and reality, has been the focus of this book: the way of the Spirit. I have sought to show Christians that there really is only one valid kind of truth, and one valid method of attaining it. Too many Christians seek to follow two masters in pursing truth, by employing a 'reliance' on the methodology of reason (in its various forms) *alongside* faith. To provide the structure for their pursuit of understanding God, they allow the method to shape the message. In other words, they end up with a view of Christian life in relation to God that looks like a philosophical system with a religious twist. This approach generates a life of rules and regulations, practices and principles, systems and programmes that tend to leave a personal, dynamic relationship with God on the side. In some cases God and his truth become a 'thing', which the believer relates to through adherence to rationally contrived doctrinal formulas.

While not denigrating or dissuading the value of reasoning, I have attempted to show that a dynamic openness to God's Spirit, and a willingness to allow God to lead the truth endeavour, will not only lead to 'the truth', but also to a life of true consistency with it. Because, when all is said and done, truth is not a thing to intellectually grasp but a personal intimacy with the God of truth; a life lived in conformity with his divine will – a life animated by the Spirit of God.

Coming to terms with such a view of truth means undoing the errors of philosophy, and the various fallacies that have been sown into the Christian understanding of truth. We addressed how reason-based approaches have misconstrued fundamental truths about God and his truth, thus hindering people from seeing it. In review, then, the errors we engaged were as follows.

The first error that we addressed was the division of spirituality and materiality through rationalistic dualism, or its seamless melding through the philosophy of monism. However, God's material world was created by the Spirit, and given all its wondrous design by the same. The Spirit not only created the material world, but in doing so ratifies the material realm as a means of the Spirit's engagement with humanity. The Spirit stands distinct from the material realm, even while intimately animating its existence. The Spirit works in the power of nature to reveal truth, as in the case of the miracles of Jesus. The Spirit also works in the circumstances and experiences of life, ordering affairs to bring about a revelation of truth. Indeed, the Spirit that created the material world, also creates in it the conditions to understand truth through it. So, as we have seen, in order to understand truth, we must not readily dismiss the revelatory power of the material realm, and the Holy Spirit's capacity to work in and through it.

The second error that limited a true understanding of truth, was the notion of the individual pursuit of truth. Taken as an individual quest, more often than not, the quest for truth turns into a theoretical game – a means of assuaging the individual's desire for certainty and security through some intellectual pursuit. But God created a community of faith (the church) as a means through which the Spirit of God works to reveal truth. To fully understand this, we must also contend with the fallacy that the church is merely an organization, and the Spirit only works through organizational structures. The church is a creation of the Spirit, and was created as a dynamic entity:

the body of Christ – a living organism, in which and through which the Holy Spirit reveals truth. The Spirit endows every member of the body of Christ with a 'gift', a special ability that is given for the edification of the whole. Not only the 'knowledge' gifts but also the service gifts work together to reveal and validate truth. Without the Spirit's community, the truth is not fully knowable.

The third error we sought to debunk related to the misrepresentation of personal spiritual experience. As suggested in Chapter 5, there is a proclivity among Christians either to rationalize experience and hence downplay its meaningful significance; or to spiritualize it and upscale its significance, such that it is deemed to be normative for everyone for all time. The Holy Spirit can and does use personal religious experiences to lead people into a new appreciation of truth. Indeed, there are clear accounts in Holy Scripture of the Spirit working in supernatural ways to break the 'hardness' of people's false beliefs and lead them into a richer understanding of God and his truths. Even more significant than what is revealed is the 'experience of revelation', in which the Holy Spirit personally convicts, guides and comforts. It is this personal engagement of the Spirit, that assists the recipient to see that truth is not merely a 'thing' to know, but a state of being arising from an intimate relationship with God.

The fourth error we sought to address was the misunderstanding of Holy Scripture's capacity to act as the regulating authority of truth. We carefully pointed out that many seek to validate Scripture's authority by way of human methods: history and tradition, etc. However, in doing so, they unwittingly shift the authority one step back to the validation process. As such, Scripture loses the primacy of its divine authority. The Holy Spirit is the only source of Scripture's authority, and it needs no validation from the flesh.

Through the process of direct inspiration, the Spirit brings the word of God into written text, as an abiding testimony to God's truth. We also affirmed that Holy Scripture was the most consistently reliable of the media that the Spirit uses to lead people into the truth. The other means though valid are unreliable: An act of nature might be a direct act of God or it might not; combined wisdom of the Christian community might be the authoritative will of God or it might not; a religious experience may be a direct work of the Spirit or it might be nothing more than a person's emotions. Holy Scripture as the Spirit-inspired word of God represents that arm of the Spirit's revelatory work that brings to bear a divine corrective on spurious forms of 'truth' revelation. Furthermore, it is the Spirit that takes the written word and makes it applicable to the life of a believer.

The final issue to be addressed in this book was the role of practice as a means of truth affirmation. Practice is a necessary component for understanding truth, which has been grossly downplayed in those advocating a more theoretical approach to truth. Practising truth, however, is more than simply doing something so that it might be empirically clarified. Rather, when a Christian under the guidance of the Spirit puts into practice their beliefs they gain a deeper appreciation of the personal nature of truth, through direct relational intimacy with God. For example, when Paul said: 'I want to know Christ and the power of his resurrection and the fellowship of sharing in his sufferings, becoming like him in his death' (Phil. 3:10), he was not suggesting he wants to 'walk a mile in Christ's shoes' to understand his world. No, there is more to it. Paul is suggesting that, in walking like Christ in the power of the Spirit, he gets to experience the presence of Christ in a way that transcends mere imitation – it is as if he experiences the presence of Christ. In suffering like Christ, and for Christ, he gets to do it with Christ, through the abiding presence of the Spirit. Practising truth in the Spirit leads a believer into a 'true' understanding of truth. Not merely propositions to affirm, but relational intimacy to embrace.

In summary then, the truth that most people seek is really a lie. Indeed, even if one could gain a grand theoretical knowledge of God through theological study, they still would not have arrived at the truth. Yes, we can affirm truth propositions about God: God is love, Jesus rose from the dead, Jesus is God, etc. are all valid propositions we can affirm. But knowing 'the' truth is more than simply knowing about a thing, even if that 'thing' is God. Coming to terms with the truth is about coming to terms with God: face to face, heart to heart, life to life. It is 'really' about entering into an intimate relationship with him, through Jesus Christ, in the power of the Spirit. When people have grasped truth in this manner, they are no longer preoccupied with the technicality of truth ideas. They are caught up in the wonder of God, and a desire to obediently walk in his ways in the power of the Spirit – for his glory. In so doing, they have found the truth, a reality in which the sovereign God animates their every thought and action. This is life in the Spirit, this is truth!

Bibliography

Achtemeier, Paul J. *The Inspiration of Scripture: Problems and Proposals* (Philadelphia: Westminster Press, 1980).
Aristotle. 'Categories' (trans. J.L. Ackrill). Pages 3–24 in *The Complete Works of Aristotle* (ed. Jonathan Barnes; Princeton, NJ: Princeton University Press, 1995).
———. 'History of Animals' (trans. A.W. Thompson). Pages 774–993 in *The Complete Works of Aristotle* (ed. Jonathan Barnes; Princeton, NJ: Princeton University Press, 1995).
———. 'Metaphysics' (trans. W.D. Ross). Pages 1552–728 in *The Complete Works of Aristotle* (ed. Jonathan Barnes; Princeton, NJ: Princeton University Press, 1995).
———. 'On the Soul' (trans. J.A. Smith). Pages 641–92 in *The Complete Works of Aristotle* (ed. Jonathan Barnes; Princeton, NJ: Princeton University Press, 1995).
———. 'Sense and Sensibilia' (trans. J.I. Beare). Pages 693–713 in *The Complete Works of Aristotle* (ed. Jonathan Barnes; Princeton, NJ: Princeton University Press, 1995).
Armstrong, C.B. *An Outline of Western Philosophy* (London: SPCK, 1964).
Augustine, *The Confessions* (Peabody: Hendrickson, 2004).
———. *On the Spirit and the Letter*, vol. 5 (trans. Peter Holmes and Rober Ernest Wallace; ed. Philip Schaff; Grand Rapids, MI: Eerdmans, 1971).
Ayer, A.J. *The Origins of Pragmatism* (London: Macmillan, 1968).
Barclay, William. *The Promise of the Spirit* (London: Epworth Press, 1960).
Barnes, Jonathan. 'Aristotle'. Pages 191–302 in *Greek Philosophers* (ed. Keith Thomas. Oxford: Oxford University Press, 1999).
Barth, Karl. *The Epistle to the Romans* (trans. Edwyn C. Hoskyns; London: Oxford University Press, 1933).

Bartholomew, Craig G., and Ryan P. O'Dowd. *Old Testament Wisdom Literature: A Theological Introduction* (Downers Grove: IVP Academic, 2011).
Berkhof, Hendrikus. *The Doctrine of the Holy Spirit* (London: Epworth Press, 1964).
Billings, J. Todd. *The Word of God for the People of God* (Grand Rapids, MI: Wm. B. Eerdmans, 2010).
Bloesch, Donald G. *Holy Scripture: Revelation, Inspiration and Interpretation* (Downers Grove: IVP Academic, 1994).
Byassee, Jason. *Reading Augustine: A Guide to the Confessions* (Eugene, OR: Cascade Books, 2006).
Calvin, John. *Institutes of the Christian Religion* (trans. Ford Lewis Battles; Library of Christian Classics, ed. John T. McNeill, vol. 1, Philadelphia: Westminster Press, 1960).
———. *Twelve Minor Prophets* (trans. John Owen; vol. Jonah, Micah, Nahum, Grand Rapids, MI: Eerdmans, 1874).
Cary, Phillip. *Augustine's Invention of the Inner Self: The Legacy of a Christian Platonist* (Oxford: Oxford University Press, 2000).
Casalis, Georges. *Portrait of Karl Barth* (trans. Robert McAfee Brown; Garden City: Doubleday, 1963).
Chapell, Bryan. 'The Main Message of Your Bible' (25 June 2016). http://www.thegospelcoalition.org/article/the-main-message-of-your-bible/ (accessed 14 Jul. 2016).
Crowell, Stephen. 'Existentialism' in *Stanford Encyclopedia of Philosophy* (ed. Edward N. Zalta; Stanford, CA: Metaphysics Research Lab, Stanford University [2015]) https://plato.stanford.edu/entries/existentialism/ (accessed 19 Apr. 2015).
Dahl, Nils A. 'Paul and the Church at Corinth.' Pages 85–97 in *Christianity at Corinth* (ed. David G. Horrell and Edward Adams. Louisville: Westminster John Knox Press, 2004.
Davey, Nicholas. 'Gadamer's Aesthetics' in *Stanford Encyclopedia of Philosophy* (ed. Edward N. Zalta; Stanford, CA: Metaphysics Research Lab, Stanford University [2016]) https://plato.stanford.edu/entries/gadamer-aesthetics/ (accessed 29 Jan. 2016).
Dell, Katharine J., and Margaret Barker. *Wisdom: The Collected Articles of Norman Whybray* (Aldershot: Ashgate, 2005).
Descartes, Rene. *Meditations and Other Metaphysical Writings* (trans. Desmond M. Clark; London: Penguin Books, 2000).

Dodd, C.H. *The Authority of the Bible* (London: Nisbet, 1928).
Dunn, James D.G. *Baptism in the Holy Spirit* (Philadelphia: Westminster Press, 1970).
Engberg-Pedersen, Troels. *Cosmology and Self in the Apostle Paul: The Material Spirit* (Oxford: Oxford University Press, 2010).
Erickson, Millard J. *Christian Theology* (Grand Rapids, MI: Baker, 1990).
Fee, Gordon D. *The First Epistle to the Corinthians* (ed. F.F. Bruce; Grand Rapids, MI: Eerdmans, 1988).
Gaffin, Richard B. *Perspectives on Pentecost* (Phillipsburg: Presbyterian and Reformed, 1979).
Garland, David E. *1 Corinthians* (Grand Rapids, MI: Baker, 2003).
———. *1 Corinthians* (ed. Robert W. Yarbrough and Robert H. Stein; Grand Rapids, MI: Baker, 2008).
Goldingay, John. *Job for Everyone* (London: SPCK, 2013).
Green, Michael. *I Believe in the Holy Spirit* (London: Hodder & Stoughton, 1974).
Grindheim, Sigurd. 'The Law Kills but the Gospel Gives Life: The Letter-Spirit Dualism in 2 Corinthians 3:5-18', *Journal for the Study of the New Testament* 84 (2001): pp. 97–115.
Heidegger, Martin. 'Being and Time'. Pages 115–46 in *Hermeneutic Tradition: From Ast to Ricoeur* (ed. Gayle L. Ormiston and Alan D. Schrift; Albany: State University of New York Press, 1990).
Hendry, George S. *The Holy Spirit in Christian Theology* (London: SCM Press, 1957).
Hogg, Murray. *The Knowledge of God: John's Gospel and Contemporary Epistemology* (Sydney, Australia: Australian College of Theology, 2011).
Hookway, Christopher. 'Pragmatism' in *Stanford Encyclopedia of Philosophy* (ed. Edward N. Zalta; Stanford, CA: Metaphysics Research Lab, Stanford University [2015]) https://plato.stanford.edu/entries/pragmatism/ (accessed 3 Jul. 2015).
Hume, David. *A Treatise of Human Nature*, vol. 1 (London: J.M. Dent & Sons Ltd, 1911).
James, William. *The Philosophy of William James* (New York: Modern Library, 1925).
Kant, Immanuel. *Critique of Pure Reason* (trans. J.M.D. Meiklejohn; New York: Prometheus, 1990).
Keller, Roger R. 'Karl Barth's Treatment of the Old Testament as Expectation'. *Andrews University Seminary Studies* 35 (1997): pp. 165–79.

Kenny, John Peter. *The Mysticism of Saint Augustine: Rereading the Confessions* (New York: Routledge, 2005).

Kierkegaard, Soren. 'Either/Or: A Fragment of Life'. Pages 19–108 in *A Kierkegaard Anthology* (ed. Robert Bretall; Princeton, NJ: Princeton University Press, 1946).

Kilpatrick, William H. 'Dewey's Influence on Education'. Pages 447–73 in *The Philosophy of John Dewey* (ed. Paul Arthur Schlipp; New York: Tudor, 1951).

Lamm, Julia A. *The Living God: Schleiermacher's Theological Appropriation of Spinoza* (University Park, PA: Pennsylvania State University Press, 1996).

Lieu, Judith M. *I, II, & III John: A Commentary* (ed. C. Clifton Black, M. Eugene Boring and John T. Carroll; Louisville, KY: Westminster John Knox Press, 2008).

———. *The Theology of the Johannine Epistles* (Cambridge: Cambridge University Press, 1991).

Lyden, John. 'The Influence of Hermann Cohen on Karl Barth's Dialectical Theology.' *Modern Judaism* 12 (1992): pp. 167–84.

Marshall, Colin, and Tony Payne. *The Trellis and the Vine* (Kingsford: Matthias, 2009).

Marshall, I. Howard. *The Epistles of John* (ed. F.F. Bruce; Grand Rapids, MI: Eerdmans, 1978).

Martin, Hugh. *Jonah* (Edinburgh: Banner of Truth Trust, 1978).

McDonald, William. 'Soren Kierkegaard' in *Stanford Encyclopedia of Philosophy* (ed. Edward N. Zalta; Stanford, CA: Metaphysics Research Lab, Stanford University [2014]) https://plato.stanford.edu/entries/kierkegaard/ (accessed 10 Jul. 2015).

McGrath, Alister E. *A Scientific Theology: Nature* (Edinburgh: T&T Clark, 2001).

McGrath, S.J. *Heidegger: A (Very) Critical Introduction* (Grand Rapids, MI: Eerdmans, 2008).

Menzies, Robert P. *Empowered for Witness: The Spirit in Luke-Acts* (Sheffield: Sheffield Academic Press, 1994).

Metzger, Bruce M. *The Canon of the New Testament: Its Origin, Development, and Significance* (Oxford: Clarendon Press, 1987).

Mitchell, Margaret M. *Paul, the Corinthians and the Birth of Christian Hermeneutics* (Cambridge: Cambridge University Press, 2010).

Moltmann, Jürgen. *The Spirit of Life: A Universal Affirmation* (London: SCM Press, 1992).

Morris, William Edward, and Charlotte R. Brown. 'David Hume' in *The Stanford Encyclopedia of Philosophy* (ed. Edward N. Zalta; Stanford, CA: Metaphysics Research Lab, Stanford University [2016]) http://plato.stanford.edu/archives/spr2016/entries/hume (accessed 15 Mar. 2016).

Munzinger, Andre. *Discerning the Spirits: Theological and Ethical Hermeneutics in Paul* (Cambridge: Cambridge University Press, 2007).

Nash, Ronald H. *The Light of the Mind: St. Augustine's Theory of Knowledge* (Lima: Academic Renewal Press, 2003).

Otto, Rudolf. *Naturalism and Religion* (trans. J. Arthur Thomson and Margaret R. Thomson; London: Williams & Norgate, 1907).

Owen, John. *The Holy Spirit: His Gifts and Power* (Grand Rapids, MI: Kregel, 1960).

Painter, John. *1, 2, and 3 John*. Sacra Pagina (ed. Daniel J. Harrington; Collegeville, MN: Liturgical Press, 2002).

Peirce, Charles Sanders. *Pragmatism as a Principle and Method of Right Thinking* (ed. Patricia Ann Turrisi; Albany: State University of New York Press, 1997).

Philip, Finny. *The Origins of Pauline Pneumatology* (Tübingen: Mohr Siebeck, 2005).

Plato. 'Phaedo'. Pages 49–100 in *Plato: Complete Works* (ed. John M. Cooper and D.S. Hutchinson; Indianapolis, IN: Hackett, 1997).

———. 'Republic'. Pages 971–1223 in *Plato: The Complete Works* (ed. John M. Cooper and D.S. Hutchinson; Indianapolis, IN: Hackett, 1997).

Pogoloff, Stephen M. *Logos and Sophia: The Rhetorical Situation of 1 Corinthians* (ed. David L. Peterson and Pheme Perkins; Atlanta, GA: Scholars Press, 1992).

Rabens, Volker. *The Holy Spirit and Ethics in Paul: Transformation and Empowering for Religious-Ethical Life* (Tübingen: Mohr Siebeck, 2010).

Russell, Bertrand. *History of Western Philosophy* (London: George Allen & Unwin, 1946).

Schleiermacher, Friedrich. *The Christian Faith* (Edinburgh: T&T Clark, 1948).

———. *The Christian Faith* (ed. H.R. Mackintosh and J.S. Stewart; 2 vols, New York: Harper & Row, 1963).

Schweizer, Eduard. *The Holy Spirit* (Philadelphia: Fortress Press, 1978).

Scott, Ian W. *Implicit Epistemology in the Letters of Paul* (Tübingen: Mohr Siebeck, 2005).

Scruton, Roger. 'Kant'. Pages 6–104 in *German Philosophers* (ed. Keith Thomas; Oxford: Oxford University Press, 2001).

Smith, Brandon D. 'Karl Barth, Christ and the OT' (25 October 2015) http://www.patheos.com/blogs/brandonsmith/2015/10/karl-barth-christ-and-the-ot/ (accessed 30 Oct. 2015).

Stacey, W.D. *Prophetic Drama in the Old Testament* (London: Epworth Press, 1990).

Strecker, Georg. *The Johannine Letters* (trans. Linda M. Maloney; Minneapolis: Fortress Press, 1996).

Taylor, Charles. *A Secular Age* (Cambridge: Belknap Press of Harvard University Press, 2007).

Terrien, Samuel. *Job: Poet of Existence* (New York: Bobbs-Merrill, 1957).

Thielicke, Helmut. *The Evangelical Faith* (trans. Geoffrey W. Bromiley; 3 vols, Grand Rapids, MI: Eerdmans, 1982).

Thiselton, Anthony C. *The Holy Spirit in Biblical Teaching, through the Centuries, and Today* (Grand Rapids, MI: Eerdmans, 2013).

Van Gelder, Craig. *The Ministry of the Missional Church* (Grand Rapids, MI: Baker, 2007).

Van Til, Cornelius. *In Defense of the Faith: A Survey of Christian Epistemology* (Phillipsburg: Presbyterian and Reformed, 1988).

Walters, Gwyn. *The Sovereign Spirit: The Doctrine of the Holy Spirit in the Writings of John Calvin* (Edinburgh: Rutherford House, 2009).

Ward, Timothy. *Words of Life: Scripture as the Living and Active Word of God* (Downers Grove: IVP Academic, 2009).

Warfield, B.B. *Calvin and Augustine* (ed. Samuel G. Craig; Philadelphia: Presbyterian and Reformed, 1974).

Watson, Julia. *Kierkegaard* (London: Continuum, 1997).

Whybray, Norman. *Job* (Sheffield: Sheffield Academic Press, 1998).

Wittgenstein, Ludwig. *The Blue and Brown Books* (Oxford: Basil Blackwell, 1960).

———. *Tractatus Logico-Philosophicus* (London: Routledge, 2001).

Yarbrough, Robert W. *1-3 John* (ed. Robert W. Yarbrough and Robert H. Stein; Grand Rapids, MI: Baker, 2008).

Notes

1 Truth and Reason

[1] Bertrand Russell, *History of Western Philosophy* (London: George Allen & Unwin, 1946), p. 50.
[2] C.B. Armstrong, *An Outline of Western Philosophy* (London: SPCK, 1964), p. 6.
[3] Armstrong, *Outline*, p. 20.
[4] Plato, 'Phaedo', in *Plato: The Complete Works* (ed. John M. Cooper and D.S. Hutchinson; Indianapolis, IN: Hackett, 1997), p. 57.
[5] Plato, 'Phaedo', p. 57.
[6] Plato, 'Phaedo', p. 58.
[7] Plato, 'Phaedo', p. 67.
[8] Plato, 'Phaedo', p. 66.
[9] Plato, 'Phaedo', p. 70.
[10] Plato, 'Republic', in *Plato: The Complete Works* (ed. John M. Cooper and D.S. Hutchinson; Indianapolis, IN: Hackett, 1997), p. 1135.
[11] Plato, 'Republic', p. 1135.
[12] Rene Descartes, *Meditations and Other Metaphysical Writings* (trans. Desmond M. Clark; London: Penguin Books, 2000), p. 19.
[13] Descartes, *Meditations*, p. 24.
[14] Descartes, *Meditations*, p. 25.
[15] Descartes, *Meditations*, p. 39.
[16] Descartes, *Meditations*, p. 44.
[17] Descartes, *Meditations*, p. 44.
[18] Descartes, *Meditations*, p. 44.
[19] 'And thus, as long as I think only about God and focus completely on him, I find no cause of error or falsehood in myself. But as soon as I turned back to myself, however, I find that I am subject to innumerable

errors. *By using the intellect I merely perceive the ideas about which I can make a judgement, and this can contain no error in the strict sense when it is considered precisely from this point of view.*' Descartes, *Meditations*, p. 46.

[20] Immanuel Kant, *Critique of Pure Reason* (trans. J.M.D Meiklejohn; New York: Prometheus, 1990), p. 12.
[21] Kant, *Critique of Pure Reason*, p. 1.
[22] Kant, *Critique of Pure Reason*, p. 26.
[23] Kant, *Critique of Pure Reason*, p. 47.
[24] Kant, *Critique of Pure Reason*, p. 62.
[25] Roger Scruton, 'Kant', in *German Philosophers* (ed. Keith Thomas; Oxford: OUP, 2001), p. 42.
[26] Scruton, 'Kant', p. 102.
[27] Armstrong, *Outline*, p. 33.
[28] Armstrong, *Outline*, p. 25.
[29] Jonathan Barnes, 'Aristotle', in *Greek Philosophers* (ed. Keith Thomas; Oxford: OUP, 1999), p. 264.
[30] Aristotle, 'Metaphysics', in *The Complete Works of Aristotle* (ed. Jonathan Barnes; Princeton: Princeton University Press, 1995), p. 1552.
[31] Aristotle, 'Metaphysics', p. 1553.
[32] Aristotle, 'On the Soul', in *The Complete Works of Aristotle* (ed. Jonathan Barnes; Princeton: Princeton University Press, 1995), p. 674.
[33] Aristotle, 'Sense and Sensibilia', in *The Compete Works of Aristotle* (ed. Jonathan Barnes; Princeton: Princeton University Press, 1995), p. 712.
[34] Barnes, 'Aristotle', p. 211.
[35] Aristotle, 'History of Animals', in *The Complete Works of Aristotle* (ed. Jonathan Barnes; Princeton: Princeton University Press, 1995), p. 789.
[36] Barnes, 'Aristotle', p. 244.
[37] Aristotle, 'Categories', in *The Complete Works of Aristotle* (ed. Jonathan Barnes; Princeton: Princeton University Press, 1995), p. 10.
[38] Aristotle, 'Metaphysics', p. 1600.
[39] Armstrong, *Outline*, p. 24.
[40] William Edward Morris and Charlotte R. Brown, 'David Hume', in *The Stanford Encyclopedia of Philosophy* (ed. Edward N. Zalta; Stanford, CA: Metaphysics Research Lab, Stanford University [2016]) http://plato.stanford.edu/archives/spr2016/entries/hume (accessed 15 Mar. 2016).
[41] David Hume, *A Treatise of Human Nature*, vol. 1 (London: J.M. Dent & Sons Ltd, 1911), p. 231.
[42] Hume, *Treatise*, p. 235.
[43] Hume, *Treatise*, p. 239.
[44] Hume, *Treatise*, p. 240.

45 Hume, *Treatise*, p. 11.
46 Morris and Brown, 'David Hume'.
47 Hume, *Treatise*, p. 14.
48 Hume, *Treatise*, p. 15.
49 Hume, *Treatise*, p. 20.
50 Hume, *Treatise*, p. 20.
51 Armstrong, *Outline*, p. 118.
52 Ludwig Wittgenstein, *Tractatus Logico-Philosophicus* (London: Routledge, 2001), p. 3.
53 Wittgenstein, *Tractatus*, p. 5.
54 Ludwig Wittgenstein, *The Blue and Brown Books* (Oxford: Basil Blackwell, 1960), p. 1.
55 Wittgenstein, *Blue and Brown Books*, p. 3.
56 Wittgenstein, *Blue and Brown Books*, p. 4.
57 Wittgenstein, *Blue and Brown Books*, p. 4.
58 Wittgenstein, *Blue and Brown Books*, p. 5.
59 Cornelius van Til, *In Defense of the Faith: A Survey of Christian Epistemology* (Phillipsburg: Presbyterian and Reformed, 1988), p. 113.
60 Peirce, quoted in A.J. Ayer, *The Origins of Pragmatism* (London: Macmillan, 1968), p. 27.
61 Peirce, quoted in Ayer, *Origins*, p. 19.
62 Peirce, quoted in Ayer, *Origins*, p. 35.
63 Peirce, quoted in Ayer, *Origins*, p. 36.
64 Charles Sanders Peirce, 'Lecture 1', in *Pragmatism as a Principle and Method of Right Thinking* (ed. Patricia Ann Turrisi; Albany: State University of New York Press, 1997), p. 116.
65 Peirce, 'Lecture 1', p. 111.
66 Peirce, 'Lecture 2', p. 150.
67 Christopher Hookway, 'Pragmatism', in *Stanford Encyclopedia of Philosophy* (ed. Edward N. Zalta; Stanford, CA: Metaphysics Research Lab, Stanford University [2015]) https:// plato.stanford.edu/entries/pragmatism/ (accessed 3 Jul. 2015).
68 William James, *The Philosophy of William James* (New York: Modern Library, 1925), p. 125.
69 James, *Philosophy*, p. 65.
70 Ayer, *Origins*, p. 197.
71 Ayer, *Origins*, p. 211.
72 James, *Philosophy*, p. 91.
73 William H. Kilpatrick, 'Dewey's Influence on Education', in *The Philosophy of John Dewey* (ed. Paul Arthur Schlipp; New York: Tudor, 1951), p. 452.

74 Kilpatrick, 'Dewey's Influence on Education', p. 459.
75 Stephen Crowell, 'Existentialism', in *Stanford Encyclopedia of Philosophy* (ed. Edward N. Zalta; Stanford, CA: Metaphysics Research Lab, Stanford University [2015]) https://plato.stanford.edu/entries/existentialism/ (accessed 19 Apr. 2015).
76 Augustine, *Confessions*, trans. R.S. Pine-Coffin (Harmondsworth: Penguin Books, 1961), p. 60.
77 Phillip Cary, *Augustine's Invention of the Inner Self: The Legacy of a Christian Platonist* (Oxford: Oxford University Press, 2000), p. 51.
78 Ronald H. Nash, *The Light of the Mind: St. Augustine's Theory of Knowledge* (Lima: Academic Renewal Press, 2003), p. 4.
79 Nash, *Light*, p. 11.
80 Augustine, *Confessions*, p. 61.
81 Augustine, *Confessions*, p. 78.
82 Augustine, *Confessions*, p. 77.
83 Julia Watson, *Kierkegaard* (London: Continuum, 1997), p. 12.
84 William McDonald, 'Soren Kierkegaard', in *Stanford Encyclopedia of Philosophy* (ed. Edward N. Zalta; Stanford, CA: Metaphysics Research Lab, Stanford University [2014]) https://plato.stanford.edu/entries/kierkegaard/ (accessed 10 Jul. 2015).
85 McDonald, 'Soren Kierkegaard'.
86 Soren Kierkegaard, 'Either/Or: A Fragment of Life', in *A Kierkegaard Anthology* (ed. Robert Bretall (Princeton: Princeton University Press, 1946), p. 33.
87 S.J. McGrath, *Heidegger: A (Very) Critical Introduction* (Grand Rapids, MI: Eerdmans, 2008), p. 2.
88 Martin Heidegger, *Being and Time* (New York: Harper & Row, 1962), p. 26.
89 Heidegger, *Being and Time*, p. 33.
90 Heidegger, *Being and Time*, p. 39.
91 Heidegger, *Being and Time*, p. 98.

2 Truth and Divine Revelation

1 John Goldingay, *Job for Everyone* (London: SPCK, 2013), p. 4.
2 Craig G. Bartholomew and Ryan P. O'Dowd, *Old Testament Wisdom Literature: A Theological Introduction* (Downers Grove: IVP Academic, 2011), p. 34.

3. Bartholomew and O'Dowd, *Old Testament*, p. 140.
4. Samuel Terrien, *Job: Poet of Existence* (New York: Bobbs-Merrill, 1957), p. 236.
5. Terrien, *Job*, p. 236.
6. Norman Whybray, *Job* (Sheffield: Sheffield Academic Press, 1998), p. 22.
7. Whybray, *Job*, p. 23.
8. Bartholomew and O'Dowd, *Old Testament*, p. 183.
9. Bartholomew and O'Dowd, *Old Testament*, p. 161.
10. Bartholomew and O'Dowd, *Old Testament*, p. 155.
11. Bartholomew and O'Dowd, *Old Testament*, p. 150.
12. Terrien, *Job*, p. 239.
13. Terrien, *Job*, p. 246.
14. Katharine J. Dell and Margaret Barker, *Wisdom: The Collected Articles of Norman Whybray* (Aldershot: Ashgate, 2005), p. 192.
15. 'The connection of rhetoric with social class is highly significant for 1 Cor. For the rhetorical situation must connect them, not only to the exigence of division, but also is the social status . . . thus, Paul is responding not to division itself, but to the values which lie behind them. Those "of Paul" have perceived him as possessing the status indicator of eloquence, or those "of Apollo's" perceive Apollo's superior in this regard.' Stephen M. Pogoloff, *Logos and Sophia: The Rhetorical Situation of 1 Corinthians* (ed. David L. Peterson and Pheme Perkins; Atlanta: Scholars Press, 1992), p. 119.
16. Pogoloff, *Logos*, p. 120.
17. Ian W. Scott, *Implicit Epistemology in the Letters of Paul* (Tübingen: Mohr Siebeck, 2005), p. 24.
18. David E. Garland, *1 Corinthians* (ed. Robert W. Yarbrough and Robert H. Stein; Grand Rapids, MI: Baker, 2008), p. 75.
19. William Barclay, *The Promise of the Spirit* (London: Epworth Press, 1960), p. 69.
20. Anthony C. Thiselton, *The Holy Spirit in Biblical Teaching, through the Centuries, and Today* (Grand Rapids, MI: Eerdmans, 2013), p. 122.
21. Thiselton, *Holy Spirit*, p. 122.
22. Scott, *Implicit Epistemology*, p. 29.
23. Scott, *Implicit Epistemology*, p. 19.
24. Andre Munzinger, *Discerning the Spirits: Theological and Ethical Hermeneutics in Paul* (Cambridge: CUP, 2007), p. 82.
25. Nils A. Dahl, 'Paul and the Church at Corinth', in *Christianity at Corinth* (ed. David G. Horrell and Edward Adams; Louisville, KY: Westminster John Knox Press, 2004), p. 95.

[26] Dahl, 'Paul', p. 95.
[27] Scott, *Implicit Epistemology*, p. 44.
[28] Margaret M. Mitchell, *Paul, the Corinthians and the Birth of Christian Hermeneutics* (Cambridge: CUP, 2010), p. 42.
[29] Gordon D. Fee, *The First Epistle to the Corinthians* (ed. F.F. Bruce; Grand Rapids, MI: Eerdmans, 1988), p. 110.
[30] Fee, *First Epistle*, p. 120.
[31] Finny Philip, *The Origins of Pauline Pneumatology* (Tübingen: Mohr Siebeck, 2005), pp. 226–227.
[32] Scott, *Implicit Epistemology*, p. 48.
[33] Murray Hogg, *The Knowledge of God: John's Gospel and Contemporary Epistemology* (Sydney, Australia: Australian College of Theology, 2011), p. 88.
[34] Hogg, *Knowledge*, p. 89.
[35] Georg Strecker, *The Johannine Letters* (trans. Linda M. Maloney; Minneapolis: Fortress Press, 1996), p. 71.
[36] I. Howard Marshall, *The Epistles of John* (ed. F.F. Bruce; Grand Rapids, MI: Eerdmans, 1978), p. 153.
[37] Robert W. Yarbrough, *1-3 John* (ed. Robert W. Yarbrough and Robert H. Stein; Grand Rapids, MI: Baker, 2008), p. 149.
[38] Yarbrough, *1-3 John*, p. 151.
[39] Judith M. Lieu, *I, II, & III John: A Commentary* (ed. C. Clifton Black, M. Eugene Boring, and John T. Carroll; Louisville, KY: Westminster John Knox Press, 2008), p. 104.
[40] Lieu, *I, II, & III John*, p. 161.
[41] John Painter, *1, 2, and 3 John* (ed. Daniel J. Harrington; Collegeville, MN: Liturgical Press, 2002), p. 252.
[42] Strecker, *Johannine Letters*, p. 134.
[43] Marshall, *Epistles of John*, p. 235.
[44] Lieu, *I, II, & III John*, p. 213.

3 The Spirit, Truth and the Material World

[1] Plato, 'Phaedo', in *Plato: The Complete Works* (ed. John M. Cooper and D.S. Hutchinson; Indianapolis, IN: Hackett, 1997), p. 58.
[2] Friedrich Schleiermacher, *The Christian Faith*, vol. 1 (ed. H.R. Mackintosh and J.S. Stewart; New York: Harper & Row, 1963), p. 234.
[3] John Lyden, 'The Influence of Hermann Cohen on Karl Barth's Dialectical Theology', *Modern Judaism* 12 (1992): p. 173.

4. Georges Casalis, *Portrait of Karl Barth* (trans. Robert McAfee Brown; Garden City: Doubleday, 1963), p. 85.
5. Karl Barth, *The Epistle to the Romans* (trans. Edwyn C. Hoskyns; (London: OUP, 1933), p. 33.
6. Jürgen Moltmann, *The Spirit of Life: A Universal Affirmation* (London: SCM Press, 1992), p. 5.
7. Moltmann, *Spirit*, p. 7.
8. Moltmann, *Spirit*, p. 7.
9. Moltmann, *Spirit*, p. 7.
10. Recent examples of scholars who have engaged this discussion are: Volker Rabens, *The Holy Spirit and Ethics in Paul: Transformation and Empowering for Religious-Ethical Life* (Tübingen: Mohr Siebeck, 2010); and Troels Engberg-Pedersen, *Cosmology and Self in the Apostle Paul: The Material Spirit* (Oxford: OUP, 2010). Rabens' position orients more toward the dualist position, though recognizes that Paul does not set forth a clear ontology of the Spirit; Engberg-Pedersen adopts an infusional view of a material spirit, which draws on Stoic monism.
11. Moltmann, *Spirit*, p. 8.
12. Alister E. McGrath, *A Scientific Theology: Nature* (Edinburgh: T&T Clark, 2001), p. 146.
13. John Calvin, *Institutes of the Christian Religion*, vol. 1 (trans. Ford Lewis Battles; ed. John T. McNeill; Philadelphia: Westminster Press, 1960), 1:XIII.14.138.
14. John Owen, *The Holy Spirit: His Gifts and Power* (Grand Rapids, MI: Kregel, 1960), p. 56.
15. Eduard Schweizer, *The Holy Spirit* (Philadelphia: Fortress Press, 1978), p. 14.
16. Rudolf Otto, *Naturalism and Religion* (trans. J. Arthur Thomson and Margaret R. Thomson; London: Williams & Norgate, 1907), p. 80.
17. Nicholas Davey, 'Gadamer's Aesthetics', in *Stanford Encyclopedia of Philosophy* (ed. Edward N. Zalta; Stanford, CA: Metaphysics Research Lab, Stanford University [2016]) https://plato.stanford.edu/entries/gadamer-aesthetics/ (accessed 29 Jan. 2016).
18. Davey, 'Gadamer's Aesthetics'.
19. Gwyn Walters, *The Sovereign Spirit: The Doctrine of the Holy Spirit in the Writings of John Calvin* (Edinburgh: Rutherford House, 2009), p. 18.
20. Calvin, *Institutes*, 1.II:2.16.275.
21. W.D. Stacey, *Prophetic Drama in the Old Testament* (London: Epworth Press, 1990), p. 267.

22 John Calvin, *Twelve Minor Prophets* (trans. John Owen; vol. Jonah, Micah, Nahum; Grand Rapids, MI: Eerdmans, 1874), p. 33.
23 Hugh Martin, *Jonah* (Edinburgh: Banner of Truth Trust, 1978), p. 69.

4 The Spirit, Truth and the Church

1 Hendrikus Berkhof, *The Doctrine of the Holy Spirit* (London: Epworth Press, 1964), p. 44.
2 George S. Hendry, *The Holy Spirit in Christian Theology* (London: SCM Press, 1957), p. 58.
3 Berkhof, *Doctrine*, p. 58.
4 Charles Taylor, *A Secular Age* (Cambridge: Belknap Press of Harvard University Press, 2007), p. 69.
5 Berkhof, *Doctrine*, p. 51.
6 B.B. Warfield, *Calvin and Augustine* (ed. Samuel G. Craig; Philadelphia: Presbyterian and Reformed, 1974), p. 484.
7 Augustine presented a conjunctive relationship between Spirit and Scripture: 'the letter of the law, which teaches us not to commit sin, kills, if the life-giving Spirit be absent'. Augustine, *On the Spirit and the Letter*, vol. 5 (trans. Peter Holmes and Rober Ernest Wallace; ed. Philip Schaff; Grand Rapids, MI: Eerdmans, 1971), p. 86.
8 John Calvin, *Institutes of the Christian Religion*, vol. 1 (trans. Ford Lewis Battles; ed. John T. McNeill; Philadelphia: Westminster Press, 1960), pp. 78–9.
9 Calvin, *Institutes*, p. 95.
10 Calvin, *Institutes*, p. 1012.
11 Calvin, *Institutes*, p. 1021.
12 Michael Green, in the reformed and evangelical tradition, views the spiritual gifts from a highly 'functional' perspective. Michael Green, *I Believe in the Holy Spirit* (London: Hodder & Stoughton, 1974), p. 118.
13 Millard J. Erickson, *Christian Theology* (Grand Rapids, MI: Baker, 1990), p. 1083.
14 Erickson, *Christian Theology*, p. 1083.
15 Erickson, *Christian Theology*, pp. 1028, 1029.
16 Craig Van Gelder, *The Ministry of the Missional Church* (Grand Rapids, MI: Baker, 2007), p. 23.
17 Richard B. Gaffin, *Perspectives on Pentecost* (Phillipsburg: Presbyterian and Reformed, 1979), p. 14.

[18] James D.G. Dunn, *Baptism in the Holy Spirit* (Philadelphia: Westminster Press, 1970), p. 40.
[19] Dunn, *Baptism*, p. 48.
[20] Dunn, *Baptism*, p. 51.
[21] Dunn, *Baptism*, p. 42.
[22] Gaffin, *Perspectives*, p. 20.
[23] Judith M. Lieu, *The Theology of the Johannine Epistles* (Cambridge: CUP, 1991), p. 27.
[24] Van Gelder, *Ministry*, p. 96.
[25] Gaffin, *Perspectives*, p. 38.
[26] Robert P. Menzies, *Empowered for Witness: The Spirit in Luke-Acts* (Sheffield: Sheffield Academic Press, 1994), p. 175.
[27] David E. Garland, *1 Corinthians* (Grand Rapids, MI: Baker, 2003), p. 626.
[28] Berkhof, *Doctrine*, p. 69.
[29] Colin Marshall and Tony Payne, *The Trellis and the Vine* (Kingsford: Matthias, 2009), p. 2.

5 The Spirit, Truth and Personal Experience

[1] John Peter Kenny, *The Mysticism of Saint Augustine: Rereading the Confessions* (New York: Routledge, 2005), p. 12.
[2] Jason Byassee, *Reading Augustine: A Guide to the Confessions* (Eugene, OR: Cascade, 2006), p. 1.
[3] Augustine, *The Confessions* (Peabody: Hendrickson, 2004), p. 32.
[4] Augustine, *Confessions*, p. 153.
[5] Augustine, *Confessions*, p. 158.
[6] Augustine, *Confessions*, pp. 159–60.
[7] Kenny, *Mysticism*, p. ix.
[8] Rene Descartes, *Meditations and Other Metaphysical Writings* (trans. Desmond M. Clark; London: Penguin Books, 2000), p. 67.
[9] Julia A. Lamm, *The Living God: Schleiermacher's Theological Appropriation of Spinoza* (University Park, PA: Pennsylvania State University Press, 1996), p. 26.
[10] Lamm, *Living God*, p. 33.
[11] Friedrich Schleiermacher, *The Christian Faith* (Edinburgh: T&T Clark, 1948), p. 13.
[12] Schleiermacher, *Christian Faith*, p. 26.
[13] Schleiermacher, *Christian Faith*, p. 21.

14 Schleiermacher, *Christian Faith*, p. 65.
15 Schleiermacher, *Christian Faith*, p. 571.
16 Schleiermacher, *Christian Faith*, p. 573.
17 Helmut Thielicke, *The Evangelical Faith*, vol. 3 (trans. Geoffrey W. Bromiley; Grand Rapids, MI: Eerdmans, 1982), p. 4.
18 Thielicke, *Evangelical Faith*, p. 5.
19 Thielicke, *Evangelical Faith*, p. 5.
20 Martin Heidegger, 'Being and Time', in *Hermeneutic Tradition: From Ast to Ricoeur* (ed. Gayle L. Ormiston and Alan D. Schrift; Albany: State University of New York Press, 1990), p. 122.

6 The Spirit, Truth and Holy Scripture

1 Donald G. Bloesch, *Holy Scripture: Revelation, Inspiration and Interpretation* (Downers Grove: IVP Academic, 1994), p. 283.
2 Bloesch, *Holy Scripture*, p. 282.
3 Bruce M. Metzger, *The Canon of the New Testament: Its Origin. Development, and Significance* (Oxford: Clarendon Press, 1987), p. 254.
4 Metzger, *Canon*, p. 252.
5 Metzger, *Canon*, p. 253.
6 Metzger, *Canon*, p. 256.
7 C.H. Dodd, *The Authority of the Bible* (London: Nisbet, 1928), p. 35.
8 Dodd, *Authority*, p. 260.
9 Dodd, *Authority*, p. xii.
10 Dodd, *Authority*, p. 260.
11 Bryan Chapell, 'The Main Message of Your Bible' (25 June 2016) http://www.thegospelcoalition.org/article/the-main-message-of-your-bible/ (accessed 14 Jul. 2016).
12 Brandon D. Smith, 'Karl Barth, Christ and the OT' (25 October 2015) http://www.patheos.com/blogs/brandonsmith/2015/10/karl-barth-christ-and-the-ot/ (accessed 30 Oct. 2015).
13 Roger R. Keller, 'Karl Barth's Treatment of the Old Testament as Expectation', *Andrews University Seminary Studies* 35 (1997): p. 167.
14 Timothy Ward, *Words of Life: Scripture as the Living and Active Word of God* (Downers Grove: IVP Academic, 2009), p. 80.
15 J. Todd Billings, *The Word of God for the People of God* (Grand Rapids: Wm. B. Eerdmans Publishing Co, 2010), p. 93.
16 Billings, *Word of God*, p. 89.

[17] Bloesch, *Holy Scripture*, p. 127.
[18] Paul J. Achtemeier, *The Inspiration of Scripture: Problems and Proposals* (Philadelphia: Westminster Press, 1980), p. 138.
[19] Bloesch, *Holy Scripture*, p. 287.
[20] Sigurd Grindheim, 'The Law Kills but the Gospel Gives Life: The Letter-Spirit Dualism in 2 Corinthians 3:5-18', *Journal for the Study of the New Testament* 84 (2001): pp. 97–115.

Spirit and Life

The Practice of Living by the Spirit

Roland J. Lowther

The Apostle Paul challenged Christians to live by the Holy Spirit. But how is such a Spirit-oriented life to be envisaged? How might it be defined? In answering these questions, this remarkable book investigates Paul's concept of living by the Spirit. The radical conclusion reached is that the Spirit-influenced Christian, engaged in a Spirit-endowed Church, aware of a Spirit-ordered world, under the authoritative guidance of a Spirit-inspired Word, lives a Spirit-coordinated life to the glory of God.

A must read for those who wish to walk in God's ways.

978-1-84227-883-3

Spirit and Gospel

The Power of God for Salvation

Roland J. Lowther

Spirit and Gospel offers clarity on the vital subject of Christian salvation. Lowther revisits Paul's gospel presentation in Romans to reveal how Paul uses a sequence of highly relevant metaphors to frame his holistic message of salvation. Whilst affirming Jesus Christ as the heart of Paul's soteriology, Lowther advocates that the relationship of the Spirit to the gospel engenders in Paul's presentation a certain coherency and potency that many Christian's fail to capture.

Spirit and Gospel enables us to see that the Holy Spirit offers not just a fresh vision of salvation, but also the wisdom to understand it, the courage to embrace it, and the power to live it.

978-1-84227-886-4

We trust you enjoyed reading this book from Paternoster. If you want to be informed of any new titles from this author and other releases you can sign up to the Paternoster newsletter by scanning below:

Online:
authenticmedia.co.uk/paternoster

Follow us:

www.ingramcontent.com/pod-product-compliance
Lightning Source LLC
Chambersburg PA
CBHW070534170426
43200CB00011B/2418